Visit us at

W W W . S

Syngress is committed to
and delivering those books in media and formats
customers. We are also committed to extending the utility of the book you
purchase via additional materials available from our Web site.

SOLUTIONS WEB SITE

To register your book, visit www.syngress.com/solutions. Once registered, you can
access our solutions@syngress.com Web pages. There you may find an assortment of
valueadded features such as free e-books related to the topic of this book, URLs
of related Web sites, FAQs from the book, corrections, and any updates from the
author(s).

ULTIMATE CDs

Our Ultimate CD product line offers our readers budget-conscious compilations of
some of our best-selling backlist titles in Adobe PDF form. These CDs are the perfect
way to extend your reference library on key topics pertaining to your area of expertise,
including Cisco Engineering, Microsoft Windows System Administration, CyberCrime
Investigation, Open Source Security, and Firewall Configuration, to name a few.

DOWNLOADABLE E-BOOKS

For readers who can't wait for hard copy, we offer most of our titles in downloadable
Adobe PDF form. These e-books are often available weeks before hard copies, and are
priced affordably.

SYNGRESS OUTLET

Our outlet store at syngress.com features overstocked, out-of-print, or slightly hurt
books at significant savings.

SITE LICENSING

Syngress has a well-established program for site licensing our e-books onto servers
in corporations, educational institutions, and large organizations. Contact us at
sales@syngress.com for more information.

CUSTOM PUBLISHING

Many organizations welcome the ability to combine parts of multiple Syngress books,
as well as their own content, into a single volume for their own internal use. Contact
us at sales@syngress.com for more information.

SYNGRESS®

Managing Catastrophic Loss of Sensitive Data

Constantine Photopoulos

KEY	SERIAL NUMBER
001	HJIRTCV764
002	PO9873D5FG
003	829KM8NJH2
004	BPOQ48722D
005	CVPLQ6WQ23
006	VBP965T5T5
007	HJJJ863WD3E
008	2987GVTWMK
009	629MP5SDJT
010	IMWQ295T6T

PUBLISHED BY
Syngress Publishing, Inc.
Elsevier, Inc.
30 Corporate Drive
Burlington, MA 01803

Managing Catastrophic Loss of Sensitive Data

Printed in the United States of America
1 2 3 4 5 6 7 8 9 0

ISBN 13: 978-1-59749-239-3

Publisher: Andrew Williams
Acquisitions Editor: Patrice Rapalus
Project Manager: Gary Byrne
Page Layout and Art: SPI

Copy Editors: Adrienne Rebello and Judy Eby
Indexer: SPI
Cover Designer: Michael Kavish

For information on rights, translations, and bulk sales, contact Matt Pedersen, Commercial Sales Director and Rights, at Syngress Publishing; email m.pedersen@elsevier.com.

Author

Constantine Photopoulos is the partner in charge of the The SOX Group's national Sarbanes-Oxley practice. He has more than 20 years' experience in the IT industry, including significant experience in managing projects spanning the full range of Sarbanes-Oxley IT compliance services. At The SOX Group, he has managed, as well as participated in, engagements at a wide variety of organizations, from Fortune 500 to emerging companies, with overall responsibility for SOX process narratives, risk and control identification, test plan development, testing, remediation, and procedure documentation. This included coordination with internal IT audit staff as well as the Big Four and other external auditors.

He has managed projects covering the following areas:

Infrastructure Data center security, backup and recovery, job processing, virus and patch management, network perimeter security, change management, problem management, database security, data transmission, remote access, and operations documentation

Application Access control, logical security, administrative accounts, segregation of duties, activity monitoring and logging, application documentation, and SAS 70 (for hosted applications)

Entity-Level IT governance, strategic planning, outsourcing and third-party services, and Software Development Life Cycle (SDLC) policies and procedures

In addition to Sarbanes-Oxley work, he has an extensive background in IT security, risk management, application software management and development, infrastructure operations, and disaster recovery/business continuity planning.

He holds a B.S. in Electrical Engineering from Massachusetts Institute of Technology.

Contents

Chapter 1

Introduction

Solutions in this chapter:

- What Is Sensitive Data?
- Data Security Breach
- Data Loss Consequences
- Prevention and Safeguards
- Response
- Notification
- Recovering from a Data Breach
- Organization of the Book

Overview

The loss of sensitive data continues to be a significant concern for both organizations as well as individuals whose information may be at risk of a breach. Organizations that experience a data breach can suffer reputational damage, loss of customer and constituent confidence, legal and regulatory scrutiny, and the direct costs of managing an incident and complying with the legal requirements to notify customers that their private information has been breached.

If a data breach involves internal business information, the competitive damage to the organization can be severe. In the case of leakage of private customer information, this damage will be compounded by eroded customer trust and brand equity.

Data breaches represent a major category of organizational failures in the eyes of many individuals. Customers, constituents, and employees demand to have their personal information well protected and, in the event that sensitive data may have been exposed, require that they be notified of such incidents. As a result, lawmakers and regulators have responded by passing laws to help identity theft victims and to require organizations to protect the security and confidentiality of their customers' and employees' personal information.

Both organizations and individuals are acutely aware of the risk from the loss of sensitive information. One of the most nefarious consequences of a data breach is identity theft, a rapidly growing crime with devastating consequences to its victims. It still poses a major risk to the public as well as to the organization that mishandles private information with which it has been entrusted.

Since the consequences of identity theft are severe, a real concern arises even if only a small percentage of parties whose information was breached end up becoming victims. Moreover, any notification of a data breach, even if it does not result in identity theft, will influence consumers' behavior and confidence and may lead to the termination of their relationship with the organization that mishandled their private and confidential information. The consequence may be damage to an organization's reputation as well as the opportunity cost of lost business. This loss of confidence can also arise within the organization itself, since the loss of confidence in the security of a particular system or data store can render it hesitant or unwilling to engage in new initiatives or ventures.

Since organizations collect and store vast amounts of personal information about their customers, constituents, and employees, they must play an important role in protecting privacy and curbing the growth of identity theft through the implementation of effective safeguards and controls and through a response plan that will provide the ability to make informed decisions during an incident in order to protect the organization and its customers. This requires the development and implementation of response mechanisms for such a crisis before one occurs.

What Is Sensitive Data?

On a general level, sensitive data can be defined as information concerning the organization's or an affiliate's prospective, current, or former customers, clients, vendors, employees, or any other nonpublic business information. Sensitive data is information whose disclosure is protected by law or regulation as well as that protected by organizational policy. This includes confidential information and Personally Identifiable Information (PII), which is an individual's name in conjunction with an identifier or account number and whose compromise could lead to identity theft or fraud.

Sensitive data can be organized into the following general categories:

- Legislatively protected data subject to legal or regulatory oversight. This includes data such as medical records and financial records.

- Personally Identifiable Information, which can reasonably identify individuals and which, if disclosed, could violate the privacy of individuals and lead to identity theft or fraud.

- Any data whose unauthorized disclosure could lead to a financial or reputational loss. This includes nonpublic intellectual property and trade secrets as well as business related data such as payroll and benefits information, work history, and budget information.

- Any combination of components of customer information that could allow unauthorized access to the customer's account, such as username and password or password and account number.

- Data whose unauthorized release would constitute a violation of confidentiality agreed to as a condition of possessing the data.

- System or user credentials whose unauthorized release could provide access to sensitive systems or resources.

- Any data protected by organizational policy.

Personally Identifiable Information

An important class of sensitive information is notice-triggering Personally Identifiable Information (PII). This type of data is tightly associated with identity theft or fraud and is subject to legislation requiring both reporting and notification of unauthorized access.

Personally Identifiable Information is any information that permits the identity of an individual to be directly or indirectly inferred, including the first name or first initial and last name, address, or telephone number, in conjunction with any one or more of the following elements, when either the name or the data element is not encrypted:

- A social security number or national identification number.
- A driver's license number or other officially recognized form of identification.
- A credit card number, debit card number, financial account number, or any required security code, access code, or password that would permit access to financial information relating to that party.
- Any additional, specific factor that adds to the personally identifying profile of a specific individual, such as a relationship with a specific financial institution or membership in a club.
- Medical information.

This general definition of PII can apply is most cases unless local jurisdiction law or regulatory guidance is stricter, in which case the organization must abide by the local jurisdiction laws or regulations.

In addition to PII, other high risk personal information includes health information, student records, employee salary and benefits data, financial information, or other personal information the disclosure of which would violate the privacy of individuals.

Confidential Business Information

In addition to customer, constituent, and employee information, sensitive data encompasses business and operational information whose disclosure would violate a legal agreement or would either deny the organization a competitive advantage or provide an advantage to its competitors. This includes trade secrets and intellectual property, operational details, organizational strategies, certain client relationships, and sensitive third-party information subject to a nondisclosure agreement.

Legally protected business information includes pending mergers and acquisitions. The premature disclosure of this information to or its use by certain parties can result in regulatory and legal penalties since it can provide the potential for insider gains in security trading.

Data Categories

Not all sensitive information requires the same level of safeguards or poses the same risk of harm in case of a breach. Categorization or classification schemes are used to identify various levels of data sensitivity. The most common schemes generally classify data into three or four categories, such as Confidential, Internal, and Public. Guidelines used to classify data include:

- Monetary, reputational, contractual, or regulatory impact if the data is compromised.

- Statutes, regulations, or policies requiring certain information types to receive special consideration with respect to unauthorized disclosure or dissemination.

- Confidentiality and accuracy of the data with respect to business functions and needs.

Data Security Breach

Despite efforts at identifying and correcting security vulnerabilities, weaknesses will remain given the difficulty in sustaining a fully secured posture. The intentional or accidental exploitation of such weaknesses to obtain unauthorized access to information can result in a data security incident or breach. More specifically, a breach can be defined as any known or suspected circumstance that results in an actual or possible unauthorized release of information deemed sensitive by the organization or subject to regulation or legislation. This can include the unauthorized acquisition, use, alteration, disclosure, retention, and destruction of data that compromises the confidentiality, integrity, or availability of sensitive information maintained by the organization or by a third-party provider under contract to the organization.

An incident can include events that do not constitute an actual compromise or breach but nonetheless pose a security risk to the organization, such as the violation of an explicit or implicit information security policy that can increase the risk of a compromise, or any adverse event whereby the confidentiality, integrity, or availability of organizational information could be threatened accidentally or intentionally.

Specific regulations and laws can also have very specific definitions of incidents, particularly of breaches that warrant notification and reporting to regulators and the affected parties.

An incident can be the result of accidental or intentional actions, by internal or external parties. However, good faith acquisition of sensitive information by an employee for business purposes is not a breach provided that the information is not used or subject to further unauthorized disclosure.

Incidents can have one or more root causes, including negligent employees, negligent third parties, malicious internal or external parties, and unaddressed process or technical vulnerabilities.

There are several ways in which data breach incidents can lead to the compromise of sensitive information. Some common ways include:

- Lost or stolen laptops or storage devices.
- Theft of intellectual property.
- Attempted or actual unauthorized access to systems or information.
- Unauthorized sharing of data.
- Improper handling or disposal of data.
- Compromised user accounts.
- Inappropriate use or sharing of passwords.
- Intentional or unintentional noncompliance with organizational security policies and processes.
- Noncompliance by a party with contractual obligations regarding the safeguard of sensitive information.

Data Loss Consequences

The consequences of a loss of sensitive information can affect both the organization and any external party whose information was compromised. The principal issue is the threat of misuse of the breached information, especially if this misuse leads to identity theft or fraud.

Impact

For the organization, a loss of sensitive information at a minimum will entail the cost of responding to and managing the incident along with the associated productivity loss. Beyond that, it can include one or more of the following:

- Regulatory or legal impact if the incident will likely result in regulatory attention, legal penalties, civil action, or governmental prosecution.

- Customer impact if the incident resulted in a disruption of customer service or in a loss of customer accounts.

- Reputational impact if the incident resulted in negative publicity and/or negatively impacted the reputation of the organization.

- Financial impact if the incident resulted in or is likely to result in a financial loss or expense.

Identity Theft

Identity theft and identity fraud refer to all types of crime in which someone wrongfully obtains and uses another person's personal data in some way that involves fraud or deception, typically for economic gain. A baseline definition can be found in the US Identity Theft and Assumption Deterrence Act of 1998, in which identity theft is described as a range of illegal activities that use a person's personal information to perpetrate a crime. The act identifies offenders as anyone who "…knowingly transfers or uses, without lawful authority, any name or number that may be used, alone or in conjunction with any other information, to identify a specific individual with the intent to commit, or to aid or abet, any unlawful activity…".

There are several forms of identity theft:

- The use of financial account identifiers to access an individual's existing accounts and make unauthorized charges or withdrawals.

- The use of identifiers such as social security or other identification numbers to open new accounts and incur charges and credit in an individual's name without that person's knowledge. These identifiers can also be used for other fraudulent activity such as impersonation.

- Criminal identity theft, which occurs when an imposter gives another individual's name and information to a law enforcement officer during an investigation or arrest. This can result in the creation of a criminal record for the victim and lead to issuance of a warrant or to denial of employment.

One reason that identity theft can be so destructive to its victims is the sheer amount of time and energy often required to remediate its consequences. Recovering from identity theft can be a lengthy, costly, and stressful process. There will be time and expense spent clearing credit reports with credit-reporting agencies, disputing charges with individual creditors, or monitoring credit reports for additional impacts of the theft.

Perhaps the most valuable piece of information for the identity thief is the social security number or national identification number. This and a name can be used in many cases to open an account and obtain credit or other benefits in the victim's name. Other data, such as account numbers and passwords, are also valuable because they enable thieves to access existing consumer accounts.

A data breach need not lead to identity theft, and identity theft often arises from compromised data obtained from sources not associated with data breaches. The chance that the exposed data will be used for that purpose depends upon a number of factors, such as the circumstances surrounding the breach, the accessibility of the exposed data, and the type of information exposed.

However, since the consequences are severe, a real concern arises even if a small percentage of parties whose information was breached end up becoming victims of identity theft. Moreover, any notification of a data breach, even if a risk analysis indicates that it will not result in identity theft, will influence consumers' behavior and confidence and may lead to the termination of their relationship with the organization that mishandled their private and confidential information. The consequence may be damage to an organization's reputation as well as the opportunity cost of lost business. This loss of confidence can arise within the organization itself, since the loss of confidence in the security of a particular system or data store can render it hesitant or unwilling to engage in new initiatives or ventures.

Organizational Costs

Data breaches can result in multiple and significant organizational costs, including:

- **Personnel** Personnel costs in dealing with the incident, including the time of all employees who participated in the response.

- **Staff productivity** Productivity loss of employees who were prevented from working, experienced a slowdown in work because of the incident, or had to be redeployed to contain the breach and mitigate its consequences.

- **Lost business** Costs related to the inability to service customers and the opportunity cost of customers terminating or modifying their relationship with the organization.

- **Victim notification** The time and expense to determine the affected parties, collect and analyze contact information, and send the notification.

- **Victim assistance** Services offered to victims to help minimize the impact of the breach, including credit monitoring, data breach monitoring, identity theft insurance, and other incentives.

- **Call center** Incremental or existing customer care center to respond to inquiries.

- **Media management** Press plan, preparation and release of press statement, and other public relations activities.

- **Consulting services** Specialties that the organization does not have in house or to supplement existing skills.

- **Legal fees** Fees associated with legal advice in managing the breach and to represent the organization during regulatory review or civil litigation.

- **Regulatory or legal penalties** Fines assessed by regulatory agencies as well as potential compensatory and punitive penalties that may be assessed civilly.

- **Reputational** This can be one of the most serious effects of a data breach due to the loss of current customers and the opportunity costs of lost future business.

- **Competitive advantage** Business effect of competitors obtaining released sensitive information.

- **Credit rating and stock price** Effect of breach publicity on stock price and credit rating.

Prevention and Safeguards

By its very definition, sensitive information must be protected from unauthorized disclosure. This protection is necessary for several reasons, including:

- Maintaining reputational integrity through customer and constituent confidence and loyalty in the organization's products, services, efficiency, and trustworthiness.

- Protecting the confidentiality of sensitive personal and financial data.

- Protecting sensitive operational data from inappropriate disclosure or use by competitors or other parties.

- Preserving the integrity of business relationships with vendors and third parties.

- Avoiding fraud.

- Avoiding litigation.

- Complying with pertinent legal and regulatory requirements relating to data and privacy safeguards.

A variety of safeguards and controls are employed to protect sensitive data. Information security controls are the technical, process, physical, and policy safeguards designed to protect sensitive data. This usually is accomplished through a multipronged approach of multiple layers of different types of protection presenting unique obstacles in order to increase the likelihood of identifying and preventing any unauthorized disclosure from occurring.

A basis upon which controls can be implemented is a data classification scheme to help the organization in categorizing information assets, defining their sensitivity and confidentiality, and identifying the appropriate level of protection. The classification scheme can help ensure that sensitive data has adequate security controls, and conversely that less sensitive data does not have unnecessary controls that can lead to access restrictions and increased costs.

Classification and confidentiality levels within the scheme define appropriate protection profiles for the data, based on the potential impact of a data breach of that information.

In addition to the classification scheme that can guide in the implementation of appropriate controls for various types of data, the organization should develop and enforce a data security policy. This will form the basis of an effective data security program. The policy provides a formal statement of the organization's approach to managing information security protecting data assets while establishing expectations for data confidentiality, integrity, and availability.

Response

Preventative activities based on risk assessments will help lower the risk of a data incident and possibly mitigate its effects, but information security policies or safeguards will not guarantee total protection of information and systems. Efforts at addressing vulnerabilities and implementing safeguards will not eliminate all weaknesses because of the great amount of resources needed to maintain security commensurate with all known or yet to be identified potential vulnerabilities.

Effective incident handling also requires the implementation of response mechanisms for such an eventuality before it occurs in order to make informed decisions that will protect the organization, its customers, employees, and partners in case of a data breach. A plan to manage detection, analysis, and response to security breaches is a strategic undertaking, which can make the difference between a catastrophic occurrence and a controlled event.

Most organizations above a certain size will need to engage in some kind of advance planning for this contingency, since the ability to respond quickly and effectively is critical to minimizing the effects of the breach. Beyond responding to the possibility of an incident, such planning may in some cases be mandated by law or regulation and may also help reduce liability by demonstrating proactive consideration for this eventuality.

A documented response program will provide a defined roadmap in case of an incident and reduce the number of decisions that need to be made under the pressure of the event, thus allowing the organization to more efficiently recover from a data security incident. The structure and scope of the response program will reflect the size and complexity of the organization.

The program will include the formation and staffing of a Data Breach Response Team responsible for managing an incident, procedures for evaluating the severity of an incident, description of appropriate measures to contain and control the breach, and notification guidelines to affected parties if an analysis indicates that the compromised data might be misused.

Notification

A key part of an organization's duty to protect sensitive information against unauthorized access is the notification of affected parties of a data breach involving their information. If an internal investigation determines that the misuse of this information has occurred or is reasonably possible, the organization should expeditiously notify the affected parties, despite the potential for embarrassment or inconvenience.

Timely notification is important to comply with legal and regulatory requirements. The appropriate handling of this duty will also help in managing the organization's reputational and legal risk, and will enable the affected parties to take protective measures against the consequences of identity theft or fraud.

Care is needed in defining appropriate notification criteria and thresholds, since a breach notification when there is little or no risk of harm might create unnecessary concern and confusion among the recipients.

The initial step in deciding whether to notify will be to determine whether notice-triggering information is reasonably believed to have been compromised by being accessed by or in the possession of an unauthorized party. Various laws and regulations define thresholds to make such a determination, and mandate that the notification occur if such thresholds are reached.

Since various jurisdictions have legal requirements regarding timing, care should be taken that each affected party is notified within the time limits of their local jurisdiction. However notification can be delayed upon the request of a law enforcement agency, if the data breach has not been fully contained, or if a public announcement may alert the perpetrator of the value of the information or otherwise compound the harm of the initial breach.

Notification contents usually are mandated by law or regulation, but should include a description of the breach, including estimated date and time, the manner in which the compromise occurred and was detected, the type and amount of personal information compromised, an assessment of the risk of identity theft or fraud, a description of the measures taken to manage the breach, any information and advice on what the affected parties can do to protect themselves, and contact information to obtain more information and assistance.

In addition to victim notification, communications with other parties may need to include employees, regulators, law enforcement, the media, and credit reporting agencies.

Recovering from a Data Breach

Once the incident has been successfully managed and all data and systems are fully operational, formal closure will help the organization take action against its cause and learn from it to improve current processes and procedures.

One of the most important closure activities is the Lessons Learned or post-incident review session. This will include all involved parties and review how effective the incident management process was. It will identify necessary improvements to existing policies, processes, controls, awareness and training, risk analysis, and other organizational practices.

The organization will also need to identify and tabulate the incident impact and costs. This can help justify the implementation of new safeguards and controls and determine a monetary amount if the organization pursues legal actions to recover damages. These costs include direct costs such as personnel involved in the breach response and lost productivity as well as indirect costs such as reputational or competitive advantage damage.

A final closure report will include a description of the incident, the response process used, the notification process used, actions taken to prevent further incidents, tangible and intangible damage and cost, and suggested policy and control changes. In addition to providing appropriate management and the board a detailed incident response accounting, the report will serve as a reference to assist in handling similar incidents, to identify potential areas of improvement in incident handling and reporting procedures, and to train new response team members.

Organization of the Book

This book is organized into chapters covering the various aspects of data breach management, from preparation through response and closure. Topics covered are outlined in the following chapters.

Chapter 2: Data Classification

Data classification is the process through which an organization categorizes its information assets and defines their sensitivity and confidentiality in order to identify appropriate levels of protection. This chapter covers security objectives; potential impact of a security breach; classification levels; data ownership and usage; the various phases of a data classification project, including risk assessment; and the data life cycle.

Chapter 3: Controls and Safeguards

The effective implementation of data controls and safeguards will help protect sensitive data by mitigating the risks to its confidentiality, integrity, and availability. This chapter covers the data security program, security controls, and the procedural and technical safeguards for various possible sources of data leakage.

Chapter 4: Data Security Policy

A data security policy forms the basis of the organization's approach to managing information security and outlines the essential requirements for protecting data assets. This chapter covers the policy development process, the contents of the policy, the implementation and continued update, and auditing and metrics to measure the success of the policy.

Chapter 5: Response Program

The development of a response program will help the organization to engage in advance planning for the possibility of a breach. This chapter will cover the objectives of the program, the implementation and structure of a data breach response team, and the development of a response plan that will establish procedures for handling data incidents as they occur.

Chapter 6: Detection and Reporting

This initial phase of the incident life cycle includes the detection of an incident and its reporting to the appropriate parties. This chapter covers detection sources and processes and the required reporting mechanism to the response team.

Chapter 7: Evaluation and Response

Breach evaluation is the process of analyzing the incident data, including the initial analysis, team escalation, information gathering, incident classification and scope, and severity assessment. The goal of the response is to take technical and procedural measures to limit the scope of the incident and to return the organization to a secure status. This includes containment, isolation, recovery, documentation, and forensics.

Chapter 8: Disclosure and Notification

Timely notification of the affected parties and victims of a data breach is important to comply with legal requirements, manage an organization's reputational and legal risk, and enable victims to take protective measures against the consequences of identity theft or fraud. This chapter covers the notification threshold, the identification of the recipients; the timing, scope, and contents of the notice; other necessary notifications, legal issues and requirements; and follow-up support.

Chapter 9: Closure

This phase provides closure for the incident by taking action against its cause and learning from it to improve current processes and procedures. This chapter covers lessons learned, incident impact and costs, root cause analysis and corrective actions plans, internal and external follow-ups, and incident closure.

Appendix A: Relevant Legislation

This section will cover legislation and regulations that address data breaches.

Chapter 2

Data Classification

Solutions in this chapter:

Introduction

One of the fundamental elements of an information security program is the existence of and adherence to a formal data classification scheme. Data classification allows an organization to categorize information assets and define their sensitivity and confidentiality. This facilitates data security by helping identify the appropriate level of protection as well as the audience that may access the data. Without a classification scheme, there is an increased risk that sensitive data will not have adequate security controls, or that nonsensitive or less sensitive data will have more controls than necessary, leading to unnecessary restrictions and increased costs. As such, classification is a prerequisite to establishing guidelines and system requirements for the secure generation, collection, access, storage, transmission, archiving, and disposal of data.

Each classification level defines a protection profile for data in the classification. The profile is used to both develop and assess internal controls and third-party contractual requirements. The definition of each profile is based on the potential impact of a data breach upon the organization, affecting the ability to accomplish its assigned mission, fulfill its legal responsibilities, and protect individuals.

The classification scheme should apply throughout the organization and include definitions of data ownership, security levels and controls, and retention and destruction requirements. In addition, classification guidelines should include conventions for initial classification and reclassification throughout the data life cycle to take into account current usage as well as environmental and regulatory changes.

The effort and cost involved in successfully classifying data can be substantial. They include the development of the scheme with appropriate controls based on each class of data, the identification and initial classification of the data, the actual implementation and monitoring of the controls and safeguards, and the continued effort by data owners to classify data. However, data classification has intrinsic value beyond data protection since it can provide a basis for an organization's maturity in information asset management.

Security Objectives

Security objectives will determine the classification level. Three data security objectives are commonly defined:

- **Confidentiality** Identifies how sensitive the data is with regard to unauthorized disclosure. It involves preserving authorized restrictions on information access and disclosure, including means for protecting personal privacy and proprietary information. A loss of confidentiality is the unauthorized disclosure of information.

- **Integrity** The assurance that data is protected from unauthorized changes, whether intentional or accidental. It involves guarding against improper information modification or destruction, and includes ensuring information nonrepudiation and authenticity. A loss of integrity is the unauthorized modification or destruction of information.

- **Availability** The timely and reliable access to and use of the systems responsible for processing, delivering, and storing information. A loss of availability is the disruption of access to or use of information or of an information system.

Confidentiality, integrity, and availability are designated as the CIA triad and serve as the foundation for information security. These objectives are controlled through the following stages:

- **Identification** Methods through which resources are recognized and claim their identities. Identification requires unique names or identifiers on a local or global basis so that access control can be enforced.

- **Authentication** Methods through which resources establish proof of identity and verify the authenticity of the identity declared at the identification stage. The aim is to obtain assurance that the identity declared actually belongs to the party claiming it.

- **Authorization** Methods through which resources are accorded, and exercise access rights and permissions that define what data they can access and what they can do with that data.

- **Accountability** Methods through which actions are traced to their source in order to establish responsibility for these actions. Accountability is provided mainly by logs and audit trails.

- **Nonrepudiation** Processes and controls necessary to prevent denial of actions. Nonrepudiation is a way to ensure that the originator of an action or message cannot later deny performing the action or sending the message and that the recipient of a message cannot later deny receiving the message.

Potential Impact

Three levels of potential impact on organizations or individuals can be defined should there be a breach of security via a loss of confidentiality, integrity, or availability.

Low

The potential impact is low if the loss of confidentiality, integrity, availability, or accountability could be expected to have a limited adverse effect on organizational operations, organizational assets, or individuals. A limited adverse effect means that the breach may result in:

- An operational impact of a type and duration that slightly degrades or does not affect the organization's ability to perform its primary functions.

- Minor damage to organizational assets.

- A minor competitive advantage.

- A minor financial loss.

- A minor loss of customer, shareholder, or business partner confidence.

- Minimal harm or inconvenience to individuals.

If the potential impact is low or limited, the data or system owner will determine whether corrective actions are required or will decide to accept the risk.

Moderate

The potential impact is moderate if the loss of confidentiality, integrity, availability, or accountability could be expected to have a moderate adverse effect on organizational operations, organizational assets, or individuals. A moderate adverse effect means that the breach may result in:

- An operational impact of a type and duration that significantly degrades the organization's ability to perform its primary functions.

- A significant damage to organizational assets.

- A significant competitive advantage with ensuing loss of market share.

- A significant financial loss.

- A significant loss of customer, shareholder, or business partner confidence.

- Moderate harm to individuals that does not involve the loss of personally identifiable information.

If the potential impact is moderate, corrective actions are needed and a plan must be developed to incorporate these actions within a reasonable period of time.

High

The potential impact is high if the loss of confidentiality, integrity, availability, or accountability could be expected to have a severe or catastrophic adverse effect on organizational operations, organizational assets, or individuals. A severe or catastrophic adverse effect means that the breach may result in:

- An operational impact of a type and duration that severely or completely degrades the organization's ability to perform its primary functions.

- Major damage to organizational assets, including major reputational damage.

- A major competitive advantage with ensuing loss of market share.

- A major financial loss.

- The loss of trade secret or patent protection.

- A negative effect on the company's stock value or venture capital support.

- A major loss of customer, shareholder, or business partner confidence.

- Severe harm to individuals, including the loss of personally identifiable information and the exposure to fraud and identity theft.

If the potential impact is high, there is a strong need for corrective measures. Although an existing system may continue to operate, a corrective action plan must be put in place as soon as possible.

Classification Levels

Various classification schemes have been developed and can be used depending on the needs of the enterprise. In general, a minimal number of levels should be adopted for simplicity and effectiveness, because if an attempt is made to provide overly granulated guidelines, the classification scheme likely will be unwieldy and will require excessively frequent changes. On the other hand, if the categories are too broad, then the guidelines for assigning impact levels likely will be too general to be useful.

Categories should be comprehensive so that each information asset fits into a particular classification, and mutually exclusive, so that each information asset fits into only one category.

As a best practice, the organization should begin by considering a basic classification scheme and then increasing or decreasing the number of levels based on mission and need. Three common classification levels are *confidential*, *internal*, and *public*.

Confidential

Confidential data is sensitive information whose unauthorized disclosure could have a serious adverse impact on the organization, including financial, legal, and reputation damage. It includes information whose disclosure would violate the privacy of customers and employees, information subject to legal and regulatory restrictions, and specific operating plans or strategies that are not public record.

Confidential data is intended for use by a specific group of individuals with a legitimate access need to perform their job functions. It is stored in a physically and logically secured environment and access is granted after a stringent review and approval process. It is encrypted during transmission or if it moves outside the secure environment. Finally, its disposal requires destruction or erasure of media so that the information cannot be read or reconstructed.

Examples of confidential information include operational details and results, earnings projections, organizational strategies, clients or client relationships, proprietary products, pending mergers and acquisitions, plans to raise capital, employee records, as well as sensitive third-party information subject to a nondisclosure agreement.

There are two important classes of confidential information. One is Personally Identifiable Information (PII), which includes a name in conjunction with a social security or other identifier number, driver's license number, account number, or credit/debit card number. The compromise of this information is of particular concern due to the danger of identity theft and to legislation requiring both reporting and notification of unauthorized access.

The second type is proprietary information, which is confidential nonpublic information related to or associated with the organization's products, business, or activities, including financial data or statements, research and development, existing and future product designs and specifications, marketing plans or techniques, and other processes and know-how. Proprietary information includes intellectual property such as trade secrets, copyrights, and patents. In addition to its own intellectual property, the organization may purchase or license that of other organizations and must abide by purchase or licensing agreements that control its release or duplication.

Confidential data can be organized into four general categories:

- Data whose unauthorized release would be a violation of a regulation or law.

- Data whose unauthorized release could cause severe reputational, operational, or financial loss.

- Data whose unauthorized release would constitute a violation of confidentiality agreed to as a condition of possessing the data.

- Account credentials whose unauthorized release could provide access to sensitive systems or resources.

Internal

The Internal classification is for information that is not sensitive to disclosure within the organization but is not intended for external distribution. This would comprise all information that requires some level of security protection but does not meet the criteria to place it in the confidential category. It includes information that is intended for use by employees when conducting business, such as policies and procedures, internal announcements, and operational reports, as well as nonsensitive third-party information subject to a nondisclosure agreement.

Public

Public data is information already in the public domain or that has been explicitly approved for distribution to the public. It is not sensitive in context or content, requires no special protection, and can be freely disseminated without potential harm. Examples are product and service information, publicly available financial information, job postings, press releases, and marketing material.

Table 2.1 includes examples of various classifications of information.

Table 2.1 Examples of Information Classification

Classification	Data Examples
Confidential	Personally Identifiable Information (name in conjunction with a social security or identifier number, driver's license number, account number, or credit/debit card number)
	Organizational strategies
	Operational details
	Earnings projections
	Clients or client relationships
	Proprietary products
	Nonpublic intellectual property
	Trade secrets
	Prepatent data
	Pending mergers and acquisitions
	Employee records
	Health records
	Regulated data
Internal Use	Policies and procedures
	Internal announcements and communications
	Nonsensitive operational reports
	Minutes of meetings
	Project reports
	Organizational charts
	Business partner data
	Regulatory audit and reporting data
	Employee directory and contact information
Public	Information on organization web site
	Product and service information
	Publicly available financial information
	Annual Reports
	Employment postings
	Press releases
	Marketing material

Data Ownership and Usage

The concept of data ownership designates individuals and entities that are responsible for various data usage and protection activities. The general approach is to establish responsibilities at three levels: *owner*, *custodian*, and *user*.

Owner

An owner needs to be identified for all data assets. This is usually the line-of-business manager whose organizational unit either originates or is the primary user of the data. The owner is responsible for classifying data according to the classification scheme and is ultimately responsible for ensuring that appropriate protection is defined and implemented.

For systems processing various types of data, the owner of the system is responsible for identifying the information types stored in, processed by, or generated by that system in order to facilitate the identification of the data owner.

If data responsibility is shared, the business unit that has the greatest operational need for the data or that requires the highest security, integrity, and availability of the data will be designated the primary owner. If an owner cannot be determined for a data asset, the Information Security Officer will perform that role.

Data owner responsibilities include:

- Judging the value and sensitivity of the data resources and assigning the proper classification level.

- Periodically reviewing the data to ensure it is still appropriately classified.

- Defining, implementing, and reviewing appropriate controls commensurate with the classification to ensure that data is properly safeguarded from unauthorized access, modification, disclosure, and destruction.

- Ensuring that security control objectives are addressed for the information as well as the systems that process and maintain the information.

- Ensuring that the system processing the sensitive information is maintained in an effective and controlled manner.

- Developing and maintaining a data security plan and ensuring that the relevant system and database are deployed and operated according to the agreed-upon security requirements.

- Developing access guidelines and approving or revoking access rights associated with information assets they own.

- Periodically reviewing these rights to ensure that they are still appropriate for the job requirements.

- Monitoring and ensuring continued compliance with organizational policies and external regulations.

- Communicating access and safeguard requirements to the data custodian and users.

- Maintaining responsibility for data disclosed or shared with another organization or third party.

In order to perform these functions effectively, data owners must begin by identifying and documenting systems and processes under their responsibility that store or utilize sensitive information. The documentation should include the system name, associated files and databases, location of the information, the responsible custodian or administrator, and authorized users.

In the case of a breach or suspected breach of sensitive information, the data owner will play an important discovery, reporting, and management role and will assist in acquiring information, preserving evidence, and providing additional resources as deemed necessary by the Data Breach Response Team. The data owner will also serve as a liaison between the organization and any third party involved with a breach affecting the organization's data.

The organization should implement a process to provide owners with the appropriate training and authority to fulfill their responsibilities. Additionally, procedures should be developed for assigning ownership responsibilities when the owner is unavailable and reassigning ownership upon a change of owner.

Custodian

A data custodian is the person or organization entrusted with implementing and managing the necessary safeguards to protect the data based on the requirements established by the owner. Custodians are responsible for protecting the information in their possession from unauthorized access as well as for performing backup and recovery functions. Custodian responsibilities include:

- Administering access requests to information properly authorized by the owner.

- Revoking access to users no longer entitled to it.

- Running regular backups and routinely testing the validity of the backup data.

- Performing data restoration from the backups when necessary.

Data owners are responsible for identifying custodians who are in possession of the information for which they are the responsible party.

User

Users are individuals or organizations who have been granted explicit authorization to access and use the information by the data owner. User responsibilities include:

- Knowing the classification level(s) of the information they access and use.

- Following the established practices and procedures around protecting that information and using it only for the purposes and in the manner approved by the data owner.

- Complying with all security measures implemented by the owner and custodian or defined by organizational security policies, procedures, standards, and guidelines.

- Maintaining confidentiality of their accounts and passwords.

- Refraining from disclosing sensitive information to other parties.

- Knowing how to contact the Data Owner, the Information Security Office, or the Data Breach Response Team for any information security questions or concerns.

- Promptly reporting security incidents or vulnerabilities.

Effective administration of user access includes account management, activity monitoring and auditing, and timely access modification or removal.

User Manager

User management is primarily responsible for notifying the owner of new user access requests, of employee transfers that involve a change of access rights or privileges, and of employee terminations that necessitate timely access revocation. Managers usually receive and distribute initial IDs and passwords for newly created user access accounts.

User managers are also responsible for ensuring that all employees in their unit are aware of appropriate security policies, procedures, and standards for protecting sensitive information and are appropriately educated and trained in these procedures.

Information Security Officer

The Information Security Officer manages the organization's information security program, including the development and implementation of security practices and compliance with policies and procedures regarding the confidentiality, integrity, and security of information assets. The Information Security Officer is responsible for:

- Defining the security requirements, controls, and mechanisms applicable to all data assets.

- Defining the methods and guidelines used to identify and classify all data assets.

- Defining the procedures for identifying data owners for all data assets.

- Defining all other data security usage, processing, transmission, storage and disposal processes and procedures.

- Performing scheduled risk assessments to evaluate vulnerabilities of and threats to the organization's data and systems.

- Developing, maintaining, and testing risk-based, cost-effective information security policies, procedures, and controls.

- Remediating any deficiencies and weaknesses in the organization's control program.

- Ensuring compliance to the policy by all users and vendors.

- Ensuring that all personnel, including contractors, receive appropriate information security awareness training.

- Facilitating the evaluation of new regulatory, legal, and best practice requirements.

The Information Security Officer will also work with and offer advice to data owners as to how they can manage their data security responsibilities. With existing systems or databases, they will help data owners meet their responsibility in complying with the Data Security Policy. With new and proposed systems, advice must be sought at the planning and development phase to ensure systems will meet the requirements before deployment.

Chief Information Officer

The Chief Information Officer (CIO) manages the organization's information technology infrastructure. As part of those duties, the CIO is responsible for:

- Ensuring that an information security program is developed, documented, and implemented to provide security for all systems and data that support the operations of the organization.

- Ensuring that information security processes are integrated with strategic and operational planning processes to secure the organization's mission.

- Ensuring that information security officers and data and system owners are given the necessary authority to secure the assets under their control.

- Designating an Information Security Officer and delegating authority to that individual to ensure compliance with applicable information security requirements.

- Reporting annually, in coordination with the other senior officials, to the executive board on the effectiveness of the information security program, including progress of remedial actions.

Data Sharing

Service Agreements or other contracts may include clauses or agreements regarding data sharing and the use, disclosure, and maintenance of data by an authorized recipient organization or third party. Data owners are not released from their responsibility for this data upon an authorized disclosure and must set the requirements for how this data can be used by the third party to whom it has been disclosed.

The agreement must contain language that defines the security level, monitoring, use, and destruction of the data based upon the data classification and requirements set by the Data owner. The recipient's data classification and controls over the data must align with any such requirements. Appropriate monitoring should be performed to ensure that all clauses of the agreement are adhered to and enforced.

Furthermore, if an agreement states that the recipient may further share the data, the subsequent recipients must adhere to the requirements of the original classification, unless the data has been de-identified or otherwise modified such that a different classification is required.

Metadata

Classification levels and other security information about particular data can be stored in associated metadata (data about data), which is labeling used to describe an information resource and define the data content. By including security information labeling as an element of the metadata, the organization can help enforce data protection policies and can reap significant benefits in terms of risk management and cost reduction. Such labeling can include access control requirements, special dissemination, handling, or distribution instructions; or other information required to enforce the data security policy.

Once the discovery process has identified the types of data and files in the organization, metadata about its sensitivity (as well as other attributes) is applied. Metadata may be maintained at the system level, table level, document level, or more granularly based on needs and capabilities. This metadata can additionally be stored in a database that can be searched and referenced. Based on metadata and content, organizations can fine-tune access controls and file privileges.

On an information security level, data labeling need not be a complex undertaking. Simple splash screens when accessing sensitive data or information stored in the file properties dialog box of sensitive files can provide an initial layer of security.

Metadata should be captured at the point of data creation. It can include the data's owner, current classification, initial classification, any event or date upon which classification may change, and any supplemental markings. Appropriate retention, protection, and disposal requirements can also be captured in an object's metadata.

Classification Project

A data classification project generally is managed by the Information Security Officer and offers a structured and systematic approach to data classification in larger environments. It generally is comprised of the following phases:

1. Create an information asset inventory.
2. Specify the classification criteria.
3. Classify the data.
4. Assess risk for each classification level.
5. Implement classification level controls.
6. Document exceptions to the classification policy.

Create an Information Asset Inventory

The first step in the implementation of any classification scheme is to develop an information asset inventory to identify, locate, and classify data requiring safeguards.

A team under the direction of the Information Security Officer will be tasked with surveying the organization's business units to determine the types and nature of information they collect and process as well as the information they access outside the organization.

Since this can involve a substantial effort, the team will identify a subset of organizational data that could present legal or security risks as the initial information to be classified. The survey will identify the following:

- Type of data and its origin
- The business unit and data owner
- A description of the intended users and uses
- The physical location of the platform holding the data
- Degree of sensitivity, including confidentiality, integrity, and availability
- Data usage, storage, and disposal
- A description of security controls
- Existing relevant policies
- Legal, regulatory, or contractual requirements governing the data
- Whether contact information is kept for all parties whose Personally Identifiable Information is stored
- Current and past material events affecting this data

To ensure that all sensitive data is identified, the team also should identify patterns indicating where sensitive information may be used and stored, including employee types or classes that have access to and use of the data, and the original source of the data. These patterns also identify questions that can be asked in determining whether a breached system is likely to have contained sensitive information.

In identifying data owners, a line-of-business focus should be applied, since data ownership is not an IT responsibility. The data owner is the business unit manager responsible for the specific system that makes the greatest use of a particular data collection. The head of a particular unit or their delegate will be able to clarify ownership for the various systems and data stores.

One method of facilitating data collection and developing the asset inventory is through surveys completed by appropriate data owners. The survey will include the following information requests:

- Server host name.

- Database type or data management tool.

- Dependencies on other systems and data.

- Application used to access the data.

- Name and contact of data owner.

- Name and contact of custodian.

- Types of users accessing this data.

- Sensitive data elements stored in database.

- For Personally Identifiable Information, type and number of individuals for whom data is stored.

- Description of all security methods used to protect the data.

- Description of possible risks and vulnerabilities.

- Description and severity of any incident involving the data.

Other methods of obtaining this information are individual or group meetings with data owners. Even though brainstorming and freeform feedback can be encouraged, these meetings should be clearly structured with a specific direction and questions in order to effectively manage the large number of meetings likely to be required.

Specify the Classification Criteria

The Information Security Manager will establish a system to classify the organization's data with respect to its level of confidentiality. It is advisable to restrict the number of classification levels to a manageable number to reduce maintenance and increase compliance.

It is possible that certain business units might require additional or different classification levels. While this can be accommodated, it should generally be discouraged to promote standardization, especially in cases where data might flow from one business unit or one system to another.

Once the classification levels are defined, a matrix will be created, which will include the various levels as well as the type of information that will fall under each level. This will guide data owners in classifying their data.

Classify the Data

The owner of each system, or an individual designated by the owner, is responsible for identifying the types of data stored in, processed by, or generated by that system. The owner will use the organizational data classification matrix as the basis for the effort. Several questions can guide the owner in determining the appropriate classification:

- What would be the impact if the data was compromised, particularly regarding monetary damage, reputational damage, and contractual or regulatory obligations?

- What are the information types that are required by statute, regulation, or policy to receive special consideration with respect to unauthorized disclosure or dissemination?

- How essential to business functions are the confidentiality and accuracy of the data?

Where applicable, a monetary value can be assigned to the data based upon the original, replacement, or recreation cost; penalties arising from legal or regulatory violations; potential revenue loss; and potential loss arising from disclosure, modification, destruction, or misuse of the information. This assigned monetary value can be used as the basis for determining the cost/benefit of protecting the asset.

The owner will select provisional classification levels, which can then be reviewed for appropriateness based on the environment, use, and connectivity associated with the data under review. Adjustments can then be made as appropriate.

Once the specific data assets are identified and classified, any resources such as systems or applications that store or process that data must also be classified. Although the appropriate classification of most data elements will be apparent to the owner, it should be kept in mind that most systems usually do not clearly segregate more sensitive from less sensitive elements. In cases where data with a higher sensitivity is stored together and cannot be reasonably and effectively partitioned away from data with a lower sensitivity, then the higher classification will apply to the entire application, database, or system, and the most sensitive data element in the collection will determine the classification category for the entire collection.

After the initial classification project, data owners should review and update categories and protection profiles on a scheduled basis to ensure that the classification remains valid by addressing new technologies, appropriateness of existing controls, new risks and vulnerabilities, regulatory or process changes, and other changes in data sensitivity.

Special Considerations

Now let's discuss some special considerations.

Aggregation

Data aggregation refers to the gathering of information in separate sets from multiple sources. Often, this data is stored in a data warehouse in a summarized form. Aggregation allows patterns in the data to emerge, and these patterns are the basis for analysis and decision making.

Data aggregates should be classified at the most secure classification level of any individual component. An additional consideration in this case is that some data may have less sensitivity in isolation than when aggregated with other data, since the sensitivity of a data element is likely to be greater in context than in isolation, as is the case with Personally Identifiable Information or when the aggregate can reveal sensitive patterns or plans.

If review reveals increased sensitivity or criticality associated with information aggregates, then the system categorization may need to be adjusted to a higher level than would be indicated by the impact associated with any individual information type in order to reflect the increased sensitivity.

Extracts

Data extracts are multiple records of information that are copied or extracted from an originating database and maintained outside of that database. Requests for data extraction are to be evaluated based on guidelines determined by the data owner. The risks from extracted sensitive data can be reduced by:

- Limiting the amount of sensitive data extracted in each record.

- Limiting the number of records in the extract to the smallest number needed.

- Deleting the extract as soon as it is no longer needed.

Impact on Other Data or Systems

Compromise of some types of data types may have low impact in the context of a system's primary function but may have much more significance when viewed in the context of the potential impact of compromising other systems or data to which the system in question is connected, or other systems that are dependent on that system's information.

If access to a data type or system might result in some form of access to other data types or systems, the sensitivity and criticality attributes of all data and systems to which such indirect access can result needs to be considered. Similarly, some information may have low sensitivity or criticality attributes; however that information may be used by other systems to enable more sensitive or critical functions.

Unstructured Data

One particularly complex issue is the classification and control of unstructured data, which is data residing outside of a database, such as files on a network, reports, and emails. A multitiered approach to security will be required, with clear policies and appropriate access control to the data as well as to the underlying file systems. The approach will include:

- **Content Inventory:** An inventory of the actual contents of shared files along with metadata gleaned from the individual file properties. For each folder, this also will include contents of subfolders as well as access rights.

- **Access Review:** A review and reauthorization of access permissions in order to restrict particular folder access to appropriate groups and individuals.

- **Data Properties:** Data with no known owners or that has not been accessed for an extended period of time should be removed from active storage. Conversely, frequently accessed files or files identified as sensitive should be moved to active database storage where possible.

Perform Risk Assessment

The scope and nature of an organization's activities as well as the scale and complexity of its operations will affect the nature of the threats it will face. A risk assessment will help identify and understand reasonably foreseeable threats as well as the likelihood and potential damage of identified threats, taking into consideration the sensitivity of the information. Assessing risk is one element of a broader set of risk management activities. Other elements include implementing appropriate policies and controls, promoting awareness, and monitoring and evaluating policy and control effectiveness.

Within the context of information security, a vulnerability is a weakness associated with an asset and represents a condition or set of conditions that may allow a threat to affect an asset, either with greater frequency, greater impact, or both. Typically a vulnerability is a consequence of flawed procedures, untrained staff, or incorrectly configured or defective technology. For a vulnerability to be exploitable it must be known to or discoverable by a threat, which is the intentional or accidental cause of an unwanted event that may result in harm to an asset.

Risk is the potential that a given threat will exploit vulnerabilities to compromise an asset's confidentiality, integrity, or availability. The security risk level is determined from the combination of the asset value and sensitivity and assessed levels of related threats and associated vulnerabilities.

A risk assessment is a prerequisite to the implementation of information security strategies and controls. It consists of the analysis of information assets in relation to potential threats and vulnerabilities, resulting in a ranking of risks to mitigate. The assessment must be sufficient in scope to identify the threats from both within and outside an organization's operations that could result in unauthorized disclosure, misuse, alteration, or destruction of information. It should also address risks to information stored on systems owned or managed by third-party providers.

Because risk cannot be eliminated entirely, the risk management process will help the organization balance the operational and economic costs of protective measures.

Assessment Elements

A risk assessment incorporates various components such as the organizational data in question, its vulnerabilities, the possible threats and their likelihood, the consequences of a compromise, and the available controls and safeguards. It generally includes:

- **Data Valuation** The criticality level of the data. This can consist of its intrinsic value, sensitivity, as well as the impact and consequences of a compromise.

- **Threat Identification** A review and understanding of the threats that could harm and thus adversely affect critical information assets. Threats will be identified and analyzed to determine occurrence likelihood and potential harm.

- **Occurrence Likelihood** The estimate of the probability that such threats will materialize and that a particular vulnerability will be exploited based on historical information and judgment of knowledgeable individuals. Likelihood can be classified as Frequent (possibility of repeated incidents),

Possible (probability of infrequent or isolated incidents), and Remote (unlikely or highly improbable occurrence).

- **Consequence Assessment** The estimate of potential immediate and aggregate losses or damage, both direct and indirect, that could occur if a threat materializes. This can also be designated as the Business Impact Assessment (BIA) and will directly affect the severity of the identified risk.

- **Vulnerability Analysis** An analysis of possible weaknesses in or absence of data security processes and controls that could be exploited by a threat.

- **Control and Safeguard Identification** The identification of implemented or needed controls to mitigate or reduce the vulnerability to a threat. This will include an examination of the effectiveness of the existing controls as well as the identification of new controls that need to be implemented.

- **Action Plan** A documentation of the results of the risk assessment including the development of an immediate and longer-term plan to address the findings. The plan should include a schedule for taking the recommended actions for each of the assessed units, or for the areas that are determined to be most susceptible to loss.

Models

There are various models and methods for assessing risk. A quantitative approach attempts to assign independently objective numeric values to the components of risk assessment and to the assessment of potential losses by estimating the monetary cost of risk and risk reduction techniques based on the likelihood that a damaging event will occur, the costs of potential losses, and the costs of mitigating actions. This approach may be suitable where risks can be quantified and provides methods to use in probability-based appraisals of return-on-security investment.

A qualitative approach addresses more intangible values of loss and typically attempts to produce scenarios so risk can be anticipated and managed. It defines risk in more subjective and general terms where explicit scales, such as high, medium, and low, are used for likelihood, consequences, and determined level of risk. It depends more on the expertise, experience, and judgment of those conducting the assessment.

Approach

Since an analysis of information security risks could be time and resource intensive, a more focused approach may involve conducting an initial high-level data risk analysis to identify risks that are common across areas, as well as unusual and potentially serious risks that may require a more detailed analysis.

The high-level analysis initially considers the business value, the sensitivity, and associated risks of the data to help determine which risks require further analysis. The general rule is that if inadequate information security can result in significant harm or damage to an organization, its processes, or its assets, then a detailed risk analysis is necessary to identify suitable control options.

A previous risk analysis can lay the foundation of the current analysis when combined with updates to risk, vulnerabilities, data and data classification, and compliance requirements. In all approaches, a comprehensive listing of potential threat sources, or risk matrix, will be used to create a risk profile for each selected information asset. It will identify the sensitivity of each asset, the possible threats as well as their probabilities, the vulnerability of the asset to the threats, and the impact of the threat. This will allow the assignment of a relative value to each event and will be used to prioritize the control and risk mitigation efforts. When assessing likelihood the timeframe for the possible event should be taken into account.

Existing inputs that can facilitate the creation of the risk matrix include any prior risk assessments, audit comments, security requirements, and security test results.

Considerations

While conducting the risk assessment and developing control recommendations, the following questions should be considered:

- What processes, controls, and safeguards currently exist?

- Are these controls effective in reducing risk to an acceptable level?

- Are these controls the most cost effective considering the sensitivity of the data and the adverse consequences if the risk occurs?

- Are there specific laws and regulations that must be complied to governing data confidentiality and integrity and are there areas of potential noncompliance?

- What new controls are needed?

- What resources are needed to implement and manage the controls?

- Who will have responsibility and accountability for managing the risk and implementing the appropriate controls?

Risk Management Options

Individual risks can be managed through a combination the following options:

- **Acceptance** An informed decision to accept the consequences and the likelihood of a particular risk. A risk can be accepted by the organization with the knowledge of the potential threats and vulnerabilities to the information asset if a risk analysis indicates that the exposure is within a certain tolerance level, if the cost of treatment outweighs the benefit, or if there is no treatment for the risk.

- **Mitigation** A selective application of appropriate safeguards and controls to reduce or eliminate the level of risk exposure or the likelihood of an occurrence, its consequences, or both. Mitigation includes the development of a data security incident response plan and the implementation of a specific response in case of a data breach.

- **Transfer** The shift or transfer of risk management and possible loss or cost responsibility or burden to another asset, another process, or another party. This can be accomplished through redesigning a service offering, outsourcing a process, insurance, service contracts, or other means.

- **Avoidance** An informed decision not to accept a risk situation. This can include elimination of the asset's exposure or even the asset itself.

Key Practices

The effectiveness of the risk assessment is related directly to the following key practices:

- **Multidisciplinary Review** An accurate evaluation of various risk and control practices requires the involvement of a broad range of subject matter experts to ensure that the assessment takes into account various approaches to and opinions about the severity of various risks, the importance of various controls, and the sensitivity and criticality of various data elements and systems. In particular, business managers generally have the best understanding of the criticality and sensitivity of individual business operations and of the systems and data that supported these operations, and usually are in the best position to gauge the impact of data compromise and misuse.

- **Systematic and Centralized Approach** A centralized and coordinated approach will help ensure risk assessment standardization, coordination, consistency, and completeness. It will also facilitate an organizational view of risks and lessons learned from the risk assessment process.

- **Defined Procedures** Defined and documented procedures for conducting risk assessments will facilitate the process and ensure a certain level of assessment consistency. These procedures will specify staff responsible for initiating and conducting assessments, specific steps to be followed, approvals needed, and reporting mechanisms.

Documentation

Appropriate documentation of the risk assessment process as well as of the particular decisions to mitigate or accept risk will ensure consistency and completeness as well as accountability. This documentation will provide a useful starting point for subsequent assessments as well as a ready source of information for managers and staff. In addition, appropriate documentation will serve to:

- Formally report the results of risk assessment activities.

- Demonstrate that the risk assessment process has been carried out correctly.

- Provide organizational managers and data owners with sufficient information to make sound risk-based decisions on resource allocation and risk mitigation.

- Provide evidence and an audit trail of decisions and actions.

- Facilitate continuing monitoring and review.

- Share and communicate information.

Update

Because risks, vulnerabilities, regulations, and processes change over time, risk assessment is an ongoing process. Organizations periodically should reassess risks and reconsider the appropriateness and effectiveness of policies and controls to make certain they are adequate to safeguard sensitive information and systems. The assessment should be repeated when changes occur that could impact the confidentiality, integrity, or availability of the data.

In the event the reassessment identifies new risks or inadequate controls, a control deficiency will be opened and tracked until compliance is achieved or mitigating controls have been implemented.

The risk assessment methodology should be updated as necessary to account for data and system changes before they are implemented or new products or services before they are offered.

Challenges

Reliably assessing information security risks can be challenging because of the imprecise nature of any estimate concerning likelihood and cost of a data compromise and because of the variable nature of risk factors.

Certain costs, such as the reputational impact from the loss of sensitive information, the possible associated legal or regulatory liability, and the possible loss of productivity that may result when new controls are implemented, are inherently difficult to quantify and estimate. This lack of reliable data may preclude a precise determination of which information security risks are the most significant and which associated controls are the most effective.

Even though the data on threat likelihood and on the costs of risk reduction techniques may be limited, this does not preclude effectively exploring, understanding, and ranking information security risks by employing qualitative methods that efficiently achieve the benefits of risk assessment while avoiding attempts to develop seemingly precise quantitative results that are of questionable reliability.

Develop Control Implementation Plan

Upon the completion of the risk assessment, a prioritized list of the risks is produced along with recommendation for corrective actions based on the level of risk and the criticality of the asset. This will provide an overview of the risk level and pattern, focus attention on the higher risk and sensitivity items, help determine immediate actions as well as future activities, and facilitate the allocation of resources.

Based upon the risk assessment, business and technical units will develop action plans for implementing the recommendations with the priorities established within short, medium, and long timeframe. The plan should include:

- Security objectives in terms of confidentiality, integrity, and availability of information.

- Risk assessment results including the designated owners of each risk.

- Existing and planned controls, with priority designation and estimated effectiveness.

- A mapping of controls to risks on a one-to-one, one-to-many, and many-to-many basis.

- Appraisal of the residual risk that remains to the information asset after control implementation.

- Implementation details, including schedule, priority, budget, and responsibility.

- Estimated implementation costs for new controls and operating costs for existing controls.

- Awareness and training needed to ensure the effectiveness of the controls.

- Scheduled risk assessment monitoring, reporting, review, and maintenance.

Should a recommendation not be implemented, a justification or Risk Acceptance (RA) must be submitted and approved to document the justification and suggest an alternative solution for reducing the risk.

Types of Classification Level Controls

A variety of policies, procedures, and controls must be evaluated and adopted to appropriately address the risks identified through the risk assessment. Several types of controls must be considered and, if appropriate, adopted. The following are examples of the types of controls that can be implemented as part of the organization's data security program.

Device and Media Controls

These are policies, procedures, and other safeguards such as encryption to protect sensitive information stored on laptops, portable storage devices, and other transportable media.

Technical Safeguards Technical procedures and systems to detect actual and attempted attacks on or intrusions into information systems or databases. These include firewalls, intrusion detection and prevention systems, penetration testing and vulnerability scanning, anti-virus and patch management, data transmission and remote access, and email controls.

Access Controls Access procedures and mechanisms data to authenticate and permit access only to authorized individuals. This includes access provisioning, accounts and password management, entitlement reviews, privileged account control, developer access to production, and physical access controls.

Systems Development Software assurance to ensure that provisions are included for built-in security of developed or acquired software.

Change Management Procedures designed to ensure that sensitive information system modifications are consistent with the institution's information security program.

Monitoring and Logging Monitoring of user activity and periodic review of access logs and entitlements.

Backup and Recovery Data backup procedures to ensure scheduled backups of sensitive data as well as periodic recovery testing of the backup data.

Third-Party Vendor Management Due diligence practices in selecting and monitoring third-party providers.

Data Disposal Appropriate disposal practices to prevent unauthorized access to or use of sensitive information once it is no longer needed for a particular business purpose.

Security Training Effective data security training to ensure that employees will effectively adhere to and carry out the organizational security policy.

Scheduled Control Auditing and Testing Risk-based audit programs to ensure the adequate implementation and effectiveness of data security policies and procedures.

Response Program Documented response program that specifies actions to be taken when the organization suspects or detects that unauthorized individuals have gained access to sensitive data.

Document Exceptions to Recommended Controls

Exceptions to information security policies and controls are appropriate only when compliance would cause adverse financial or reputational impact that would not be offset by the reduced risk occasioned by compliance. Data owners should clearly understand that a control deficiency in one data collection or system can jeopardize other systems because erroneous data may be inherited and security compromised.

With the assistance of the Information Security Officer, data owners should prepare a Risk Acceptance (RA), which describes the risks, the reasons for the lack of compliance with a policy or standard, a justification for why the exception is warranted, the compensating controls implemented to address the risk, the expiration date of the exception, and review procedures. The RA also will clearly identify the acceptance of responsibility for the risks associated with the exception. Typically, RAs are required for all instances of significant or material noncompliance with the classification policy or recommended controls.

If the risk exposure is exclusively related to a business unit's data or systems, the business unit head is responsible for deciding if the risk should be accepted. If the risk exposure affects multiple business units, the responsibility for the accepting the risk escalates to higher management levels, typically the chief information officer, for a decision.

After the RA is completed and signed by the responsible manager, it is submitted for review and approval to the information security office, risk management group, relevant audit staff, and other interested parties. A consensus is reached to approve or deny the exception, or suggest additional compensating controls to reduce the exposure.

Approved exceptions should be reviewed on a scheduled basis. The reevaluation determines if the exposure still exists, what progress has been made to mitigate the exposure, and if the acceptance of the exposure is still appropriate.

The Data Life Cycle

Data must be secured throughout the data life cycle, including receipt or generation, storage, access and use, distribution and transmittal, maintenance, and disposal. Since the sensitivity of information can change over its life cycle, the classification may change as well as the data moves through the various life cycle stages. A risk assessment can identify those change factors and help in adjusting resources and controls to safeguard the information as its criticality changes. Even though the classification may change throughout the data life cycle, each discrete type of data should belong to only one classification level at any one stage of the life cycle in order to facilitate the efficient and cost-effective implementation of controls an safeguards.

For each stage of the life cycle, the assessment will help determine:

- The form in which the data exists.
- The physical and logical locations at which the data exists.
- The access and processing levels and permissions required.
- The risks and vulnerabilities.
- The implemented or desirable controls, including existence and effectiveness.

This assessment will provide a baseline that can be used to develop and implement controls that should be applied at each phase of the life cycle.

Information protection throughout the life cycle should be viewed as separate from systems protection since in many cases data will routinely flow in and out of the trusted organizational network through numerous access points.

Summary

- A data classification scheme will help an organization to categorize information assets and define their sensitivity and confidentiality in order to identify the appropriate level of protection.

- Data security objectives will determine the classification level and include confidentiality, which identifies how sensitive the data is with regard to unauthorized disclosure; integrity, which is the assurance that data is protected from unauthorized changes; and availability, which consists of the timely and reliable access to systems and data.

- The potential impact of a data security breach can be classified as Low, Moderate, or High, depending on the resulting level of harm to the organization and individuals.

- Common data sensitivity classification levels include Confidential, for sensitive information whose unauthorized disclosure could have a serious adverse impact on the organization; Internal, for information that is not intended for external distribution; and Public, for information in the public domain or that has been explicitly approved for distribution to the public.

- Data ownership is used to designate individuals and entities responsible for data usage and protection activities. The Data Owner is the line-of-business manager responsible for classifying data and for ensuring that appropriate protection is defined and implemented. The Data Custodian implements the necessary safeguards to protect the data based on the requirements established by the owner, and the Data User is granted authorization to use the data for a particular business purpose.

- The first step in any classification scheme is the development of an information asset inventory to identify, locate, and classify data requiring safeguards.

- Data will be classified by the owner taking into account confidentiality, impact of compromise, and legal requirements.

- A risk assessment will help identify reasonably foreseeable threats as well as their likelihood and potential damage, and is a prerequisite to the implementation of information security strategies and controls.

- Based upon the risk assessment, safeguards and controls will be implemented and managed in order to protect organizational data assets.

- Policy and control exceptions are appropriate in case the cost or impact of implementation is not offset by the reduced risk occasioned by compliance.

- Data must be secured throughout its life cycle, including generation, storage, access, use, transmission, maintenance, and disposal.

Chapter 3

Controls and Safeguards

Solutions in this chapter:

- **Data Security Program**
- **Security Controls**
- **Technical Safeguards**
- **Access Control**
- **Activity Logging and Monitoring**
- **Software Assurance**
- **Change Management**
- **Disaster Recovery/Business Continuity Planning**
- **Training and Awareness**
- **Auditing**
- ☑ **Summary**

Data Security Program

An organization's data security program will enable the management and control of identified data security risks. It can significantly influence reputational, operational, legal, and strategic risks by limiting the organization's vulnerability to data compromise and maintaining third-party confidence and trust.

The data security program includes data classification and the associated risk assessment, an information security strategy to mitigate the risks, the implementation of controls to protect the data, monitoring and testing of the controls to verify that they are appropriate, effective, and performing as intended, and a process to continuously gather and analyze new threats and vulnerabilities in order to update the risk assessment, strategy, and controls.

The successful implementation of a data security program will depend on several factors, including:

- Security policies, procedures, and controls based on business objectives.

- A security approach consistent with organizational culture.

- Visible management support and commitment.

- A thorough understanding of security requirements based on a risk management approach.

- Implementation and testing of controls.

- Appropriate policy and standards distribution, training, and education.

Security Controls

Information security controls are the technical, process, physical, and policy safeguards designed to protect sensitive data by mitigating the identified and assessed risks to its confidentiality, integrity, and availability. The selection and specification of controls is accomplished as part of an organizationwide risk management and information security program and is typically dependent on risk mitigation objectives balanced by implementation cost.

Management Responsibility

Senior management has the responsibility to ensure integration of security controls throughout the organization by ensuring the security program is governed by organizational policies and practices that are consistently applied, enforcing compliance with the security program across the organization, and ensuring an effective information security awareness program has been implemented.

In order to delineate clear lines of responsibility and accountability for information security risk management decisions, management should designate one or more individuals as information security officers, who will be responsible and accountable for administration of the security program. To ensure appropriate segregation of duties, the information security officers should report directly to the board or to senior management and have sufficient independence to perform their assigned tasks.

While information security officers may ultimately be responsible for the management of the security program and the implementation of appropriate safeguards, a system of internal control is not a separate and distinct system within an organization, but the embodiment of all the plans and devices that assure reasonable control over risks and operations. Accordingly, the responsibility for good internal controls rests with the management of the individual business units and not with any external unit. The same managers who are responsible for day-to-day operations and decision making are also responsible for ensuring the presence and effectiveness of internal controls.

Defense in Depth

Since it is practically impossible to eliminate all vulnerabilities in the organizational infrastructure, security should integrate and coordinate the capabilities of people, operations, and technology to establish multiple security countermeasures to protect the confidentiality and integrity of information assets. This multilayered defense strategy, called defense in depth (DiD), is an Information Assurance construct in which multiple related actions and controls are applied to minimize failures and compromises and their propagation.

Defense in Depth involves a multipronged and tiered approach in defense mechanisms. It is designed on the principle that multiple layers of different types of protection presenting unique obstacles will increase the likelihood of being able to identify and prevent an attack from occurring. Each protection layer has unique characteristics, presenting successive obstacles for an intruder to overcome. This will not only reduce the risk of security breaches, but allow an organization time to detect and respond to an attack, therefore reducing and mitigating the breach's impact.

Achieving Information Assurance through DiD requires a focus on three primary elements:

- **People** This includes senior level management attention, assignment of specific roles and responsibilities, commitment of resources, training of critical personnel, and personal accountability.

- **Technology** Multiple and layered technological defenses outside, at, and within the perimeter, including encryption, firewalls, intrusion detection, transmission and remote access controls, and antivirus and patch management.

- **Operations** The activities required to sustain an organization's security posture on a day-to-day basis, including security policies, risk assessments, security and vulnerability reviews, process controls, and incident response planning.

Control Identification

The challenge for organizations is to determine the appropriate set of security controls, which if implemented and determined to be effective in their application, would comply with the stated security requirements by mitigating the impact or likelihood of each identified threat. For each security category, a variety of controls are necessary for a comprehensive and robust security framework.

The following considerations should be addressed during control selection and implementation:

- What are the necessary controls to adequately protect organizational information?

- Have the selected security controls been implemented or is there a realistic plan for their implementation?

- What is the required level of assurance that the selected controls are effective as implemented?

The major factor that will influence the selection of safeguards and controls is a risk-based cost/benefit analysis. Other factors include ease of use, transparency to users, compatibility with existing controls, and integration with overall security management tools.

Control identification is accomplished most effectively as an organizationwide exercise, which considers the protection requirements for the various classes of information. This is especially relevant since many controls may depend on other controls and processes for proper functioning.

Control identification and implementation is performed generally by a specialized team under the direction of the Information Security Office. However data owners are ultimately responsible for the proper functioning of security controls affecting their data.

Types of Controls

Controls can be categorized by what they are and what they do. The following three broad categories define the main objectives of effective security implementation:

- **Physical Controls** Security measures, devices, and means to control physical access to a defined structure.

- **Technical Controls** Technology-based measures to control logical access to sensitive information.

- **Administrative** or **Process Controls** Policies, procedures, and processes to define and guide user actions and restrictions in dealing with sensitive information.

Within these major categories, controls can be defined by what they do, including:

- **Preventive** Preventive controls act to limit the likelihood of a threat by preventing intentional or unintentional unauthorized disclosure of sensitive information.

- **Detective** Detective controls detect and report actual or attempted unauthorized events by helping identify harmful actions as they occur.

- **Corrective** Corrective controls respond to security incidents and terminate harmful events or reduce their damage.

Baseline Approach

A baseline approach to control implementation requires the establishment of a minimum set of information safeguards against the most common threats. An appropriate and justifiable baseline can be developed based on industry practice or public standards, and existing safeguards can be compared with the baseline. A gap analysis will identify applicable controls that need to be implemented.

The benefit of the baseline approach is a simplified risk assessment. However there are several risks in using this approach, including:

- The baseline does not identify all the organization's assets or accurately reflect its environment.

- Nonstandard threats or vulnerabilities are missed by the baseline.

- The gap analysis does not accurately reflect the variation between existing and required controls.

- The baseline is used as a simple checklist and acts as a substitute for all risk management.

- The baseline may be excessive for the security risk exposure as a whole or as related to a particular control.

As a result, a baseline should not be adopted without ensuring that it is appropriate to the organization's risk profile and circumstances. However, it can be useful in identifying information security strengths and weaknesses, since the result of a security baseline analysis can enable the organization to evaluate its information security posture and identify areas for improvement.

Constraints

Several constraints may arise during control implementation and may need to be resolved on a control-by-control basis. These include:

- **Time** The acceptable implementation time period based on asset sensitivity, criticality, vulnerability, and risk exposure criteria.

- **Financial** Because of conflicting demands on financial resources, a proposed control may be partially implemented and management is prepared to accept the residual risk until additional funds become available.

- **Technical** Technical and compatibility constraints can hinder the effective implementation of controls to an existing systems or data.

- **Cultural** Individual resistance to particular controls may render them ineffective, especially if staff feels that the control hinders their work and as a result develop workarounds.

- **Legal** Legal and contractual factors may mandate or bar the selection and implementation of a particular control.

- **Skills and Training** Some controls may not operate correctly if people with the necessary skills, competencies, and training are not available.

Laptops

Lost or stolen laptops represent a significant source of data compromise and are the most frequently reported information security incidents. Any sensitive data stored on a lost or stolen laptop and potentially compromised will most likely have a much greater value than the replacement cost of the actual laptop.

As a general rule, sensitive data should not be stored on laptops or any devices that can leave a secure environment. If there is a legitimate business need to store such data on a laptop, access or downloads should be logged at the source so that there is a record of what information was copied, to where, when, and by whom.

The security requirements implemented on laptops that may potentially store sensitive information should be comparable to network-based security. These include:

- Full-disk encryption to prevent unauthorized parties from retrieving the data or from extracting domain-based credentials and user account profiles that allow access to organizational network resources. Encryption passwords should adhere to complexity standards to minimize cracking risk. The organization should consider implementing systemic disk encryption solutions that do not rely on employees' discretion as to what data to encrypt.

- Any technology that can restrict usage of the laptop to a designated individual.

- Remote tracking and data reset features that once activated will ensure that files are not readable or recoverable.

- Frequent connection to the corporate network to receive the latest software patches, antivirus files, and firewall patterns.

- A prohibition on altering system software or hardware configuration unless specifically instructed to do so by IT Services.

- A prohibition on loading additional application software onto the laptop unless specifically approved by IT Services.

- Scheduled backups of all important information on the laptop.

- Implementation and adherence to a policy describing the risks of laptop loss as well as the responsibility of the user.

- An implemented policy for specifically authorizing certain laptops to process sensitive information.

- Procedures for appropriate physical securing, proper and inconspicuous packing during transportation, and general alertness to minimize risk of theft and loss.

Sufficient attention should be given to property management. This includes conducting periodic inventories of accountable property, ensuring that departing employees return all property that had been issued to them, and adequately documenting the destruction of outdated, damaged, or excessed laptops, including sanitization of all sensitive information prior to disposal.

Portable Storage Devices

Portable storage devices such as flash drives present particular challenges because their small size increases the possibility of physical loss with the attendant data loss. Additionally, the size combined with the ease of use can allow malicious insiders to inconspicuously copy large amounts of data.

Particular care should be paid to these devices since they can also impact data and network security through the intentional or unintentional bypass of perimeter defenses such as firewalls and antivirus software and introduce viruses and malware into the network.

The organization should outline in its acceptable use policy guidelines on using portable storage devices by specifying the parameters within which they can be used. Sensitive data should not be stored on a portable storage device unless the appropriate procedure is implemented and followed for obtaining management authorization for the placement of sensitive data on the device. This can be enforced through automated means that can detect when such a device is connected to an organizational resource.

If the use of these devices is allowed by the organization, data owners will have the primary responsibility authorizing the use and storage of sensitive data on them. Controls will include:

- Provisions for training to increase awareness of the need for security in this area.

- Limiting access to authorized devices or users.

- Blocking communication with specific information resources.

- Disabling file- and print-sharing functions.

- As in the case of laptops, encryption to protect any sensitive data on the device.

- Passwords that conform to the requirements and guidelines of organizational password policies.

- A prohibition on transferring sensitive data to another device not in compliance with the policy.

- Inventory and audit trail of the sensitive data used by specific individuals on specific portable devices.

- Ensuring that there is a backup of data within a secured storage environment.

- Labeling all portable devices for individual identification, such as an asset or property tag or banner containing appropriate contact information and instructions on how to return the portable device.

- Ensuring that any loss, theft, or unauthorized access is reported promptly and appropriately.

Transportable Media

Numerous business processes may require the transfer of information via transportable media such as backup tapes. The organization should evaluate all transfers of physical media containing sensitive information to discontinue unnecessary or redundant transfers either through the elimination of the transfer or through migration to network-based transmission. This determination can be made by considering the potential risk represented by the transfer, the size of the transfer, the related business process, any infrastructure limitations, legal, regulatory, or counterparty constraints, and associated costs.

If the organization determines that these transfers cannot be terminated or transmitted in-network and that physical transfers are necessary, the following controls should be implemented:

- Sensitive data in transport should be encrypted using approved encryption algorithms where feasible.

- An exact copy of the data should be maintained in case of loss or damage.

- A complete record of transport should be maintained including contents, origin and destination, time shipped and received, who handled it during transport, and condition upon arrival.

- A Risk Acceptance should be filed when the transfer is noncompliant or encryption is not possible due to regulatory issues or other reasons.

A primary compensating control for the transfer of unencrypted physical media containing sensitive information is the use of an approved secure courier service. The media must be properly packaged in a tamper-evident container and all transfer pickups and deliveries should be logged and documented, including volume serial number, tracking number, pickup or delivery time and date, as well as the name and contact information of the individual who transported the package(s).

Under certain circumstances, and where deemed appropriate and prudent, a staff member may transport unencrypted media containing sensitive information. The media must be properly packaged, the staff member must maintain physical control over the media at all times, and must obtain written acknowledgement of receipt from the recipient.

E-mail

Now we'll discuss internal and external controls for securing e-mail communications.

Internal Controls

Any electronic communications containing sensitive information should be encrypted any time it is sent outside the organization. In addition, particularly sensitive communications should be encrypted at all times, even when sent internally. Staff members should be aware of the secure e-mail encryption requirements, have an approved encryption solution installed on their desktops, and be aware of how and when to use it. In certain instances, automated and policy-driven encryption can be used to protect the confidentiality and integrity of sensitive data when in transit without the sender's intervention.

More generally, an e-mail acceptable use policy should be implemented to clearly describe applicable restrictions on the transmission of sensitive information via e-mail.

Since it relies on open ports, a particular risk of e-mail is that it allows malicious outsiders to circumvent perimeter defenses such as firewalls through the e-mail architecture. E-mail-born viruses and malware can compromise sensitive data with the added risk of spreading to partners, vendors, and competitors.

E-mail security solutions can be installed at the network boundary or at the mail server layer to filter mail based on preconfigured or configurable standards. These include content filtering for inbound mail, traffic monitoring, and reporting. Additionally, solutions can be deployed to monitor outbound e-mail to detect information patterns and restrict the transmission of sensitive information from users not specifically authorized to transmit it.

External Controls

E-mail and Internet-related fraudulent schemes present a substantial risk to the reputation and customers of any organization that is impersonated. Current and potential customers may mistakenly perceive that weak information security resulted in security breaches that allowed access to confidential information. In addition, customers who fall prey to fraudulent schemes face a real and immediate risk from malicious parties who will normally act quickly to gain unauthorized access and commit identity theft.

If warranted, an organization should consider enhancing security programs to address possible e-mail fraudulent schemes. This may include periodic notification to alert customers of known e-mail-related fraudulent schemes and to remind them to report any such requests, monitoring accounts individually or in aggregate for unusual activity, and in general avoiding sending any e-mails that request confidential information.

Technical Safeguards

In this section, we'll discuss various technical safeguards for securing systems within an organization's environment.

Firewalls

A firewall is a system, device, or collection of components configured to manage and regulate data flow between networks of different trust levels by permitting, denying, or proxying data. Although firewalls usually are placed between an internal network and an external untrusted network such as the Internet, they can also be used to create different subnets of the organizational network.

Typically, firewalls block or allow traffic based on static or dynamic rules. Static rules are preconfigured, while dynamic rules can be the result of automated coordination between the firewall and an intrusion detection system.

For a higher security environment, a possible firewall implementation is a DMZ, which is a neutral accessible zone separated by a firewall between it and the organization's private network and another firewall between it and any external access point or network. By putting all publicly accessible services on the DMZ, which constitutes a separate logical security domain, and allowing external parties to initiate connections to services on the DMZ only, the organization can ensure that its data and systems are not directly accessible from any external source.

A firewall policy will establish the organization's expectations for how the firewall should function and stems from an ongoing security risk assessment process. It establishes a formal process for approving and testing all external network connections, as well as rules for incoming and outgoing traffic, continuing management, and changes to the firewall configuration. These rules will cover:

- Firewall types, topology, and architecture.

- Functional requirements, including access controls, baseline configurations, rules and filters, services, content restrictions, and security and authentication details.

- List of services and ports necessary for business.

- Permissible traffic, including protocols, data, and applications permitted.

- Management and maintenance, including configuration auditing and testing.

- Traffic monitoring.

- Justification and documentation for any risky protocols allowed, including reason for use of protocol and security features implemented.

- Procedures for addressing requests to bypass firewall security for specific protocols or services required for business purposes.

A review of firewall logs can alert administrators to changes to firewall policy, addition or promotion of administrative accounts, and network activity, including permitted and denied connections.

Intrusion Detection and Prevention Systems

Intrusion detection and prevention systems (IDS) are access control mechanisms that allow or disallow access based on a data traffic analysis. They monitor the events occurring in a system or network, analyze them for signs of possible incidents involving unauthorized access or actual or imminent threats of policy violation, log and report incident activity, and attempt to stop the intrusion or mitigate the effects of the detected issue. This is done either directly or by reconfiguring a firewall or making other changes to the security environment. The organization should ensure that:

- Intrusion detection systems are placed at any location where traffic from external entities is allowed to enter controlled or private networks
- Host-based intrusion detection is placed on all sensitive systems even if they do not allow external access.
- Administrators regularly analyze logs.
- Intrusion detection signatures are frequently updated.

IDS logs can record activities such as access to privileged accounts, unusual outbound connectivity, as well as administrative access to the IDS system.

Penetration Testing and Vulnerability Scanning

Penetration testing is used to evaluate the security of a system, network, or database by simulating an attack by a malicious user. It can help determine potential vulnerabilities that may result from improper configuration, technical flaws, or operational and process weaknesses. Once security issues are uncovered, their impact is assessed and a remediation plan is developed.

The test plan should detail the scope and procedure of the test in the context of assessed threats to organizational data. Depending on the test objective, resulting action may include:

- A detailed technical report on data and system vulnerabilities.
- The outcome of the test in business risk terms.
- Short-term and tactical recommendations.
- Long-term and strategic recommendations.
- A data security improvement action plan.

The frequency of testing should be determined on the basis of risk analysis and when significant changes are implemented.

Unlike the more manual approach of a penetration test, vulnerability scanning uses automated host or network-based tools to help assess security weaknesses and risks. The tools can be run on a scheduled or ad-hoc basis and will generate a report identifying each discovered vulnerability and potential risk.

Data Transmission

Sensitive data transmission, whether through FTP, system to system, or web form submission, should be performed only over a trusted path or medium with controls to provide confidentiality, integrity, and authenticity of content. All connections from an internal system or database to other systems outside the accreditation boundary should be authorized only through the use of system connection agreements, and the connection should be monitored and controlled on an ongoing basis.

Strong cryptography and security protocols should be used to safeguard the data during transmission over open, public networks. The transfer of personal information from external parties to the organization, usually through a web site, should be accomplished via secure servers using high-level encryption.

The risks from wireless networks should be evaluated carefully and appropriate controls implemented. Default network names and administrator passwords should be changed before activating the network. Address filtering can specify which physical computer addresses can connect to the network.

Wireless network transmitting sensitive data should be security enabled and transmissions should be encrypted using protected access. Additionally, strong authentication and configuration controls should be implemented at the access point and on all clients, and unauthorized access points and clients should be monitored.

Remote Access

Remote access is any access to an organizational information resource by a user or system communicating through an external, nonorganization-controlled network or connection. The organization may deem it necessary to provide remote access to data and systems for remote workers or to support operations at remote locations. In some cases, remote access is required periodically by vendors to make regular or emergency system support.

Because of the increased risks associated with access from outside the trusted perimeter, the organization should implement policies and processes governing the conditions under which remote access is granted and terminated. Remote access should be granted based on authorized business needs, limited to the minimum privileges needed, and require management approval, with all approvals periodically reviewed and justified.

Any system remotely logging into an organizational network should have adequate antivirus and firewall protections, have all the mandated security and configurations settings, and be properly patched. As a general practice, only devices that have been configured by organization or vendor devices that meet these requirements should be authorized to connect to the internal network.

All communications between remote users and organizational networks should be through a virtual private network (VPN), which can provide a secure communications channel across a public network. Appropriate VPN security includes:

- Encryption of all transmitted data.

- Multifactor authentication requiring factors beyond general usernames and passwords to gain access.

- Strong password and account policies.

- Automatic session time-out after a certain period of inactivity and disconnection after a certain number of incorrect logon attempts.

- Logging and analysis of remote communications.

In cases where a vendor may require remote access to a system or data for maintenance or diagnostic purposes, the vendor must implement a level of security at least as high as that implemented on the data or system being serviced, unless the component being accessed is removed from the overall system and sanitized with regard to sensitive information and also tested for potentially malicious or erroneous updates before being reconnected to the system.

External System Connections

The organization may need to provide access to and from external information systems that are outside the accreditation boundary and for which there is no direct assurance over the application of security controls or the assessment of their effectiveness. In such circumstances, the organization should verify the employment of necessary security controls on the external system or have approved connection or processing agreements with the entity hosting the external system.

Interconnection security agreements are established between the organizations that own and operate the connected systems to specify the connection requirements and describe the security controls that will be used to protect the systems and data. These controls will be adhered to by both parties and will be based on risk and data sensitivity.

Additional considerations for interconnected systems include an effective change management process to coordinate planned system changes that could affect the interconnection and prompt notification by both sides of security incidents and system disruptions in order to facilitate a coordinated response.

Antivirus and Patches

All servers and workstations should be configured with antivirus software, which should be automatically updated from the vendor's site at least daily. In addition to persistent protection, the antivirus software should perform a complete system scan on a scheduled basis. Individual workstations should not be able to disable local antivirus software or updates.

The organization should implement procedures for handling virus infections that cannot be automatically cleaned. Such procedures can include isolating the affected device, manually attempting to remove the virus, or complete reinstallation or reconfiguration.

Centralized configuration files and identical group policies should be used to configure all workstations to an appropriately high level of security. In addition to decreasing the risk of a virus infection, this practice will also simplify general support.

Since viruses and intruders can exploit existing operating system vulnerabilities, it is important to configure all operating software to automatically receive the latest upgrades and patches. In addition, a system should be in place to scan all devices for missing patches and automatically initiates patch remediation without administrator involvement.

Isolation and Minimization

By restricting host systems to enterprise applications and operating system components, and isolating individual services to separate hosts, a potential compromise can be limited to the individual system or service and the impact on other critical services would be limited.

As part of a defense-in-depth protection strategy, the organization considers partitioning sensitive data or systems into separate domains or environments. Any connections should occur through managed interfaces consisting of appropriate boundary protection devices arranged in an effective architecture.

More generally, communities of services, systems, data, and users that operate in different security roles or zones should be isolated in separate but interconnected groups, with monitoring and controls at the external boundary and at key internal boundaries.

In the system configuration context, the principle of minimization essentially states that all software, services, protocols, or other functionality that is not required by the system or not necessary to perform a particular function should either be disabled or not installed to eliminate the possibility of compromise. In addition to increased security, this best practice can also improve performance and simplify administration.

Access Control

Access to data should be controlled through a process that ensures that user access rights reflect defined and documented business needs and job requirements. All users must be uniquely identifiable, job requirements should be attached to user identities, access privileges for each system and data group should be identified, and access rights must be in line with defined and documented business needs and should reflect the concepts of least privilege and segregation of duties.

Access Provisioning

Organizations should have an effective process for identifying new users and recording, approving, and administering access rights. New access requests will be submitted by user management to the data or system owner for approval and processing. In certain cases, the assignment of rights may be established by the employee's role or group membership, and managed by preestablished authorizations for that group. Vendors or contractors may be granted access based on their relationship with the organization.

The data owner will review and evaluate the request based on job function, data sensitivity, least privilege, and segregation of duties. Once approved, access will be configured by the data custodians or system administrators, who should not also be end users of the system in question.

The provisioning process should include an efficient mechanism for notifying the granting authority when a user's status or role changes. This, along with system changes, will prompt a review and update of access rights. In addition, upon user leave or termination, access control privileges should be revoked in a timely manner.

In addition to normal operations, the assignment of authentication and authorization credentials should include business continuity planning responsibilities.

Authentication

Authentication is the verification of identity by a system or database based on the presentation of unique credentials to that system. Authentication contributes to the confidentiality of data and the accountability of actions performed on systems by verifying the unique identity of a user.

Passwords are a primary method used to control access to resources and are the most common authentication mechanism. Other mechanisms include token mechanisms and biometrics. Authentication that relies on more than one credential is called multifactor authentication and is generally stronger than any single-factor methods. To determine the need for this approach, the organization should perform a risk assessment of the particular access need. If the risk assessment indicates that the use of single-factor authentication may be inadequate, it should implement multifactor authentication, layered security, or other controls reasonably calculated to mitigate risk.

At a minimum, any access to sensitive organizational assets should require a unique account with an associated password. Passwords assigned to user accounts that access sensitive data should adhere to certain password management best practices, including:

- Adhering to complexity requirements such as minimum length, avoidance of common words or terms, avoidance of personal or factual information, and inclusion of various types of characters.

- Changing the initial administrator-issued password on new accounts before first use.

- Aging implementation, which requires password changes at set intervals commensurate with the risk level of the account.

- Avoiding use of the same account and password for multiple applications or purposes.

- Avoiding sharing, writing down, or electronic storage of passwords.

- Prohibiting password reuse for a specified number of generations.

- Ability for an administrator to change or reset a user password at any time.

- Clear guidance for handling lost and compromised passwords.

Accounts should be automatically logged off after a predetermined period of inactivity and locked out due to extended lack of use. They should also be locked out due to repeated unsuccessful logon attempts. These automatic lockouts are usually temporary and automatically released after a predetermined time period. To increase security against unauthorized logon attempts, the authentication error feedback should not specify the particular component in error, but rather return a general error message.

Any password system must balance the password strength with the user's ability to remember and maintain a stronger password and more secure password. When the balancing produces a password that is not sufficiently strong, a different authentication mechanism should be considered.

All account, password, and other user authentication information should be protected from unauthorized access or modification. An end user account should not provide access to components other than the application front-end in order to prevent the bypassing security and sign-on controls. Conversely, administrative accounts should not be used to perform end user functions. All files containing passwords or other authenticators must be encrypted and the passwords must not be transmitted in clear text.

Entitlement Reviews

An entitlement review is a periodic assessment of actual entitlement privileges and permissions to systems and data to ensure that access to particular information assets is proper and limited to the needs of the assigned role or job function as dictated by the user's manager. It allows the determination of which users have access to which systems and information, and whether that access complies with the organization's security policies. The review should examine the levels of access each individual has, conformity with the concept of least privilege, whether all accounts are still active, and whether management authorizations are current.

Entitlement reviews should be performed on a scheduled basis, with the review frequency determined by the information risk assessment. In addition, an entitlement review should be performed whenever there is a change in user status, including transfer or reassignment to another business unit, change of job responsibilities within the same business unit, leave of absence or disability leave, conversion from nonemployee to employee, and employment termination. For particularly sensitive databases or resources, the review process should be automated to report changes in permissions to the appropriate manager.

Each business unit should implement a documented process to review and verify user entitlements on a scheduled basis. An individual or group who does not perform the actual reviews should be assigned to oversee the entitlement review process. This individual or group, usually from security or compliance, will have the following responsibilities:

- Ensuring that business managers do not review their own access.

- Confirming that transferred and terminated employee entitlements were appropriately changed or revoked.

- Ensuring accurate and appropriate entitlements.

- Escalating overdue reviews and exceptions.

- Coordinating any process improvements based on issues that arise during the entitlement review process.

Privileged Accounts

Privileged accounts are functional IDs used for system administration and operation. These accounts have very few security restrictions, so they can allow a user to make unauthorized changes or to gain access to sensitive data, whether inadvertently or by design. In addition, as they are usually associated with a group or role and not directly attributable to an individual, there can be limited, if any, accountability.

Since privileged accounts are critical to operating system and application availability, and are sometimes the only IDs allowed to perform certain functions, it is usually not possible to disable or delete them. It is therefore important to manage the risks associated with them by defining their appropriate use, ownership, and control.

Account Ownership

Each privileged account should be assigned to an owner who will be able to assign the account to an administrator but who will remain responsible for all activities performed with the account. For a system processing sensitive data, the owner will be the data or application owner, who will be able to assign the account to the administrator or DBA supporting the application or database.

Upon an account owner's termination or transfer, the account should be transferred to a new owner, who will perform an entitlement review to ensure that all accounts are assigned properly.

Account Assignment and Usage

An account owner can authorize the use of a privileged account by a staff member based on:

- **Justification** The reason access is required.
- **Risk Profile** The system criticality multiplied by the account access level.

- **Least Privilege** The minimum privilege required to fulfill the person's job function.

- **Segregation of Duties** Separation of certain areas of responsibility to reduce the opportunity for unauthorized modifications or misuse.

Based on these criteria, the account owner will determine the level of access associated with the account. For particularly sensitive accounts, multifactor authentication such as smart cards or the simultaneous logon by two users should be required.

A detailed record should be kept of what privileges have been given to whom, when, and for what purpose.

Managing Account Passwords

Privileged account passwords must be changed at scheduled intervals commensurate with the risk level of the account as well as when the account owner or any authorized user leaves the organization or changes job responsibilities.

Password management best practices also require that passwords have a certain minimum length and adhere to complexity rules. In addition, password aging, inactivity threshold, and unsuccessful password attempt lockout should be implemented.

Activity Logging and Monitoring

For general security purposes and in order to demonstrate compliance to regulatory and data privacy requirements, it is essential to log and monitor all activity performed with privileged accounts. The audit log should record the user ID, log on and log off times, and activity of every session.

These activity logs should be reviewed by the account owner on a regular basis, with special attention being paid to the use of these accounts to create new user accounts or to elevate the privileges of other accounts.

Policies and Procedures

Clear policies and procedures must be in place to manage and control administrative access. They should include the following:

- **Separate User and Administrator Accounts** Users who are also administrators should have a regular account for typical end user tasks and a separate account for administrative tasks only. The passwords for these two accounts should not be the same.

- **Use Privileged Accounts Only for Relevant Tasks** The signing on to an application or database with a privileged account to perform tasks that do not directly require it should be prohibited. This will reduce security risks and prevent malicious software from running with the same privileges as the administrator.

- **Rename the Default Administrator Account** This will remove the obvious indication that this account has elevated privileges.

- **Create a Decoy Administrator Account** To add an additional layer of protection and keep any would be hackers busy, a new account named Administrator with no special privileges should be created. Its usage should be monitored for unexpected activity such as logon failures.

- **Minimize the Number of Privileged Accounts** The number of privileged accounts should be kept to an absolute minimum. This will increase control and security and reduce the administrative burden.

- **Periodically Expire Privileged Accounts** Expiration dates should be placed upon administrative accounts and they should be periodically expired to eliminate unused accounts.

- **Closely Manage Vendor Software Default Passwords** Sometimes the privileged account is the default account delivered in vendor software. These accounts present a particular risk as they are widely known and are usually the first ones that an unauthorized user will try. If possible, these accounts should be removed or obscured. Additionally, the default passwords for these accounts should be immediately changed when the software is installed.

Developer Access to Production

There are certain circumstances under which developers need access to production data or systems in order to debug a particular feature in a live system or to use realistic production data for test purposes. Since developers do not usually have the same access privileges as business users of the data and can present a particular risk because of their in-depth technical knowledge of a system, a program should be implemented to order to strengthen controls over their access to controlled information systems and to sensitive production data in nonproduction environments.

Where sensitive data is stored or used in testing or other nonproduction environments, such data must be protected using controls comparable to those used to protect this information in production environments against unauthorized access, copying, or viewing. In addition, policy should require that before such data is moved or copied to a nonproduction environment it needs to be irreversibly redacted or masked so it is no longer sensitive. Two important considerations during the masking process are (1) to ensure that each resulting data element is realistic in matching the format of the corresponding source data element and (2) that referential integrity is maintained across relational databases so that the same data element is masked in the same manner across instances.

Persistent access by developers to production systems for debugging purposes should be disallowed and replaced by the use of emergency IDs, which are emergency temporary accounts used in a support capacity allowing access to a controlled information system. In order to minimize the inherent loss of efficiency in continually issuing special IDs for certain access purposes, the organization should implement a provisioning process that includes specific authorization criteria, predefined access profiles, predefined primary and proxy approvers, and strict time-limited access.

Physical Access

Physical safeguards, policies, and procedures should be implemented to limit physical access to sensitive information, systems, related facilities, and equipment from unauthorized intrusion as well as natural and environmental hazards.

Physical security risks can be mitigated through zone-oriented implementations, which are physical areas with differing security requirements, which are a function of the sensitivity of the data contained or accessible through the zone and the information technology. The requirements for each zone should be determined through the risk assessment.

Policies and procedures should specify the methods used to control physical access to restricted areas, ensure that access rights are defined based on business need, and that individuals with authorized access are identified by title and/or job function. Management should review the lists of individuals with physical access on a scheduled basis. The access procedures should also cover special access during disaster recovery or emergency mode operations.

Access procedures should include visitor controls, such as sign-in access logs, visitor badges, and escorts by authorized personnel. Where appropriate, physical safeguards should be implemented for individual workstations accessing sensitive data.

Other physical control considerations include:

- **Power** Stable and uninterruptible power supply for all critical components, including automated emergency shutoff due to a device-specific or endemic malfunction.

- **Environmental Management** Regulated temperature and humidity controls as well as automated administrator notification in case indicators deviate from a specified range.

- **Fire Suppression** Fire detection and suppression devices and systems that are automatically activated in the event of a fire. The devices should provide automatic notification of any activation to the organization and emergency responders.

- **Water Damage** Protection from water damage by ensuring that master shutoff valves are known, accessible, and working properly. Additional measures can include raised flowing for critical equipment.

For outsourced datacenters, audits should ensure that the third-party provider has implemented the required security practices and has appropriately secured all organizational infrastructure documentation.

Application and data processing functionality can also be offered by hardware and software located in various user departments. These are commonly housed throughout the organization without special security or environmental controls, and are thus less secure than devices and applications located in a data center or server room. In such situations, overall building or work area security becomes more important. The level of security should depend on the sensitivity of the data that can be accessed and on the significance of applications.

Activity Logging and Monitoring

Activity logging and monitoring will help assess policy compliance, identify intrusions and breaches, and support an effective response program. The degree of logging and monitoring is risk-driven and increases with data accessibility sensitivity.

Activity Monitoring

Systems and databases should log and monitor user activity performed. The scope and level of audit logging and analysis activity will depend on the sensitivity of and risk associated with the particular data or system, and should be expanded whenever there is an indication of increased risk to assets.

Logs capture data and process events through log entries denoting information such as log on and log off times, the party accessing the sensitive data, access or change occurrences with their date and time, and success or failure indication.

They can provide a record of access and authentication events, configuration changes that can compromise data confidentiality and integrity, and record details of inbound and outbound data transmission traffic.

All activity logs should be reviewed and analyzed by the account owner or designated administrator on a scheduled basis for indications of inappropriate or unusual activity, and suspicious activity or suspected violations should be investigated.

In addition to actual review and analysis, certain logging systems can develop statistical profiles of user access behavior on a continual basis and detect anomalous activity based on the profile.

Logging policies should include guidelines for log review intervals, retention standards, and response time expectations.

Baseline Logging

Organizations should implement a baseline level of logging on all system and database activity, and a higher baseline level of logging on critical systems and databases. This should include high risk activities such as privileged account and administrative-level behavior, direct access to sensitive data stores, privilege escalation, failed login attempts, and failed database operations. Automated triggers should be set to alert appropriate personnel of unusual activities with security implications. All sensitive systems and databases should be checked on a scheduled basis to verify that logging is functioning properly and adheres to standards.

Centralized Log Management

To facilitate the review and analysis of the logs, a copy of audit information from various devices, systems, and databases should be consolidated into a centralized log management repository which will aggregate, normalize, and provide reports and queries. Having all pertinent log entries available in one place and format will help identify policy violations, internal and external data and system compromise, and provide the foundation for forensic analysis.

Centralized logging will greatly facilitate event correlation, since the various logs may each contain indications of the same event or activity.

This consolidation also provides an element of redundancy should any log data become corrupted, provides secure storage for logs, and reduces the impact of log unavailability in the case of a compromised system or database.

Protection of Log Files

Whether at the source system or database or at the aggregate repository, the audit information should be protected from unauthorized access, modification, and deletion. This can be accomplished by limiting audit log access to those with a job-related need and promptly backing up audit log files to a centralized log server or media that is difficult to alter. Attention should also be paid to ensure that sensitive data is not included in the log.

Since malicious technical insiders may attempt to conceal their actions by altering system or database logs, organizations should architect their systems for log integrity. Any direct access to logs should occur by designated security principals through multifactor authentication. Additionally, events should be audited for both success and failure to determine whether any attempts are made to erase the contents of a log.

Storage

Policy should be defined for the storage, overwriting, and maintenance of all event logs, especially on how to deal with full event logs. In order to facilitate any subsequent investigations of data security incidents, sufficient audit record storage capacity should be allocated and auditing should be configured to reduce the likelihood of such capacity being exceeded. This will ensure that logging information is not overwritten and that the audit logs are retained for a period of time consistent with organizational, regulatory, and legal record retention policies. In addition, log retention may be helpful in analysis because older log entries may indicate incident precursor activity or previous undetected instances of similar compromise.

Software Assurance

A significant number of reported security incidents result from exploits against defects in the design or code of software. Software can contain erroneous or intentional code that introduces vulnerabilities and security risks into systems and applications. These hidden access points can provide unauthorized access to systems or data, unauthorized communications capabilities, and unauthorized abilities to change the software.

Ensuring the integrity of internally developed and purchased software will help protect the infrastructure from threats and vulnerabilities and reduce the overall risk of data compromise. To ensure system confidentiality and integrity, it is critical that provisions be included for built-in security of the developed or acquired software by considering the development process, the source code, and the history and reputation of the developers or vendors.

One of the organizational objectives of a Software Assurance Program is to shift the software security stance from patch management to software assurance. Security awareness during development allows designers and developers to apply security principles throughout all the phases of the Software Development Life Cycle and can raise overall software quality and security from the start rather than through the reliance on applying patches after vulnerabilities have been identified.

Software assurance encompasses the following components:

- **People** Education and training for developers and users.
- **Processes** Guidelines and best practices for the development of secure software.
- **Technology** Tools for evaluating software vulnerabilities and quality.
- **Acquisition** Specifications and guidelines for acquisition and outsourcing.

From the process perspective, several security considerations need to be taken into account during system development or purchase. Each phase should assess the business impact of unauthorized disclosure or accidental or deliberate corruption or deletion of business information. Specifically, considerations include security, control, and privacy issues during the requirements and design phase; the implementation of appropriate access controls, audit trails, and activity logs during the development phase; and thorough data security testing during the test phase. A primary testing objective is to ensure that sensitive information is not displayed in a manner where a user can view or access information that they are not authorized to view or access. Additionally, attention should be paid to data migration to ensure that sensitive data is not inadvertently disclosed and that all data is correctly mapped.

For purchased software, all vendor default settings, accounts, and passwords should be changed since these passwords and settings may be generally well known and easily determined via public information. All unnecessary services, protocols, or other functionality should be disabled.

As a necessary best practice, the organization should ensure that the development and testing environments are separate from the production environment. Applications that have been tested thoroughly and are functionally complete can be promoted to the production environment by following the organization's promotion process. Additionally, separation of duties should be implemented between development, test, and end user personnel.

Once a system has been rolled out and operating, the organization should continuously monitor performance to ensure that security controls are effectively implemented and that they remain consistent with preestablished security requirements.

An important software assurance issue is web security. Poorly tested web sites can allow unexpected inputs to pass and weaken security measures. An additional vulnerability exists at the process level since organizations cannot usually train external users or clients accessing their web sites in the basics of access control and security. Particular attention should be paid to thorough testing of web sites and applications on the access, error handling, confidentiality, and integrity levels.

Change Management

Change Management is the process by which changes to systems and databases are managed and documented. The primary objective is to maintain the integrity of the data and system while providing an orderly process for implementing changes needed by organizational units. Weak change management procedures can corrupt systems and data and can introduce new vulnerabilities.

Secure and managed environments require that implementation of changes be predictable and repeatable, following a controlled process that is defined, monitored, and enforced. A successful change management strategy combines internal processes, clearly defined personnel roles, and tools for managing the change process. Risk mitigation is an important part of the change management methodology and the results and effects of changes should be evaluated with an assessment of the risks involved.

The organization should develop and document formal change management procedures covering both normal and emergency changes to systems processing sensitive information. The procedures should include the following requirements:

- All changes are initiated through formal change requests, which include specific requirements, scope, justification, and authorized approvals.

- After you initiate a change request, the effects that the change may have on the system, data, or other interrelated systems are evaluated.

- Responsibility and accountability for creation, approval, and application is segregated.

- Business and technical risks are assessed prior to change implementation and a priority assigned based on urgency, potential benefits, and the ease with which changes can be implemented.

- A Security Impact Analysis is conducted to determine the extent to which changes to data or systems will affect the security posture of the data or systems.

- Any parties affected by the change are notified prior to change implementation.

- All changes are tested in a test environment prior to production implementation.

- Back-out procedures should be developed for all significant changes prior to rollout.

- An emergency change process is operational for emergency changes.

- Changes are monitored to assess the efficacy of change management policies.

A change management process can also be key in distinguishing benign from malicious activity during data breach incidents, since it will allow the response team to use change management information to verify rapidly whether suspicious indications are caused by authorized activity or by an actual event.

Backup and Restore

An organizational data backup and restore process is implemented to copy production data preemptively for restoration purposes in the case of an event that results in the loss or compromise of the data. Restoring the integrity of compromised data will be performed from a verified and validated backup source after an accidental deletion or corruption of data, hardware failure, or facilities damage affecting the storage device.

Strategies for data backup and appropriate backup methodologies are based on the criticality of the data. The primary risk is the inability to recover the data in case of a disaster or other disruptive event. This can be caused by incomplete or sporadic performance of backup procedures, unreliable backup media, or the inability to access off-site backup material. Written standards should document backup procedures, delineate specific responsibilities, and ensure uniform performance throughout the organization.

Backup best practices include the following:

- Full or incremental data backups should be performed on a daily basis.

- Monthly backup cycles should be maintained for archival purposes and to allow restoration from a clean slate in case a past corruption or compromise is not detected for a long period of time.

- The backup media should be stored in a secure location limited to authorized personnel.

- The backup media should rotated offsite on a weekly basis using a third-party provider.

- The backup system should provide an automatic indication or notification of successful or unsuccessful backup.

- A daily exception report of backup failures should be reviewed and issues resolved on a timely basis.

- Backups should be tested on a quarterly basis for recoverability, including reloading all backed up data and identifying any missing resources that are required to successfully complete the recovery.

A distinction should be drawn between Backup and Restore and data archiving, which refers to the process of long-term storage of inactive data for regulatory or record retention purposes.

Disaster Recovery/ Business Continuity Planning

Effective disaster recovery/business continuity planning (DR/BCP) establishes the basis for an organization to maintain and recover business processes when operations have been disrupted unexpectedly. Its objectives are to minimize financial loss; maintain ongoing operations; and mitigate the strategic, reputational, operational, financial, and legal effects of the disruption.

Events that trigger the implementation of a business continuity plan may have significant security implications, and business continuity plans should be reviewed and tested as an integral part of the security process. Risk assessments should consider the risks that appear in business continuity scenarios and the security posture that may be established.

Business continuity plan review should include the following security considerations:

- Security at the alternate facility.

- Physical and logical access controls for the new production systems and databases as well as for the inactive systems and databases when processing is transferred temporarily to an alternate facility. These controls must be defined for both users and administrators.

- Access provisioning and review methods for users during the emergency.

- Changes in the effectiveness of automated controls such as firewalls and intrusion detection systems due to resource availability and facility and systems changes that may exist when alternate facilities are placed in use.

- Changes in the effectiveness of security processes such as incident response planning under these circumstances.

Disposal

Once sensitive information is no longer needed for a particular business purpose, and once a mandatory retention period has expired, appropriate disposal practices should be implemented to prevent unauthorized access to or use of the information by preventing it from being practicably retrieved. Disposal and media sanitization practices should provide reasonable assurance, in proportion to the confidentiality of the information, that the information cannot be read or reconstructed. Disposal encompasses not only the discarding or abandonment of the information, but also the sale, donation, or transfer of any medium upon which the information is stored.

Sanitization is the process used to remove information from information system media. Sanitization techniques—including clearing, purging, and destroying media information—prevent the disclosure of organizational information to unauthorized individuals when such media is reused or disposed.

Measures

Disposal measures will be based on the sensitivity of the information, the nature and size of the organization's operations, the costs and benefits of different disposal methods, and relevant technological changes. Measures will include shredding, burning, or pulverizing paper records and destruction or erasure of storage media. Media sanitization techniques can be used to ensure that residual data does not remain on media after erasure and cannot be retrieved or reconstructed.

Responsibility

This means designating a single individual, department, or function to be responsible for disposal facilitates accountability and promotes compliance with disposal policies. Depending on the amount and sensitivity of the information to be disposed, it might be advisable to enter into and monitor compliance with a contract with another party engaged in the business of record destruction to dispose of material in an appropriate manner. The competency and integrity of the disposal company can be determined through the review of an independent audit of its operations and references from reliable sources.

Recording

Where practical, the disposal of sensitive data should be logged in a Record of Destruction or similar form, including the party responsible for and performing disposal, the date, medial type, and method of disposal.

Insiders

Insiders have a significant advantage over external parties in the ability to access and use sensitive organizational information in an unauthorized manner. They have or can more easily gain the knowledge to bypass security measures designed to prevent unauthorized access. They may also be aware of flaws and vulnerabilities in internal processes and technology. Insider attacks fall into the following categories:

- **Sabotage** This can be performed by current or former employees or contractors who intentionally exceed or misuse an authorized level of access with the intention of harming a specific individual, group, or the organization. These insiders are usually disgruntled employees motivated by a desire for revenge for a perceived or actual negative event such as termination, supervisor disputes, transfers or demotions, and salary or pay dissatisfaction.

■ **Fraud** Insiders who commit fraud with the intention of deceptively obtaining a certain gain are usually motivated by financial considerations, either for direct additional income or in return for payment from another party.

■ **Theft of sensitive information** These insiders may be motivated by the financial gain accruing from using the information in a fraudulent manner. Others may be disgruntled employees who choose to embarrass employers by revealing the information.

■ **Compromises due to carelessness or negligence** Data breaches due to insiders can be caused by careless employees or well-meaning users who lack the necessary security training and awareness for their job function. Users who have legitimate access to information may not exercise due care and inadvertently share this information with unauthorized parties. Even though fraud or theft is unlikely to result from data leakage under these circumstances, the prevalence of these types of breaches can eventually result in a significant incident.

Insider attacks usually involve unauthorized access either directly or through a compromised user or administrative account, shared account, or system account. These compromises can be detected due to system irregularity, nontechnical means such as notification by other employees or customers, and log review. They can be prevented through a layered approach consisting of policy and technical control enforcement. The following practices will help reduce the risk of insider attacks:

■ **Segregation of duties** Separation and division of certain areas of responsibility for critical functions among multiple employees to reduce the opportunity for unauthorized modifications or misuse by limiting the possibility that one individual could commit unauthorized actions without the cooperation of another individual within the organization. By segregating duties, the organization will minimize the risk that a combination of functions under the responsibility of a single individual can be combined to result in a security violation.

■ **Rotation of duties** This control, similar in concept to segregation of duties, is intended to prevent or detect misuse by minimizing over-dependence on a single staff member, thus increasing the probability of detecting policy violations or actual fraud.

- **Least privilege** The minimum privilege and resource access required to fulfill the person's job function. This limits the scope of possible threats by reducing the number of privileges that may potentially be abused.

- **Log monitoring** System or database log monitoring and review will help detect unauthorized access, even though consideration must be given to the fact that attempts may be made to conceal actions by modifying the logs.

- **Administrative account control** The use of administrative or privileged accounts should be closely managed and logged, and shared privileged accounts should be disabled.

- **Effective access provisioning and review** The provisioning process should include an efficient mechanism for updating access levels when a user's status or role changes. This is especially relevant upon user termination, where all internal and external access control privileges should be revoked in a prompt manner.

Social Engineering

Social engineering is any manipulation of a person, usually through social interaction, to obtain unauthorized information. By using persuasion, aggression, or other interpersonal skills, the unauthorized party will attempt to encourage a legitimate user or other authorized party to provide sensitive information or authentication credentials.

Risks associated with social engineering can be mitigated through a security program that includes ongoing awareness and training, as well as effective policies and procedures for employees, vendors, and partners. The challenge is to encourage a security culture that is collaborative, structured, and ingrained throughout the organization's processes and people without fostering an unnecessary level of distrust.

Training can help employees understand the potential risk of social engineering threats, provide them with the tools they need to recognize and respond to these threats, and understand why their role within the security culture is vital to organizational health. Employees in higher risk positions such as help desk staff and system administrators may benefit from specialized training.

In addition to training, strong third-party identification procedures should be implemented, especially for employees that interact with external parties. These will be used to properly authenticate the identity of the other person prior to engaging in a discussion about confidential information. This may include requesting identification information at more than one juncture during the conversation.

Third-Party Vendors

Organizations are increasingly using vendors and service providers for a variety of services, such as data center and network operations, HR and payroll, data backup, and remote help desk. Some of these services require that the vendors and third parties access, maintain, process, or are otherwise permitted access to confidential information, including an organization's sensitive customer and employee data, creating a situation where vendors essentially have the same access to this information as authorized internal employees.

Because a significant number of sensitive data breaches occur through the access to this data by outside parties, and due to heightened regulatory concern, vendor selection and supervision must become integral parts of organizational risk management strategies, especially since outsourcers typically serve multiple clients and may have security implementations that do not adequately take into account the value of the information.

The organization should exercise appropriate due diligence in selecting its service providers, including developing a process to perform vendor risk assessments based on the criticality and sensitivity of the outsourced process and data. This should include importance of the outsourced function, the nature of the activities the vendor will perform, and the inherent risk of each activity.

To ensure proper management of the due diligence process, a questionnaire can be developed covering vendor history, financial condition, personnel practices, information security policies and procedures, business continuity, and other relevant areas. This will ensure that all key areas of the due diligence process are addressed in a uniform manner.

Once a vendor has been selected, the organization should:

- Review and approve the service provider's information security policy and program.

- Enter into and enforce a contract with the service provider that requires the implementation of appropriate measures designed to protect against unauthorized access to or use of sensitive information accessed or maintained by the service provider. These include security controls for the protection of sensitive information, limiting data access to authorized staff, and defining the way in which the vendor is permitted to further outsource to other third parties.

- Include in the contract the requirement that the service provider take appropriate actions to address incidents of unauthorized access to the organization's sensitive data, including notification to the organization as soon as possible following any such incident.

- Monitor its service providers to confirm they are satisfying their contractual obligations through audits and reviews conducted by qualified internal or external independent parties. Vendor security assessment must be performed when the vendor begins performing functions that have access to confidential information and on a scheduled basis thereafter, usually yearly. They must be reperformed before the next scheduled review basis in case of a vendor security incident, changes in infrastructure or information technology platform used to process confidential information, or the use of subcontractors not previously identified by the third party that have been granted access to confidential information.

- Where a sufficient level of trust cannot be established in the external services and/or service providers, the organization should employ compensating security controls or under certain circumstances accept the greater degree of risk to its operations and information assets.

- Take steps to cure a violation or terminate the contract if the organization determines that the third-party vendor has violated a material term of the contract regarding information security.

- Upon termination of the outsourcing contract, ensure that the third-party vendor returns or destroys without maintaining any copies all sensitive information received from, created, or received on behalf of the organization. If such a return or destruction is not feasible, the vendor must extend the protections of the contract and limit further uses and disclosures for as long as the information is maintained.

An additional level of caution and consideration should be exercised if security services themselves are outsourced to obtain greater expertise, a greater range of services, or to decrease cost. Since the organization retains the same responsibilities for security as if those services were performed internally, it should ensure it has sufficient expertise to oversee and manage an outsourced security service relationship, both on a contract level for contract compliance and on a security level to sufficiently understand the scope and nature of the service, react in a timely manner when the services provided are not at the appropriate level, no longer coordinate with the internal security controls, or no longer provide the risk mitigation desired.

Training and Awareness

Effective training in data security and privacy practices, both on an initial and refresher basis, is a critical component of the information security program and is essential for ensuring that employees can effectively adhere to and carry out policy.

Establishing and maintaining a robust and relevant information security awareness and training program as part of the overall information security program is the primary conduit for providing employees with the information and tools needed to protect the organization's information assets. It will help teach users how to protect the confidential information that has been entrusted to them. In addition, it is critical to timely breach response in the event of a breach or compromise.

Training programs will help create a culture of security appropriate for the organization as determined by an enterprisewide risk assessment and tied to the organization's mission, values, and critical assets.

The organization should develop, disseminate, and periodically review and update a formal documented security awareness and training program that addresses purpose, scope, roles, responsibilities, and compliance. In addition to the general data security training and awareness, programs can also be developed for particular systems or data stores.

On a general level, a training program should encompass the following:

- The organization's vision and mission relating to the protection of information resources, including the importance of information security and the ways in which it forms part of critical asset protection.

- Applicable laws, regulations, policies, and procedures.

- Data classification requirements.

- Data life cycle security considerations, including limiting the data that is collected, accessed, or displayed to that which is essential for the function to be performed, data protection during usage, processing, and storage, and effective methods of disposal.

- An overview of risks and safeguards.

- Roles and responsibilities, including clear guidelines on the correct use of the organization's information and what each particular group of users is authorized to access.

- The implication of security incidents to both the organization and the individual.

- Reporting requirements and procedures for unauthorized access, disclosure, or modification of information.

- An overview of the data security incident management program, including workflow and other relevant features.

Training can be conducted in a classroom setting, remotely, and periodic issuance of security awareness literature. Training and awareness material can also be made available on internal networks that can be accessed by employees.

The training program should distinguish between audiences since not everyone needs the same degree or type of information security awareness. In addition to general data security issues, training programs can be developed for:

- End users about existing policies and procedures in order to provide a sound basis of understanding before granting access to sensitive information.

- Remote or mobile users.

- Specific departments or groups with security sensitive positions as well as specific systems.

- IT development and support personnel with technical security training needs, including planning and implementing security for new systems that will use sensitive information.

- Information security and audit staff who are tasked to implement or review security policies and procedures.

An effective security awareness and training program requires proper planning, implementation, maintenance, and periodic evaluation, including scope definition and objectives, program development, administration, and periodic evaluation.

Once the program has been implemented, a process to monitor compliance and effectiveness should be designed to capture key information on program activity. This will allow an assessment of the program as to its adherence to established goals and standards. Gap identification will drive any corrective action, which may take the form of formal reminders and additional awareness and training. Security awareness surveys can also measure the awareness level and highlight any areas needing improvement.

Compensating Controls

If a prescribed or recommended control cannot be effectively implemented or would cause adverse impact that would not be offset by the reduced risk, it may be necessary to specify and employ compensating controls, which are employed in lieu of a recommended control and provides equivalent or comparable protection for the data.

The effectiveness of a compensating control is dependent on the specifics of the environment in which the control is implemented, the surrounding security controls, and the configuration of the control. Compensating controls must meet the intent and rigor of the original control requirement and be commensurate with the additional risk imposed by not adhering to the requirement.

If a compensating control is implemented, the data owner should provide a rationale of the decision and a description and justification of the manner in which the control provides an equivalent security capability or level of protection. This is accomplished through Risk Acceptances (RAs), which describes the risks, the reasons for the lack of compliance, a justification for why the exception is warranted, the compensating controls implemented to address the risk, the expiration date of the exception, and review procedures.

Auditing

Risk-based audit programs should be conducted by internal and/or external auditors to ensure the adequate implementation and effectiveness of data security policies and procedures. Audits involve the review of existing controls with the objective to provide management assurance that the controls implemented are effective and to report any deficiencies together with the appropriate recommended actions.

In addition to possessing the appropriate skills and experience, auditors should be independent from the unit or organization being audited to ensure unbiased results and opinions. To minimize disruptions to business activities, the scope, approach, and timing of the audits should be planned and agreed with appropriate management.

Auditors should conduct sufficient review in the following areas to provide a basis for evaluating the overall data security program.

Data Security Policy

- Does the organization have a written data security policy?

- Has the policy been approved by upper level management?

- Are the scope and contents of the policy appropriate given the size and complexity of the organization and its operations?

- Does the policy contain the objectives of the program, assign responsibility for implementation, and provide methods for compliance and enforcement?

- Is the policy periodically updated to reflect changes in the operations, processes, and systems, as well as changes in the threats or risks to the organization's sensitive information?

- Does the organization report to its board or an appropriate committee of the board at least annually on the overall status of the information security program?

Risk Assessment

- Has all sensitive data been identified, including location and methods for storage, processing, transmission, and disposal?

- Has all sensitive data been classified?

- Has all sensitive data been assigned a data owner?

- Have reasonably foreseeable internal and external threats that could result in unauthorized disclosure, misuse, alteration, or destruction of sensitive information been identified?

- Has the organization assessed the likelihood and potential damage of these threats?

- Does the organization update the risk assessment on a scheduled basis?

- Additionally, does the organization update the risk assessment prior to major changes to data, systems, or new external conditions?

Controls

- Have measures been taken to limit the amount of sensitive information collected, maintained, or processed to the minimum amount necessary for a particular business purpose?

- Are there appropriate logical and physical access controls on sensitive data?

- Are the concepts of least privilege and segregation of duties considered when granting access to sensitive information?

- Is sensitive data encrypted during transmission or in storage?

- Has a change management process been implemented to ensure that modifications to sensitive systems are consistent with the organization's information security program?

- Have third-party and vendor controls been implemented for any third party collecting, accessing, or processing sensitive information?

- Are monitoring and logging procedures in place to detect unauthorized access to sensitive information?

- Has a breach response program been developed and staffed in cases where the organization suspects or detects unauthorized access to sensitive information, including appropriate notification to affected parties and regulatory agencies?

- Have employees been trained to implement the data security program?

Testing

- Does the organization regularly test the effectiveness of key controls, systems, and procedures of its information security program?

- Are tests conducted by independent staff or are test results reviewed by independent staff?

Third Party Providers

- Does the organization provide or allow access to sensitive information to any third-party service providers?

- For third-party providers with access to sensitive information, has the organization conducted appropriate due diligence in the selection process, taking into consideration data security?

- Are third-party providers with access to sensitive information required by contract to implement appropriate information security programs and measures?

- Does the organization monitor its third-party providers with access to sensitive information to confirm that they are maintaining appropriate security measures to safeguard the organization's sensitive information?

Testing

An information security program should include regular testing of key controls, systems, and procedures in order to obtain assurance and confidence that the security implemented controls are operational and effective in their application. Testing will determine the extent to which the controls are implemented correctly, operate as intended, and produce the desired outcome with respect to meeting data security requirements. This review is designed to identify control weaknesses, identify actions that are needed to correct these weaknesses, monitor the implementation of necessary corrective actions, and periodically assess or test the adequacy of controls.

The frequency and nature of the testing is determined by the risk assessment and adjusted as necessary to reflect changes in both internal and external conditions. Testing is based on a test plan, which includes the list of controls to test, a timeline, testing responsibility, and testing methods, including the actual testing instructions or test scripts. The number and complexity of the test scripts will be determined by the organizational size and complexity as well as by data sensitivity and risk.

Control testing occurs by reviewing samples of the control. Table 3.1 is the recommended sample size for test documentation based on control frequency.

Testing exceptions should be documented, noting whether the test failed due to design or operational deficiency. Upon investigation of each exception, remediation actions should be initiated. These are guided by a plan of action that documents planned, implemented, and evaluated remedial actions to correct deficiencies noted during the assessment and testing of the security controls and to reduce or eliminate known vulnerabilities. Controls should be retested upon completion of the remediation effort once a sufficient sample population becomes available.

The tests should be conducted by staff independent of those that develop or maintain the security program. Whether third parties should be used to either conduct tests or review their results will generally depend on regulatory compliance regulations, previous audit processes and results, whether independent organizational resources are available, and general expense and reliability considerations.

Testing documentation should be maintained for activities conducted in connection with internal control reviews, testing and remediation actions. The documentation should include the personnel involved in the test, the key factors considered, the evaluation methods used, and the conclusions reached. Documentation should be of sufficient detail to permit effective supervisory or oversight review. Independent reviewers should be able to examine and understand the documentation and determine how the original reviewers reached their conclusions.

Table 3.1 Control Testing Sample Size

Frequency of Control	Sample Size
Daily	25
Weekly	12
Semimonthly	5
Monthly	3
Quarterly	2
Semi-Annually	2
Annually	1
Automated	1
Recurring (multiple times a day)	40

Updating

In this section we'll discuss actions organizations should take to ensure that their security is up-to-date.

Security Program

The organization should review and reevaluate its security program on a scheduled basis to determine the extent of any required adjustments to its components. It will need to consider the scope, impact, and urgency of any new or changing threat or vulnerability and any changes to the information sensitivity in order to reassess possible risk and update the security process and controls accordingly.

More systemic events like mergers and acquisitions, new business endeavors, outsourcing agreements, new critical systems, or updates to existing systems will warrant an immediate review prior to the normal scheduled review.

Controls

The implementation of effective controls and safeguards is an ongoing process, whereby the effectiveness of controls at a specific point in time is just one indicator of the overall security framework. A program to audit, reassess, and update controls and safeguards on a regular basis allows the organization to react effectively to changing vulnerabilities, technologies, and business processes and conditions.

Summary

- A data security program will allow the management of data security risks and can limit the organization's vulnerability to data compromise.

- The data security program includes data classification, risk assessment, risk mitigation strategy, controls to protect the data, monitoring and testing of the controls to verify that they are effective, and a process to continuously gather and analyze new threats and vulnerabilities.

- Information security controls are the technical, physical, administrative, and policy safeguards designed to protect sensitive data.

- As part of a Defense in Depth strategy, a variety of controls are necessary for a comprehensive and robust security framework.

- Lost or stolen laptops represent a significant source of data compromise. If sensitive data must be stored on a laptop, full-disk encryption should be used to prevent unauthorized parties from retrieving the data.

- The small size of portable storage devices such as flash drives increases the possibility of physical loss with the attendant data loss.

- The organization should evaluate all transfers of physical media containing sensitive information to discontinue unnecessary or redundant transfers. Sensitive data in transport should be encrypted.

- An e-mail acceptable use policy should be implemented to clearly describe applicable restrictions on the transmission of sensitive information via e-mail.

- A variety of technical safeguards should be used for data security, including firewalls, intrusion detection systems, and vulnerability scanning.

- Sensitive data transmission should be performed only over a trusted path or medium with cryptographic controls.

- The organization should implement policies and processes governing the conditions under which remote access is granted and terminated, and all communications should be through a virtual private network that can provide a secure communications channel across a public network.

- All servers and workstations should be configured with antivirus software that is automatically updated on a daily basis with new virus definitions.

- Organizations should have an effective process for adding, modifying, and removing user access to data resources.

- Passwords should adhere to complexity and aging requirements.

- Periodic assessments and reviews of entitlement privileges and permissions to systems and data should be performed.

- Privileged and administrative accounts should be tightly controlled.

- Persistent update access by developers to production systems should be removed and read access should be granted on a case-by-case basis.

- Physical safeguards, policies, and procedures should be implemented to limit physical access to sensitive information, systems, related facilities, and equipment.

- Activity logging and monitoring will help assess policy compliance and identify intrusions and breaches.

- Each phase of the Software Development Life Cycle should assess the business impact of unauthorized disclosure or accidental or deliberate corruption or deletion of business information.

- The organization should develop and document formal change management procedures covering both normal and emergency changes to systems processing sensitive information.

- Once sensitive information is no longer needed, appropriate disposal practices should be implemented to prevent unauthorized access to or use of the information by preventing it from being practicably retrieved.

- Practices that will help reduce the risk of insider attacks include segregation and rotation of duties, least privilege, log monitoring, administrative account control, and effective access provisioning and review.

- Risks associated with social engineering can be mitigated through a security program that includes ongoing awareness and training, as well as effective policies and procedures for employees, vendors, and partners.

- Vendor selection and supervision must become integral parts of organizational risk management strategies since sensitive data breaches can occur through the access to this data by outside parties.

- Establishing and maintaining a robust and relevant information security awareness and training program as part of the overall information security program is the primary conduit for providing employees with the information and tools needed to protect the organization's information assets.

- Risk-based audit programs should be conducted to ensure the adequate implementation and effectiveness of data security policies and procedures.

- Regular testing of key controls will determine the extent to which they are implemented correctly, operate as intended, and produce the desired outcome with respect to meeting data security requirements.

- The organization should review and reevaluate its security program on a scheduled basis to determine the extent of any required adjustments to any of its components.

Chapter 4

Data Security Policy

Solutions in this chapter:

- **Standards and Procedures**
- **Benefits**
- **Goals and Trade-offs**
- **Policy Development Process**
- **Contents**
- **Related Policies**
- **Policy Implementation**
- **Update and Maintenance**
- **Compliance Audit**
- **Metrics**
- **Management Board Approval**

☑ **Summary**

Introduction

A data security policy forms the basis upon which an effective data security program is developed and managed. It is a formal statement that sets out an organization's approach to managing information security, outlines the essential requirements for protecting data assets, and establishes management's expectations for data confidentiality, integrity, and availability. It guides the formulation of standards and procedures that specify uniform and specific data security processes and actions. It will also be used as the underlying structure to develop controls to protect the data infrastructure and to collect and evaluate metrics that measure security effectiveness.

The development of a data security policy is part of a comprehensive risk management process that includes a detailed understanding of the current organizational environment, an assessment of existing and potential threats and vulnerabilities, the development and implementation of controls to mitigate the impact of threats, and the ongoing evaluation of control effectiveness with the attendant update and revision of the policy to reflect the environment.

Some of the underlying principles of the data security policy are:

- Support of the organizational mission and ability to conduct operations.

- Protection of the information resources, reputation, and legal position.

- Consistency with other institutional policies, regulations, and contracts.

- Assurance that the security measures are commensurate with the sensitivity and value of information resources and the actual threats to those resources.

- Conformance to best practices at similar organizations.

- Accountability for access to and use of information resources.

- Adaptability to address changing circumstances and regulations.

The policy must clearly define the various areas of responsibility, and once implemented, must be communicated to and understood by all affected parties. In addition to providing guidance, the policy will serve as a demonstration of management's commitment to protect information against unauthorized access and use, meet current and forthcoming regulatory and legislative requirements, and require adherence to a common security architecture in order to promote an enterprise view of the security relationship among various business units.

Individual business units within the organization may adopt additional information security requirements that are specific to their operations provided that such requirements are consistent with the policy. More specific policies governing certain types of information that must be legally protected will take precedence.

Standards and Procedures

Policies are implemented through standards, guidelines, and procedures, which offer specific approaches to implementing policy and meeting organizational goals.

Standards are a set of mandatory requirements to be used to conform to policies (as well as to laws and regulations) and represent the rules that will be used to implement the policies. They are typically collections of system-specific or procedural-specific requirements that must be met and specify uniform use of specific technologies, parameters, or procedures when such uniform use will benefit an organization.

Though not mandatory, guidelines provide recommendations as to how the policies can be implemented in cases where the imposition of standards is not achievable, appropriate, or cost-effective. They provide a guide to achieving the expected results outlined in the policy. They are used to ensure that specific measures are not overlooked, although they can be implemented in more than one way.

Standards and guidelines specify technologies and methodologies to be used to secure data. A basic combination will represent a baseline to be used to create a minimum level of security necessary to meet policy requirements.

Procedures are the specific practices for complying with the standards and guidelines that follow the policies and outline the tools and processes used to carry out the policy and to accomplish particular security-related tasks. Procedures thus help achieve the goals of the policy and include the detailed steps to be followed to accomplish a particular task or goal.

The implementation and adherence to the appropriate procedures will demonstrate a commitment to the data security policy and demonstrate due diligence in maintaining the principles of the policy. Procedures should be documented to enable a repeatable process to achieve similar results for similar tasks.

By distinguishing between policy and its implementation, the organization can promote flexibility and cost-effectiveness by offering alternative implementation approaches to achieving policy goals.

Benefits

In addition to outlining and clarifying organization expectations, a documented and distributed data security policy offers the following advantages:

- Establishes clear, consistent, and uniform security processes.

- Provides employees the assurance that they are performing their duties in conformity with organizational directive.

- Provides a baseline of performance expectations and guidelines to measure actions.

- Sets predefined boundaries within which employees can make task decisions without management reference.

- Ensures that the costs of security controls are weighed against the benefits and are within bounds set by management.

- Ensures compliance to data protection laws and regulations and limits organizational liability in case of compromise by demonstrating management commitment to information security.

- A strong data security policy can provide a competitive advantage for organizations engaging in business-to-business activity because these types of customers generally demand higher security standards to protect the integrity of their own sensitive information.

Goals and Trade-Offs

The organization's data security posture and resulting policy will be driven by the cost of security versus risk mitigation. Tangible and intangible costs must be weighed against perceived risk of compromise in order to maximize the impact of the security investment and to minimize the gap between competing objectives.

A balance needs to be struck between increased security and decreased productivity. If the organization determines that access benefit is outweighed by the risk, it may be advantageous to eliminate it rather than try to secure it. This involves several considerations and tradeoffs, including:

- **Access offered versus security** Each level and granting of access to data and systems carries certain security risks.

- **Ease of use versus security** Each level of security implemented can decrease ease of use and productivity.

- **Functionality versus security** Security may affect the system functionality, both from a feature and performance perspective.

Tone and Perspective

The Data Security Policy, like all security policies, should be written in a manner that makes it usable by its audience. In order to effectively achieve this goal, the following elements should be adhered to during the drafting of the policy:

- **Clarity** All members of the intended audience should be able to easily understand any section of the policy that applies to them. This can be achieved through avoidance of jargon and the use of concise sentences. In addition to clarity of language, the policy should also offer clear definitions of security processes and areas of responsibility.

- **Consistency** A consistent approach and response to various security issues will ensure that the policy is applied in a uniform manner under different circumstances. In addition to providing the correct response, it will avoid situations where parties may feel unjustly treated through inconsistent policy application.

- **Implementability** The policy must be implementable through specific procedures, standards, and guidelines. A policy that cannot be practically put into practice will be essentially useless.

- **Enforceability** Any written policy must have enforcement mechanisms, whether through controls, review and oversight, automated functions and tools, or with sanctions where actual prevention is not feasible.

Policy Development Process

Because of the broad impact of the data security policy on the organization, a structured development process and appropriate feedback will help ensure policy adequacy and comprehensiveness.

Organize a Policy Development Team

The development of the data security policy is predicated upon the participation of various individuals who can offer specific expertise to the team. Stakeholders and subject matter experts must be identified and consulted to ensure that the policy reflects the requirements and goals of the organization. Minimal representation should include:

- **Information security** An Information Security Officer will manage the policy development project and, as the policy owner, will be charged with the custodianship of the policy as well as with the overall responsibility for distribution, implementation, and maintenance. The policy owner will also serve as a primary point of contact for questions or update requests.

- **IT operations** IT staff will have specific knowledge in the technical aspects of data security and can provide guidance on the feasibility of specific solutions.

- **Legal** Legal counsel can provide advice on relevant data protection and breach notification statutes and ascertain the legal obligations the organization must discharge. Legal counsel can also review the policy to ensure that it complies with other organizational policies and procedures, that it conforms to legal and regulatory requirements, and that it is generally legally enforceable.

- **Internal audit** Auditors will be involved in monitoring compliance once the policy is in force and can help ensure that it is enforceable in terms of their procedures.

- **Business management** Managers from various business units will provide input about the types of data in the organization as well as with risk identification and control implementation.

- **Organizational management** A member of organizational management will serve as the executive sponsor of the policy. The sponsor will be responsible for final approval of the policy and demonstrate management commitment to data security.

Obtain Management Sponsorship and Approval

An effective data security policy requires the leadership and involvement of the organization's senior management. Management will:

- Provide the leadership and accountability for policy development.
- Allocate personnel and financial resources to policy development.
- Establish acceptable risk levels based on the risk analysis.
- Review and approve the policy and institute a program to ensure that it remains effective.

Because the policy will cross organizational boundaries, management support is critical in order to ensure its adoption and implementation throughout the entire organization and to help resolve any interorganizational issues that may develop.

Outline Major Organizational Activities

The organization's size, activities, regulatory environment, and numbers and types of information systems will shape management's security goals and establish data security principles. A thorough understanding of the business activities will allow the policy development team to determine the organizational security principles and core values. This understanding will provide a preliminary indication of the types of data and its sensitivity, the possible risks, and the necessary controls. It will also determine any legal or regularity concerns that must be addressed through the policy.

Identify and Classify Data

Data classification will allow the organization to categorize information assets and define their sensitivity and confidentiality. Security policies will be applied in accordance with that categorization in order to ensure the appropriate level of protection as well as the audience that may access the data. This categorization is done to ensure that sensitive information as well as legally protected information is appropriately safeguarded.

The types of data and their security classifications will become an integral part of the policy statement and will drive the controls and safeguards to be implemented.

Identify Threats

A threat profile will identify the type of threats that exist in a particular environment, what the probability is of a threat manifesting itself into an actual problem, and what the ramifications, costs, and consequences are of those threats being realized.

A risk assessment will help identify and understand foreseeable threats along with their likelihood and potential damage, taking into consideration the sensitivity of the information.

Determine Appropriate Controls

A variety of procedures and controls must be evaluated to address the identified risks and threats. In developing control recommendations, a data flow analysis will identify vulnerabilities during data creation, usage, transmission, storage, and disposal, and will help determine the type and placement of the various controls.

Controls are determined based upon the risk assessment, which will prioritize the risks and provide recommendations for corrective actions based on the level of risk and the sensitivity of the information. Data security controls are also driven by compliance to laws and regulations and to relevant ethical standards.

Develop the Policy

Once all the requisite information is collected, an initial draft of the policy is produced with sufficient detail to support review by relevant parties, including those units not represented on the policy development team. This will include any identified stakeholders and subject matter experts in order to ensure that the policy's scope and contents reflect the requirements and goals of the organization.

Reviews can be conducted individually or through meetings. Feedback is then forwarded to the policy owner for normalization and incorporation. In addition to the technical and procedural contents, attention should be paid to ensure that this and subsequent releases are consistent in style and content with other organizational policies. There may be the need for several draft iterations before a final document can be presented to appropriate management for approval.

Obtain Needed Approvals

Periodic reviews should be conducted with responsible management throughout the development process in order to clarify scope, contents, responsibilities, and ownership. These reviews will include a policy impact assessment describing how the policy will affect the organization and what actions are necessary to be compliant with the policy. It will list the major business and technical impacts of implementation, compliance, and enforcement.

A comment period is appropriate to receive all possible stakeholder feedback before publication. Finally, senior business and security management should sign off on the policy before distribution.

Contents

As a general rule, the contents of the policy should include an introduction or statement of purpose, goals and scope, a definition of data security, the actual statement of the policy, including data classification and ownership, the safeguards and controls framework, the roles and responsibilities of the various affected parties, enforcement and exceptions, the management of security breaches, as well as contacts, related documents, and definitions.

Statement of Purpose

The statement of purpose will provide a concise statement of what the policy is intended to accomplish as well as the factors that necessitate the development and implementation of the policy, including legal and regulatory concerns. It will present a general description of the policy and locates it within the organization's security framework and the hierarchy of other information security documents. It provides an overview of an organization's data security principles, risk control objectives, privacy and security practices, legal and compliance issues, and consequences of data security compromises or privacy violations.

Goals

Once the issue and purpose are stated and related terms and conditions discussed, this section is used to clearly state the organization's position, goals, and justification, which can be helpful in gaining compliance with the policy. The managerial objectives of the policy include:

- Ensuring that all employees, contractors, and relevant third parties have a proper awareness and concern for information security and an adequate appreciation of their responsibility and obligation for the protection of data assets.

- Providing a framework giving guidance for the establishment of standards, guidelines, and procedures for handling sensitive data to ensure its confidentiality, integrity, and availability.

- Complying with legal, regulatory, and contractual requirements.

- Establishing a baseline data security stance.

Scope

The scope outlines the policy's applicability, including who and what is covered by it. It defines the data to which the policy applies and the people or organizations who are stakeholders in it, including who must observe the policy and who must understand the policy in order to perform their duties.

In general, the policy will apply to all employees, consultants, business partners, and third-party vendors who access or use organizational data. It will set forth specific responsibilities for those who have primary responsibility for information resources, individuals who use those resources, and individuals who have management or supervisory responsibility. The organization should confirm that in the case where external parties access sensitive information, their security policies meet internal security requirements, or that the risk from policy variance is understood and mitigated.

The policy will apply to all information resources, including those used under license or contract, as well as the systems and databases that store or access them. It also should apply to all locations from which the data is accessed, whether internal or external. In some instances, it may be appropriate for a policy to name specific assets, such as major sites, installations, and large systems.

The scope will also define any exceptions to the policy, including business units or geographical locations that might be subject to other approved data security policies.

Privacy Principles

This describes the organization's obligations with respect to the collection, use, disclosure, and retention of sensitive personal information, especially Personally Identifiable Information (PII). In this context, privacy refers to the expectation and rights of individuals to the protection and secure handling of their personal information.

Maintaining the privacy of personal information is critical since it usually is protected by legislation and regulations that provide specific requirements on collecting and processing personal data and impose penalties for noncompliance. Additionally, a breach of privacy can potentially have significant negative consequences on customers and employees whose information was breached, including the possibility of identity theft and fraud.

The organization's privacy principles will outline the balance between the proper collection and use of customers' or employees' personal information. The obligations are outlined in guidelines that can include:

- Informing parties of the nature, purpose, and use of the information collected. This should be done at or before the time the information is collected. It will also be done before the information is used for new purposes not previously identified.

- Describing the individual's privacy rights under applicable laws.

- Describing the choices available before disclosing information as well as obtaining explicit consent regarding the collection and use of the information, with clear and simple instructions on granting consent. The will include a description of the process an individual should follow to exercise these choices or to change them at a later date subject to legal or contractual restrictions.

- Ensuring that the information is collected only for the identified and consented purposes.

- Retaining the information for only as long as necessary to fulfill the stated purposes.

- When feasible, providing individuals with access to their personal information for review and update. This includes explaining how individuals may gain access to their personal information, any costs associated with obtaining such access, the means by which the information may be updated, any reasons why access may be denied, and an escalation and dispute resolution procedures in these cases.

- Describing whether and with whom the collected information may be shared. This should be stated in such a manner that the individual can reasonably understand the circumstances under which this information will be disclosed, especially when required by law or regulation.

- Informing whether personal information is collected from sources other than the primary party, such as credit reporting agencies.

- Describing the safeguards applied to the collected information. These include security controls to prevent the unauthorized disclosure of the information as well as quality controls to ensure maintenance of accurate and relevant information for the purposes identified.

- Taking reasonable steps to ensure that any third party to which it discloses customer information has safeguards that are adequate to fulfill any representations made by the organization regarding the security of the information or the manner in which it is handled.

- Implementing and monitoring compliance with privacy policies and procedures and addressing privacy-related complaints.

Policy Statement

This section describes the particulars of the data security policy and provides the foundation for the development and implementation of specific guidelines and procedures. It will provide guidance for the various phases of the data life cycle, including generation, usage, transmission, transportation, storage, archiving, and disposal. It will also cover procedures for safeguarding organizational data processed by third parties or made available to vendors.

For each phase, the policy statement will outline administrative, technical, and physical safeguards appropriate to the size and complexity of the organization and the nature and scope of its activities. The policy statement includes the following safeguards.

Data Classification

A detailed overview of the organization's data classification scheme, of the various levels and categories, and of the criteria for classifying data into a particular category. The classification criteria should be outlined as the data security policy will provide guidance to data owners during the classification process. For each level, examples should be provided to illustrate an appropriate approach.

More specifically, criteria for confidential data should be clearly described. This will include data whose unauthorized release would be a violation of a regulation or law, could cause severe reputational, operational, or financial loss, or would constitute a violation of confidentiality agreement. It will also include account credentials and passwords. It should also address classification and protection of Personally Identifiable Information (PII) since this constitutes an important and legislatively protected class of confidential data.

The classification level will drive the development and implementation of appropriate controls based on the potential impact of a data breach upon that data.

Data Ownership

A definition of the roles of individuals and entities that are responsible for various data usage and protection activities as well as a description of the methodology used to determine those roles. This section will describe the responsibilities of data owners, including classifying data according to the classification scheme and ensuring that appropriate protection is defined and implemented. It will also describe the data custodian role of implementing and managing the necessary safeguards to protect the data based on the owner's requirements. Finally, it will ensure that users follow the established data protection practices and procedures.

Risk Assessment

A description of the various risks to data confidentiality, integrity, and availability along with an assessment of those risks. The risk assessment will be a prerequisite to the implementation of data security controls. Based on the sensitivity of the information, it will help identify and understand reasonably foreseeable threats as well as the likelihood and potential damage of these threats.

Based on the analysis of assets in relation to potential threats and vulnerabilities, the risk assessment will produce a risk matrix, which will rank the risks to mitigate and outline the potential damage that could occur should the risk materialize as well as the effective actions to mitigate or reduce the damage.

The assessment must be sufficient in scope to identify the threats from both within and outside an organization as well as risks to information managed by third-party providers.

Data Collection

The types of and manner in which information can be collected, as well as guidelines for limiting the collection of sensitive information to reduce the opportunity of compromise. This should explicitly limit the collection of private or sensitive information to the extent deemed reasonably necessary to serve a legitimate business purpose, and will outline the proper balance between the collection and use of customers' or employees' information.

Data collection practices are set and refined in order to minimize the type and amount of sensitive data collected. This can be based on an organizational review of collection points to determine the reason the data is collected and stored. Any reason that does not have a clear business purpose should be addressed.

One particular area of concern is the practice of using Personally Identifiable Information to ensure that an individual can be uniquely identified across organizational databases. Unique internal identification numbers should be used instead to minimize the storage of sensitive information and the attendant risk of compromise.

Data Access

A review of approved access controls and data security safeguards during usage, including permitted access methods, user authentication practices, entitlements and appropriate levels of access, access authorizations, changes and revocations, activity logging and tracking to ensure the retention and review of user and administrator activity, and scheduled access level reviews.

The policy will include a description of the process that ensures that user access rights reflect defined and documented business needs as well as the concepts of least privilege and segregation of duties. Other areas covered will include access provisioning for an efficient mechanism for providing access to new users, changing access rights when a user's status or role changes, and revoking access control privileges in a timely manner upon user leave or termination.

An important component of data access control is password management best practices, including complexity requirements such as minimum length, inclusion of various types of characters, password aging, password reuse, and guidance for handling lost and compromised passwords.

Data access control will also cover scheduled entitlement reviews, which are periodic assessments of permissions to systems and data to ensure that access is proper and limited to the needs of the assigned role.

This section will also describe physical access safeguards and procedures to control physical access to sensitive information, systems, and related facilities.

Transmission and Distribution

Transmission modes and safeguards for sensitive data, including approved email use, encryption processes, and remote access. This section will cover the monitoring and control of connections from internal to external systems. This includes cryptography and other security protocols to safeguard data during transmission over public networks. It will also cover the risks from wireless networks as well as appropriate controls.

Email policies should also be specified, especially mandating the encryption of sensitive information sent via email.

Because the risks associated with remote access, this section should include an overview of the policies and processes, including the use of Virtual Private Networks, governing the conditions under which remote access is granted and used.

Data Transportation

Security controls and requirements for sensitive data that is transported by individuals on laptops or personal storage devices as well as the parameters within which they can be used. These may include full-disk encryption to prevent unauthorized parties from retrieving the data or from extracting domain-based credentials and user account profiles. For laptops, it may also include a scheduled connection to the corporate network to receive the latest patches and antivirus updates, a prohibition on altering system software or hardware or on loading additional application software, and scheduled backups of all important information on the device.

Provisions should be made for training to increase awareness of the need for security in this area and for obtaining management authorization for the placement of sensitive data on the device.

For business processes that require the transfer of information via transportable media such as backup tapes for storage and archiving, a continual review process to discontinue unnecessary or redundant transfers is necessary. If the transfer cannot be terminated and the physical transfer is necessary, description of controls to ensure that sensitive data in transport is encrypted using approved encryption algorithms. The transfer process should include maintenance of a transport record with contents, origin and destination, and time shipped and received.

Third-Party Use

Controls over third-party access and use of sensitive information, including consent of primary parties represented by the information to share such information, due diligence in selecting third-party providers, review and approval of the third-party information security policy and program, contractual security obligations, and monitoring through audits and reviews.

The section will include due diligence guidelines in selecting service providers, such as the performance of vendor risk assessments based on the criticality and sensitivity of the outsourced process and data. It will also include review and approve the vendor's information security policy and program, monitoring and enforcement of provisions in the vendor contract requiring the implementation of appropriate security and data protection measures, and actions to address incidents of unauthorized access to organizational data maintained by the vendor.

Backup and Recovery

Strategies and methodologies for backup and recovery procedures, controls, and responsibilities based on the criticality of the data.

This section will include provisions for regular backups, storage, safeguarding of backup media, and scheduled recovery testing. It will also include backup encryption requirements for sensitive data.

Disposal

Information has a finite life cycle, and retaining sensitive data longer than needed by an organization or statutorily required adds to the risk that the data will be compromised. This section will provide guidelines to ensure that information that is no longer of use is disposed of properly and securely.

It will cover appropriate disposal practices to prevent unauthorized access to or use of the information by preventing it from being practicably retrieved, not only in the case of the discarding or abandonment of the information, but also the sale, donation, or transfer of any medium upon which the information is stored. These disposal practices include sanitization of storage media and shredding of paper records.

Responsibilities for appropriate disposal will also be outlined to facilitate accountability and promote compliance with disposal policies. Disposal responsibilities may include the services of a third-party disposal company.

This section can also include a description of specific information periods and timelines as determined by the organization's needs and by legal and regulatory requirements.

Roles and Responsibilities

All members of the organization share in the responsibility for protecting information resources for which they have access or ownership. However, the definition and documentation of roles and responsibilities will clarify scopes and levels of authority and help establish formal communication channels. It will also assign accountability for specific functions and foster a coordinated team effort to safeguard information.

Additionally, this definition will enable management to better allocate organizational resources to external firms or consultants by clarifying specific areas of responsibility and ensuring that all important tasks are appropriately assigned to various resources.

This section outlines the specific roles and responsibilities of each organization and/or identifiable user population. The relationships among various roles and groups may need to be defined in order to reduce ambiguity related to areas of responsibility or authority.

Organizational Management

Management's responsibility is to protect the organization's information resources by implementing best practices that achieve an effective balance between cost and risk.

It is ultimately responsible for security strategy, for providing the resources and means to implement an effective policy, and for establishing a security-aware culture.

Unit Management

Managers of individual units will ensure that they and their staff are aware of legislative and regulatory requirements, threats, controls, and practices relevant to their area. They appoint data owners and ensure that protective and detective controls are in place and operating effectively.

Information Security Officer

The Information Security Officer is responsible for enterprise data security, including the management of the organization's information security program and the development and implementation of security practices. Responsibilities include defining the controls applicable to data classification levels, ensuring compliance to the data security policy, facilitating information security training and awareness programs, and consulting with staff members on information security issues.

Data Owner

A data owner is designated by management or is the party having acquired, developed, or created information resources for which no other party has ownership. The data owner is responsible for classifying their data according to the defined classification scheme, for ensuring that appropriate protection is defined and implemented, and for implementing procedures for access authorization according to the particular information classification.

Data Custodian

The data custodian is designated by the data owner to protect information according to the guidelines established by the owner.

User

A user is granted explicit authorization to access and use the information by the data owner and is responsible for complying with the access guidelines established by the data owner. It is the responsibility of every user with access to sensitive data to be aware of the confidential nature of the information and the disclosure and distribution limitations that apply.

User Manager

User management will notify data owners of new user access requests, as well as of access changes and revocations. They will also ensure that all current and future staff are instructed in their security responsibilities.

Operations and Infrastructure

Operational personnel and system administrators will implement and manage the technical aspects of network, database, and system access.

Development

Project managers and developers will ensure that data security guidelines are adhered to during the system development and implementation. These guidelines include security, control, and privacy issues during the requirements and design phase, access controls, audit trails, and activity logs during the development phase, and data security testing during the test phase.

Audit

Internal audit will perform compliance reviews once the policy is implemented. This will help identify operational deficiencies, ensure that any underlying problems are rectified, and offer recommendations for preventing problems in the future.

Internal audit can also help ensure that security policies and procedures are enforceable by providing input during the implementation process.

Human Resources

Human Resources will advise on personnel issues, in particular if employees are the victims of a breach or are suspected of causing the breach. They can also assist with staff communications, policy compliance enforcement, and on the protection of employee information.

Legal

The legal department can provide advice on relevant data protection legislation and its effect as well as general legal exposure and liability. It can ensure that the policy is consistent with relevant legislation and regulations as well as with other organizational policies. The legal department is also responsible for regulatory agency or law enforcement coordination in cases of reportable violations.

On an ongoing basis, the legal department should be cognizant of major contracts that the organization enters, which may have an impact or effect on sensitive data, as well as remain aware of other organizations' privacy policies as they may affect internal processes.

General Responsibilities and Obligations

In addition to duties and responsibilities assigned to the various roles, all employees should abide by the following guidelines:

- Any information that cannot clearly be classified or whose classification status is not known should be deemed confidential and protected from disclosure.

- Sensitive or nonpublic information should not be used for personal gain, in particular for the trading of securities.

- Sensitive information should be communicated only to those persons who need to know it for a legitimate business purpose.

- Sensitive information in the possession of other staff persons or business units should not be sought or obtained unless there is a legitimate need to know.

- Confidential information of any former employer should not be brought into or used in the organization without the prior written consent of the former employer.

Reporting Data Security Breaches

A statement of how and to whom any suspected or confirmed data security breaches should be reported. This will include:

- A description of the various types of sensitive data, especially Personally Identifiable Information.

- A definition of a reportable incident, which occurs when an unauthorized person is believed to have gained access to sensitive data that or when an authorized person misuses that data. This definition will provide clear guidelines on the kinds of events to report.

- Information to include in the report based on the type of compromise.

- Defined points of contact with details and availability, as well as a general hotline or other means of contact.

- The reporting mechanism and specific procedures to follow for recording and reporting the event, including management and Incident Response Team notification.

Enforcement

Policy enforcement is critical due to the serious nature of data breaches, the regulatory compliance environment, and the scrutiny of internal and external audits. The enforcement section will explain organizational expectations regarding adherence to the policy and provide instructions on reporting violations. It will outline how and to whom a violation should be reported, include a statement of the action to be taken by the organization in the event of noncompliance, and describe the various types of violations with consequences and possible disciplinary actions. The process should implement a tiered structure of sanctions that accounts for the magnitude of harm and possible types of inappropriate activity.

Disciplinary or corrective action may be based upon the following:

- Failure to implement and maintain security controls for which an employee is responsible and aware.

- Exceeding authorized access to or intentional disclosure of sensitive data to unauthorized parties.

- Failure to report any known or suspected loss of control or unauthorized disclosure of sensitive data.

- For managers, failure to adequately instruct, train, or supervise employees in their security responsibilities.

Because noncompliance to the policy can be unintentional, it is important that along with enforcement, the organization make provisions for orientation, training, and a grace period from the implementation of the policy until full compliance.

Exceptions

There will be situations where the strict application of a policy might significantly impact the operations or services of a business unit, such as in the case where a critical system cannot support required security features or where compliance costs are disproportionate relative to the potential risk. An exception to the policy can be requested to accommodate specific requirements. This section will provide a documented process for requesting and approving exceptions to the policy by describing the procedures for determining, requesting, documenting, and approving policy waivers or variances based upon a particular unit's business needs.

Risk Acceptances are used to document and request policy exceptions. They include:

- Description of the requested exception.
- Reasons for noncompliance.
- Justification for why the exception is warranted.
- Assessment of risk associated with noncompliance.
- Plan for alternate means of risk management or compensating controls implemented to address the risk.
- Anticipated length of noncompliance.
- Review date to evaluate progress toward compliance.

Once a business unit head decides that the exception is warranted, the Risk Acceptance will be reviewed and approved/conditionally approved/denied by the Information Security Officer.

Distribution

Procedures for the dissemination of the policy, including distribution to new and current users. These procedures will include distribution tracking as well as the receipt of acknowledgements from users that they have read, understood, and agreed to abide by the policy.

This section will also describe the mechanism for obtaining additional copies of the policy, including a web site for electronic downloads.

Contacts

A list of individuals or organizations to contact for further information, guidance, and compliance along with their contact information. This will include the policy owner (generally the Information Security Officer) for questions about specific content, technical contacts for security technology implementation and use, and the incident response team or help desk to report a data security incident.

Related Documents

References to any additional documents that particular groups may need to know about in order to complement, supplement, or help explain provisions of the policy.

These can include other security policies, internal standards, guidelines, procedures, and external reference documents.

Definitions

The definitions of the terms used in the policy to a level appropriate to reduce usage ambiguity. Definitions from external sources should include the reference document from which the definition was extracted.

Within the context of the Data Security Policy, special attention should be paid to accurate definitions for a data breach, data owner and custodian, data classification levels, response plan, and Data Breach Response Team.

Acknowledgment

An acknowledgement section to ensure that all parties have read the policy, understand the contents, and agree to abide by it.

Related Policies

Policy development originates in a layered process from high level principles and plans beginning at a strategic level that considers the organization's fundamental security goals. To be effective, a policy should be consistent with other existing directives, laws, organizational culture, guidelines, procedures, and the organization's overall mission.

The organizational Information Security Policy will set the strategic direction and scope of the organization's security posture. This executive-level document will guide the development and management of the security program by describing and assigning responsibilities for organizational security programs. The Information Security Policy will serve as the umbrella under which issue-specific security policies will be developed.

The Data Security Policy will exist within a hierarchy and framework of other organizational security and acceptable use policies and will be integrated into and consistent with these policies. These additional issue and systems-specific policies can include:

- **Access Control** Logical access controls to ensure the confidentiality and integrity of information and systems, including access provisioning for granting, modifying, and revoking access, authentication, entitlement reviews, privileged accounts, and developer and administrator access to production.

- **Password Usage** Password best practices including length, complexity, aging, reset, invalid sign-on attempts.

- **Email Acceptable Use Policy** Email purpose and status as an organization resource, employee responsibilities when using email in day-to-day working activities, nonbusiness use, monitoring and expectations of privacy, codes of conduct, prohibited and unacceptable content and use, sensitive information transmission.

- **Intellectual Property** Delineates the rights and obligations of individuals and the organization with regard to internally developed or externally licensed intellectual property.

- **Incident Response Policy** Formation of a response team, incident reporting, assessment, and response, external and internal notifications.

- **Firewall** Firewall types and topology, baseline configurations, rules and filters, services, content restrictions, security and authentication, permissible traffic, management and maintenance, Traffic monitoring, auditing and testing, procedures for addressing requests to bypass firewall security.

- **Intrusion detection system** Requirements for network and host IDSes, events and alerts indicating intrusions, responses to intrusions, roles, responsibilities, and authority for administrators, security personnel, and users.

- **Virus and Patch Management** Server and workstation virus and patch management, scheduled and automatic updates and scans, procedures for handling infections that cannot be automatically removed.

- **Encryption** Approved algorithms and products, guidelines for usage, key management.

- **Backup and Recovery** Backup and recovery procedures, including scheduled backups, backup media onsite storage, offsite rotation, failed backup notification and rerun, scheduled restorations for data integrity testing.

- **Record Retention** Organizational, regulatory, and legal requirements for retention periods for various types of records.

- **Data Transmission** Security and encryption protocols, wireless access.

- **Remote Access** Management approval, access review, access mechanism, security, and encryption.

- **Information Disposal** Disposal measures based on information sensitivity, internal and outsourced disposal functions, logging.

- **Third-Party Vendor Management** Vendor selection, vendor risk assessments, review and approval of vendor information security policy and programs, contracts and service level agreements, monitoring.

- **Asset Management** Lifecycle management of the IT assets from acquisition to installation, operations, and disposal. Acquisition responsibility and process, hardware and software standard configurations, approved vendors, tracking and inventory procedures, software licensing, transfers, reallocation, and disposal.

- **Change Management** Regular and emergency change management procedures, including change initiation and change requests, business and technical risk assessment, security impact review, notification, testing, back-out procedures, change monitoring.

- **Problem Management** Problem management procedures, logging and categorization, escalation procedures, repetitive problems.

- **Software Development Life Cycle** Software development and purchase methodology, including individual phase description, inputs, end products, responsible parties, and required approvals. Security considerations in project requests, feasibility studies, business requirements, functional and system specifications, development, testing, migration, and production.

- **Physical Security** Physical access and security, including general organizational and data center security to limit physical access to sensitive information, systems, related facilities, and equipment from unauthorized intrusion as well as natural and environmental hazards.

- **Disaster Recovery and Business Continuity Planning** Procedures for recovering and restoring partially or completely interrupted critical functions within a predetermined time after a disaster or extended disruption, including regaining access to data, infrastructure, and other organizational processes.

Many of these policies build upon other related policies that must be referenced within their contents. These references can help limit contradictions between separate policies and simplify compliance management through the ability to trace high-level policy requirements to specific guidelines in lower-level policies.

Although security requirements are seldom contradictory, they may not always be complementary. As a part of the initial development and the periodic policy review, policies should be sufficiently coordinated to ensure effective implementation of a variety of convergent security objectives.

All related policies should be structured using a standard format so that they can be effectively coordinated and updated. This will help enforce consistency and ensure that all policy documents include standard required elements such as such as the author, version, and effective date.

As in the case of the data security policy itself, all policies must have a policy owner ultimately responsible for the creation, distribution, and update, be properly disseminated to the affected parties, be reviewed on a scheduled basis, and provide a mechanism through which feedback can be efficiently received and incorporated.

Policy Implementation

Policy implementation is a process that begins with the formal issuance of the policy. It goes beyond a one-time statement or directive and involves communication, orientation, training, and discrete steps toward compliance.

The initial step is the distribution of the policy to all the affected parties, and its issuance should be publicized through a variety of means to ensure high visibility, since nearly all employees will in some way be affected and major security issues are being addressed. The visibility aids implementation by helping to ensure the policy is fully communicated throughout the organization.

Orientation sessions for new as well current employees will help instill the importance of data security and explain the implications of the policy. More formal training classes can be offered, especially to those employees whose activities will be most affected by the policy. It may also be necessary to develop supporting guidance on how to effectively implement the data security policy across the organization. This subsequent guidance should be consistent with the policy and should not supersede it unless the policy itself is being modified.

A mechanism should be implemented to track the distribution of the policy as well as the receipt of acknowledgements from users that they have read the policy. This tracking should include the date of acknowledgement and the policy version.

Beyond the initial distribution and training, the policy should be readily available for access from a specified site, usually the Information Security Office site.

Update and Maintenance

Over time, policies and procedures may become inadequate because of changes in organizational mission, operational environment, threats and vulnerabilities, inadequate compliance, or changes in technology, infrastructure, or business processes.

The organization should ensure that its data security policy is sufficiently current to accommodate the information security environment, organizational mission, and operational requirements. A policy review and revision cycle should be implemented in order to achieve this goal. This review process will also demonstrate management's commitment to the security program.

After it has been formalized, the data security policy should be reviewed and updated at scheduled intervals. It is the responsibility of the policy owner to facilitate this review and to establish the mechanisms for updating the policy, including the process, the people involved, and the people who must sign off on the changes.

In addition to the schedule review, there are various events that can trigger the need to review and update a policy, including:

- Technology and process changes
- Process or business changes
- Material changes in business practices that may implicate the security of sensitive information
- New regulatory or legal requirements
- Internal feedback
- Independent reviews
- Relevant audit information
- Reported information security incidents
- Violations of the policy indicating a shortcoming in a particular area.
- Editorial, content, or reference changes
- Policy expiration

A mechanism should be put in place to allow managers to request or suggest policy changes and to review those requests in a timely manner for possible inclusion.

The data security policy, like all other organizational policies, should have a version number to indicate version in force and maintain a version history. This will also serve as an update reminder if a significant amount of time has elapsed between updates.

Along with the version, each policy should have an effective date and an expiration date. This will help users determine the current applicability of the policy as well as the next update date. These dates should conform to the organization's objectives regarding policy update cycles.

Changes to the data security policy should be made based on the organization's change management policies and procedures.

Compliance Audit

Auditing is a key means of contributing to good governance and accountability by ensuring policy compliance and assuring management that the organization's data is being appropriately protected. Audits are designed to provide an independent assessment of risks, testing and evaluation of the state of data security controls; uncover gaps that may require remediation; and provide recommendations for improvement. In addition, they evaluate the organization's efforts to comply with laws and regulations and ensure that organizational practices are in line with industry standards.

At the beginning of the policy development project, the Information Security Officer will coordinate with internal audit to determine how soon after policy publication compliance will be expected and audits based on the policy will be conducted. This will allow the various units to identify any deviations or gaps from the policy within their area. The grace period for compliance will provide users with enough time to implement the necessary processes and controls and will ensure that the policy is enforceable.

In addition to internal or external audits, self-assessments provide a method to determine the current status of the data security program and policy compliance, systematically identify programmatic weaknesses, and, where necessary, establish a target for improvement.

Metrics

Metrics facilitate decision making and improve performance and accountability through the collection, analysis, and reporting of relevant data about the status of measured activities. They facilitate improvement in those activities by applying corrective actions based on observed measurements, justifying investment requests, and targeting funds specifically to areas in need of improvement.

Metrics will provide an indication of the organization's progress and maturity in meeting its data security policy goals. They enable continuous improvement by providing an objective way of scoring the status of a particular security item. In addition, management's request for metrics will communicate the importance of policy compliance across the organization. Metrics fall into three classes:

- Implementation metrics to demonstrate progress in implementing policies and procedures and individual security processes and controls.

- Effectiveness metrics to measure the effectiveness and monitor the results of particular security controls.

- Impact metrics to measure the positive and negative impact of information security on the organization. These metrics can provide the most direct insight into the value of the data security policy.

Compliance metrics should be collected and documented in a predefined format to ensure repeatability and standardization and to guide collection, analysis, and reporting activities. Some key metrics include:

- **Awareness** Including signed compliance statements, orientation, and training completion.

- **Technical Compliance** Compliance levels of key technologies based on risk.

- **User Compliance** User compliance levels including data classification, documented access reviews, and policy violations.

- **Audit Reviews** Percentages of audit finding and resolutions.

Metrics can also be used to measure the organization's maturity level and provide targets for improvement. Particular security items and controls can be rated based on an indicated level in achieving progress toward a particular objective. Maturity levels can generally be set as follows:

- **Level 1** An asset is at level 1 if there is a formal documented policy that establishes a continuing cycle of security planning, risk management, review of security controls, lifecycle management, access controls, rules of behavior, and training.

- **Level 2** This level is achieved when formally documented procedures are developed based on the policy. These procedures focus on implementing specific security controls and provide the foundation for an accurate and complete understanding of the security program implementation. Level 2 requires actual procedures for a continuing cycle of risk assessment as well as control implementation and monitoring.

- **Level 3** At this level, the security procedures and controls are implemented in a consistent manner as opposed to ad hoc approach applied on an individual or case-by-case basis. Procedures are reinforced through an effective training and awareness program tailored for varying job functions.

- **Level 4** Level 4 requires the continual evaluation of the adequacy and effectiveness of security policies, procedures, and controls while ensuring that effective corrective actions are taken to address identified weaknesses. The evaluations should include tests and examinations of key controls and timely remediation of any deficiency.

- **Level 5** The highest maturity level is achieved when a comprehensive security program is an integral part of the organizational culture. With management support, an ongoing program is implemented to identify and institutionalize best practices, including continual improvement to policies, procedures, and controls, and the integration of security planning within the technical and operational infrastructure as well as within each stage of the asset lifecycle.

In order to be effective, metrics must use data that can realistically be obtained from existing processes and data repositories, and measure processes that already exist and are relatively stable. A weighed scale can be used to differentiate the importance of selected metrics based on the overall risk mitigation goals and to ensure that the results accurately reflect existing security program priorities.

In measuring organizational performance, trends are often more useful than individual measurements since they can help determine whether the organizational security compliance maturity is improving or declining.

In addition to the preceding objectives, metrics can be used to measure risk reduction as a function of security investments, to benchmark the organization's efforts by comparing them with the ones of other entities in its field, and to demonstrate measurable compliance to relevant laws, regulations, and policies.

Management and Board Approval

Good information security governance requires that an organization implements appropriate information security policies and controls to support its mission. This is the process of establishing and maintaining a framework to provide assurance that information security strategies are aligned with and support business objectives, are consistent with applicable laws and regulations, and provide appropriate assignment of responsibility.

Governance responsibility ultimately rests with the organization's executive board. As such, management should provide the board or an appropriate board committee a written report on the information security program at least annually. Organizations with more complex operations may find it necessary to provide information to the board on a more frequent basis. Similarly, more frequent reporting may be appropriate whenever a material event or significant modification affecting data security occurs. The content of the report will vary depending upon the nature and scope of activities as well as the different circumstances that arise during the implementation and maintenance of the security program.

The executive board should approve the written information security policies and oversee the development, implementation, and maintenance of the information security program, including assigning specific responsibility for its implementation and reviewing reports from management.

Summary

- A data security policy is a formal statement that sets out an organization's approach to managing information security, outlines the essential requirements for protecting data assets, and establishes management's expectations for data confidentiality, integrity, and availability.

- Policies are implemented through standards, guidelines, and procedures, which offer specific approaches to implementing policy and meeting organizational goals.

- A documented and distributed data security policy establishes uniform security processes, provides employees the assurance that they are performing their duties correctly, provides a baseline of performance expectations, and ensures compliance to data protection laws and regulations.

- A data security policy development team will include participation from Information Security, IT operations, legal, internal audit, business and organizational management, and other relevant subject matter experts.

- The organization's size, activities, regulatory environment, and numbers and types of information systems will shape management's security goals and establish data security principles.

- The policy statement of purpose will provide a concise statement of what the policy is intended to accomplish as well as the factors that necessitate its development and implementation.

- The policy should apply to all employees, consultants, business partners, and third-party vendors who access or use organizational data.

- Privacy principles describe the organization's obligations with respect to the collection, use, disclosure, and retention of sensitive personal information, especially Personally Identifiable Information (PII).

- The policy will include guidance on data classification, data ownership, risk assessment, data collection, access, transmission and distribution, third-party use, backup and recovery, and disposal.

- The definition of roles and responsibilities will clarify scopes and levels of authority and assign accountability for specific functions.

- The policy will describe the process of how and to whom any suspected or confirmed data security breaches should be reported.

- Policy enforcement is critical due to the serious nature of data breaches, the regulatory compliance environment, and the scrutiny of internal and external audit.

- To be effective, the data security policy should be consistent with other existing directives, laws, organizational culture, guidelines, procedures, and the organization's overall mission.

- Policy implementation begins with the formal issuance of the policy and involves communication, orientation, training, and discrete steps toward compliance.

- A policy review and revision cycle should be implemented in order to ensure that the data security policy is sufficiently current to accommodate the information security environment, organizational mission, and operational requirements.

- Auditing is a key means of contributing to good governance and accountability by ensuring policy compliance and assuring that the organization's data is being appropriately protected.

- Metrics facilitate decision making and improve performance and accountability through the collection, analysis, and reporting of relevant data about the status of measured activities.

- Metrics will provide an indication of the organization's progress and maturity in meeting its data security policy goals and improve performance and accountability.

- Data security responsibility ultimately rests with executive management and the organization's executive board, which will ensure that the organization implements appropriate information security policies and controls to support its mission.

Chapter 5

Response Program

Solutions in this chapter:

- Data Breach Response Team
- Developing the Response Plan

☑ Summary

Introduction

Given the volume of sensitive information collected and used by organizations to carry out their functions, it is almost inevitable that at one time or another a loss of control of such information will occur. Even though preventative activities based on the results of risk assessments and general best practices can lower the number of such incidents, not all incidents can be prevented, and no information security policies or safeguards will guarantee total protection of information and systems.

Despite efforts at identifying and correcting security vulnerabilities, weaknesses will remain given the difficulty in sustaining a fully secured posture, and focusing solely on prevention may not be enough to insulate an organization from the effects of a security breach. Over the long term, a large amount of resources is needed to maintain security commensurate with all potential vulnerabilities, so that even the best information security program may not identify every residual vulnerability and prevent every incident, especially since new previously unidentified threats will occur.

An important step in responding to a breach is to engage in advance planning for this contingency. A data breach response program should be a key part of an organization's information security infrastructure since the ability to respond quickly and effectively is critical to efforts to minimize the effects of the breach. An incident response capability is necessary for rapidly detecting incidents, minimizing loss and destruction, mitigating the weaknesses that were exploited, and restoring data and services. The goal is to maintain coordination and focus by executing a predefined set of response steps and minimizing reliance on immediate decisions made under pressure.

In addition to a best practice approach, data breach response programs may be mandated for certain regulated industries and may reduce certain areas of liability in the case of a breach by demonstrating proactive planning and consideration for this eventuality.

Objectives

Because a data security breach is a unique type of event, a documented risk-based response program presents the opportunity for developing a strategy and blueprint for action during an incident, minimizing the chance that important activities will fall through the cracks. It can provide a well-defined, organized approach for handling potential threats and for taking appropriate action. A formal incident response capability will provide the following benefits:

- Outline a defined roadmap for responding to data security incidents appropriately and systematically.

- Allow the organization to quickly and efficiently recover from data security incidents, minimizing loss or theft of information and disruption of services.

- Minimize the costs associated with the actual response by utilizing staff and resources more efficiently and reducing wasted or ineffective effort.

- Use information gained during incident handling to better prepare for handling future incidents and to provide stronger protection for systems and data.

- Deal properly with legal issues that may arise during incidents, including the establishment of controls for proper retrieval and handling of potential evidence.

- Mitigate downstream regulatory and legal liability for failure to exercise due care in response to a data security incident.

- Avoid compounding the reputational damage caused by the initial breach through inaction or faulty response.

- Establish an infrastructure of security professionals who can quickly respond to data and system breaches and protect against security compromises.

- Provide opportunities for improving organizational knowledge and contributing to continuous process improvement.

Establishing, documenting, and maintaining an incident response program will allow the organization to maintain situational awareness during a significant breach, since many people may play a role in the incident response and may need to communicate rapidly and efficiently with various internal and external groups.

Structure

The structure of the response program should be appropriate to the size and complexity of the organization and the nature and scope of its activities. The components of an effective response program include:

- Incident prevention through the establishment minimization of the risk of data security incidents by ensuring that appropriate safeguards and controls are implemented throughout the organization.

- Incident preparation through the establishment of an incident response capability.

- Formation, staffing, and training of a core response team that will have primary responsibility for managing the incident.

- Establishment of clear procedures for assessing the nature, scope, and impact of the incident and identifying what information has been accessed or misused.

- Measures to contain and control the incident to prevent further unauthorized access to or misuse of customer information, while preserving records and other evidence.

- Building relationships and establishing suitable means of communication with other internal as well as external groups.

- Notification to affected parties when warranted.

Business Impact Analysis

A risk analysis will allow the organization to identify and measure various threats and their likelihood and will be used as the basis for implementing appropriate controls to mitigate those threats. A Business Impact Analysis (BIA) is an assessment of the impact of various types of compromises on the organization. It uses the list of threats and vulnerabilities identified in the risk assessment, but differs through the assumption that installed controls have been bypassed or are ineffective and that a compromise occurred.

The BIA will be an essential element in the development of a response plan. Understanding the compromises that the organization may be vulnerable to and the type of damage that may occur will help in ensuring that the response plan is comprehensive and appropriate to the organizational infrastructure and operations.

Data Breach Response Team

A key practice in preparing for a potential incident is establishing a team that is specifically responsible for responding to data breach incidents. A Data Breach Response Team (DBRT) is an internal group established to provide an effective and orderly response to a data security incident. It receives, reviews, and responds to incident reports and activity, manages the incident lifecycle, assists in recovery, and closes incidents. The DBRT's objectives are:

1. Incident evaluation, analysis, response, containment, and eradication in accordance with organizational policy and legal requirements.

2. Negative impact mitigation for the organization, its clients, or other parties.

3. Disclosure, affected party notification, and timely communication to appropriate parties.

4. Lessons learned and follow-up implementation to reduce the risk of similar occurrences.

In addition to reactive services, which are triggered by a data breach event or report, the DBRT can perform proactive services, which provide assistance and information to help prepare, protect, and secure systems and data in anticipation of possible events and thus directly reduce the number of future incidents. Such services include policy development, training and awareness, risk analysis, vulnerability assessments, security auditing, and security-related information dissemination.

When selecting a team structure and staffing model, several factors should be considered, including the size of the organization, scope and type of operations, the geographic diversity of major resources, cost, and available staff expertise.

Benefits

The main purpose of forming a DBRT is to better position the organization to respond to a given incident by developing a team that can effectively carry out the defined response program by assigning roles and responsibilities to ensure that incident handling and reporting is comprehensive and efficient. A structured team can provide the following benefits:

- **Coordination** Individuals who are members of a team and who report to a specified team leader will more effectively carry out designated tasks at the specific times required.

- **Expertise** Preplanning can ensure that individuals with specific subject matter expertise are identified and can offer appropriate knowledge to apply during an emergency.

- **Efficiency** Collective wisdom and established communications channels will increase efficiency and help the response efforts remain on track.

- **Bridging of Organizational Barriers** The predefined authority vested in the team will help overcome organizational barriers more effectively than any single individual, particularly since team members are sourced from a variety of departments and business units.

- **Internal Communications and Preparedness** A data breach and incident response capability enhances internal communications and the readiness of the organization to respond to any type of incident, not just security incidents. Internal communications will be improved and contacts preestablished with public affairs, legal staff, law enforcement, and other groups.

Organization

The DBRT is generally composed of a core group of senior officials designated to make decisions regarding the organization's response to a data security incident. Members of the core group are intended to have decision-making authority and to take responsibility for ensuring that courses of action being considered have been reviewed appropriately with the relevant constituency of each member.

The group convenes in the event of a loss or suspected loss of sensitive information to conduct a risk analysis to determine the severity of the incident and manage the organization's response based on the nature and scope of the incident. Depending on the nature of the incident, an incident specific support team will complement the effort of the core team by providing expertise and personnel from the business units affected, especially data owners and custodians.

Most of the members of the response team will have regularly assigned organizational duties, since it is usually impractical for any but the largest organizations to maintain a standing team specifically dedicated to data breach management. In addition to organizational size and nature of business activities, a standing team might need to be continually maintained in cases of significant previous breaches that have attracted regulatory attention or increased reputational exposure.

In order to implement a DBRT, management must identify key employees within various units whose specialized knowledge, training, and experience would qualify them to address data incidents. Such experts would include senior personnel from information security, technology operations, risk management, internal audit, legal, and public affairs. A survey of which incident management and data security activities are already occurring in other parts of the organization and who is responsible for performing these activities can expedite the planning and design process of building a formal response capability. As a practical matter, staffing will depend on available in-house or contracted expertise, organization size, technology base, severity or complexity of possible data breaches, and funding.

In addition to internal and external resources that have been pre-identified for use during the response to an incident, the response team director should also have the authority to rapidly request and obtain additional resources as needed for incidents whose scope may overwhelm available staff.

Team Members

Each team member will have particular duties depending on their background and role within the team. In general, one or more team members will:

- Act as a central coordinator to receive all reports of actual or suspected data security incidents, including monitoring automated reporting mechanisms as well as hotlines.

- Triage incidents and make initial severity assessments.

- Direct escalating incidents that pose a significant threat to the organization to the team director for further attention.

- Perform assigned duties during incident investigation, management, and closure.

- Ensure the completeness, accuracy, and communication of incident documentation.

- Analyze and document root cause.

- Determine, in concert with the impacted business units or sectors, the necessity for creating and implementing a Corrective Action Plan.

- Produce Lessons Learned and training and awareness documentation.

- Assist the General Counsel in the compilation of any regulatory report concerning the incident.

- Develop content for the Data Incident Management web site on the organizational network.

Team Director

A team director, generally a senior manager from information security, will have the delegated authority to carry out incident response activities and will manage the team and coordinate the overall response and recovery activities during simulations and walkthroughs as well as during an actual incident. This manager will also make the final determination of whether an incident or suspected breach poses a significant enough risk to convene the team and activate the response plan.

The director will necessarily be a senior employee with significant technical and managerial experience and strong leadership qualities, both in order to lead and motivate a team under external pressure as well as to be able to make critical decisions without the consensus and approval usual under normal circumstances. The director is responsible for ensuring compliance with the response process, including:

- Determining the severity assessment of triaged incidents.

- Apprising executive management of very high severity incidents or incidents that have significant legal, regulatory, or public impact.

- Initiating the response process and gathering the team.

- Managing the Data Breach Response Team and the incident response process.

- Coordinating all relevant processes across the organization to ensure an effective response.

- Engaging appropriate internal and external parties.

- Acting as a liaison to the business managers whose systems or data have been impacted or whose operations may be affected as a result of the incident or of the incident response process.

- Acting as the main point of contact for evidence collection in order to reduce threats to its integrity due to multiple handling.

- Ensuring appropriate actions are taken to close incident investigations.

- Making recommendations based on findings and lessons learned.

- Tracking follow-up documentation related to an incident, including Root Cause Analysis, Lessons Learned, and Corrective Action Plans.

- Managing the creation and distribution of incident metrics to senior management at the business and corporate level.

- Ensuring that team members have and will continue to acquire the required knowledge and skills set for their roles.

- Working to improve the incident management program as needed.

Functional Membership and Duties

The Data Breach Response Team will include a core group composed of the Chief Security Officer, General Counsel, Director of Public Affairs, and a senior business line manager. This core group will oversee the management of tasks related to resolving the incident. The director will determine whether to convene the core team and will establish a schedule of meetings with relevant participants to plan the work of the team. In certain instances, the director may designate a working group to gather facts in advance of determining whether to convene the team.

Depending on the incident, this core group will be supplemented by temporary team members who are subject matter experts for the particular data, systems, and business issues involved in the incident. These temporary team members usually are assigned at the request of the director and serve for the duration of the incident. They can include the Chief Information Officer or delegate, technical and information security specialists, auditors, human resources staff, the data owner of the breached information, and any other organizational or industry-specific personnel. In smaller organizations, one person can assume one or more of the following roles.

Chief Security Officer

The Chief Security Officer (CSO) will serve as the director of the Data Breach Response Team and will be responsible for managing the necessary tasks to assess, contain, control, and mitigate the effects of the breach and prevent further unauthorized access to or use of sensitive information. In addition, the CSO will determine the role of each team member in a particular incident investigation, calling upon external subject matter experts as needed, and act as the primary liaison to executive management and other relevant parties.

As the team director, the CSO will also manage pre- and postincident activities such as training, walkthroughs, post-mortems, and general organizational preparation.

Chief Privacy Officer

The Chief Privacy Officer (CPO) is the senior executive within the organization responsible for managing all activities related to the adherence to the organization's policies and procedures covering customer and employee privacy. If the breach relates to Personally Identifiable Information or other private data, the CPO will advise on the existing privacy-related procedures and on relevant laws and regulations.

Legal Counsel

The General Counsel or other legal representative shall be responsible for providing legal support and guidance in response to a suspected or actual breach. This responsibility includes:

- Determining whether referral of a breach to regulators, law enforcement, or other external entities is warranted.

- Determining whether a particular breach has reached the affected party notification threshold.

- Advising of possible downstream liability such as when a compromised system is used to access another organization's data or when internal systems are being used for malicious activity.

- Advising on privacy issues.

- Specifying whether evidence should be collected for future legal proceedings and ensuring that evidence gathering, chain of custody, and preservation are appropriate.

- Serving as the official legal representative in any formal administrative or judicial proceedings that might arise as a result of a suspected or actual breach.

Public Affairs

The Public Affairs department shall be consulted when any incident needs to be reported externally. It will have the primary responsibility for developing and crafting a media communications plan to ensure consistent messages. This will include press statements, addressing media inquiries, monitoring media coverage and distributing accordingly, and providing talking points for other staff members who may communicate about the issue with external constituencies.

Additional duties in relation to data breach incident preparation will include monitoring sensitive data and privacy breaches of other organizations and how they respond.

Human Resources

Human Resources will provide advice in situations where an incident implicates the conduct of employees. This representation ensures that proper procedures are followed should an employee be found to be purposely or unwittingly the source of an incident, or the actual victim of the incident.

Chief Information Officer

The Chief Information Officer (CIO) shall be responsible generally for providing information technology guidance in responding to a suspected or actual breach, including identification and relevance of controls protecting the data. The CIO will facilitate the engagement of IT technical and staff resources in order to provide the team with in-depth knowledge of technical operations and configurations. This will include providing access to necessary hardware and software as well as specialized personnel such as systems and database administrators. These resources will also help minimize the impact of the incident to end users.

Audit

IT auditors will assist in understanding the cause of the incident, ensuring that procedures are complied with, and working with other team members to control the incident. Additionally, financial auditors will help assess the damage incurred in terms of monetary value for insurance or law enforcement purposes.

Data Owner

Data owners for any compromised system or data are the party most knowledgeable about the sensitivity, function, and structure of information and ultimately responsible in determining the effect of the breach on critical assets under their management. If personal information is involved, the data owner will determine who might be affected. In addition to the data owner, a senior business manager from the affected business unit should be available to discuss specific program and policy issues relevant to the breach.

Other Resources

Other resources and staff from within and outside the organization that may participate in the response should be identified and their roles defined before an incident in order to solicit and ensure their availability and cooperation during the response process.

Skills

Members of the DBRT will be skilled in particular areas of expertise based on individual backgrounds. In addition, all members should possess good interpersonal and communication skills since they may be required to communicate with the constituency and other team members in high-pressure circumstances, where misunderstandings can escalate and detract from the effectiveness of the response effort.

All members of the team should have a thorough knowledge of the incident response plan as well as an understanding of basic security principles, risk analysis with the effect of various threats upon vulnerabilities, implemented organizational controls, and data classification and sensitivity.

External Expertise

Since many attacks are technology based and require specific technical expertise to recognize and address, it is likely that only a subset of the team members may have the requisite skills to identify certain compromises, understand the full impact, and provide insight to the rest of the team. This skill set might need to be supplemented by subject-matter experts from outside the team with an in-depth understanding of organizational technology, who can provide technical guidance as well as training to team members. This additional level of expertise is a resource that can help to broaden the technical capabilities of the team.

If the organization does not have the internal expertise, it should develop relationships with external parties that can offer anticipated skill sets. Agreements should be put in place to outline the scope of any analysis and the restrictions on shared information.

Charter

The Team Charter formally establishes the team and documents its responsibility to respond to data security incidents. The Charter also delegates the authority to implement necessary actions and decisions during an incident, usually to the director of the team. The Charter includes:

- A Mission Statement, which describes the overall purpose, goals, and objectives of the team, including incident management, data and evidence collection, liaison with regulatory and law enforcement authorities, incident closures and post-mortems, data security assessments and audits, policy development, and security training and awareness. This can define the interaction with the constituency during the incident handling process.

- The Organizational Structure, which delineates the team's organization, management and reporting structure, roles, responsibilities, and place within the organization.

- The Level of Authority, which outlines the circumstances under which and the extent to which the team can intervene in the operational business units and systems without obtaining formal approval from appropriate managers. Predefined levels of approval required to perform response activities based on sensitive information classification will ensure that all members of the team are empowered to act effectively and will increase response efficiency. Because a data security incident is not a budgeted item, authority levels should also be defined for expenditures associated with the response. This section should include the identity of the sponsoring senior manager who authorizes the actions of the DBRT.

A clear statement of the DBRT's policies and charter will identify how the team fits within the organizational structure, help the constituency understand how best to report incidents, and what support to expect afterward. It will help to quickly resolve boundary disputes and other potential conflicts over who should handle an incident and the appropriate level of authority.

Availability

Data breach response capability needs to be available on a continual basis. Generally this is achieved by scheduling designated team members to act as primary and secondary central coordinators to receive reports of actual or suspected data security incidents and by monitoring reporting mechanisms.

Each member of the core team, especially the director, also should designate alternate members who can fulfill their responsibilities in case of expected or unexpected unavailability.

Most members of a data breach team do not exclusively perform team duties but have other job responsibilities or roles, including areas such as security, audit, human resources, legal, public affairs, and other key governance and operational areas. Organizational procedures should allow the ability and authority to rapidly disengage from their primary responsibilities to perform any necessary team duties during an actual breach.

Training

Staff training is necessary to bring new and existing team members up to the necessary skill level to perform their function within the team and to ensure that the overall team skill set level is up to date with emerging trends, technologies, and best practices.

Individual training requirements will be based on each team member's responsibilities, both from the perspective of the overall skills needed for each team member as well as the general skill coverage required for the team as a whole. Since a number of people may fulfill a role defined in the response plan, the training program should ensure that a sufficient number of trained and qualified team members are available to meet the needs of the plan.

In addition to training in individual tasks and responsibilities, cross-training should be provided to ensure that each team member can perform at last part of the tasks of another team member. For this purpose, a list of the most critical breach response tasks should be developed. Individuals with primary responsibility should be supplemented with other individuals with secondary responsibility in those tasks.

Particular attention should be paid to training all members of the team about issues concerning data sensitivity since they may come into contact with such data as part of the response. It may be necessary to predefine and preapprove data access levels. For governmental organizations, this may require the appropriate security clearance.

Team Support

Technical and procedural support should be implemented and available to allow the team to respond rapidly and effectively to data security incidents. This will include the details of the organization's data and other assets, links to business functions, team productivity resources such as dedicated servers and workstations, conference and meeting facilities, administrative support, specialized tools to detect and analyze data activity anomalies, and appropriate software to manage the tasks associated with the incident response.

An important component of team support is the provisioning of administrative accounts that allow privileged access to infrastructure, application, and data components. This will allow designated team members to have the proper credentials to perform emergency administrative functions necessary to incident management.

Communications

Effective communication among team members during an incident is critical, especially since the team may be operating in a time-sensitive, reactive mode. The team director needs to have a current and complete understanding of the response activities in order to plan the best possible course of action. Information will flow through the team director, who will then distribute it appropriately along with any instruction.

Crafting a clear communications plan can help in successful incident response. The plan should include methods of communication, type of information to collect and forward, and appropriate recipients along with their secondary contacts.

Information Disclosure

An information disclosure policy should be defined to provide guidance to team members regarding the type of information that can be disclosed to parties external to the response team. Generally, all information reported or gathered will be held in confidence and only shared with other team members to facilitate the response.

Even if another party has given an explicit consent to share the information, any disclosure exceptions should be made by the team director by taking into account disclosure restrictions that might be placed by organizational policy as well as by other organizations.

Constituency Awareness

Several means can be used to make the constituency aware of the existence of the Data Breach Response Team, of it mission, as well as of contact criteria. These can include incorporating this information as part of general security awareness and training as well as periodic notification, whether as a standalone bulletin or as part of other data security advisories.

A program web site will serve as an information repository to make awareness information available to the constituency in an efficient format by allowing users to review and download information without requiring assistance. The web site can include:

- Description of the DBRT
- Procedures for reporting suspected incidents
- Contact information
- Guidelines on threat and incident identification
- Public copy of the incident response plan
- Data security as well as other relevant policies
- Availability and scheduling of training and awareness programs
- Security self-tests and assessments

Funding

Organizational management may wish to centrally fund the cost of DBRT staffing and activities since data security breaches can have ramifications across the organization. This approach will also allow the team to independently investigate incidents free of departmental resource constraints and will avoid duplication of response efforts by the individual business units. Business units who have specific needs and higher risk profiles may consider implementing their own teams in coordination with a central team.

Funding levels are determined by the organizational size, complexity, business model, risks, and team structure. Costs can be reduced by minimizing the number of permanent team members and using available resources on an on-call basis. Additionally, outsourcing certain functions for which the organization does not have internal expertise may be beneficial.

Outsourcing

Data breach response may be partly or wholly outsourced if the size of or expertise available within the organization do not allow the creation of a team composed entirely of internal staff. Outsourcers may possess deeper knowledge of certain aspects of security relating to data loss that internal resources and may also be able to correlate events among customers so that they can identify and manage threats more quickly and more effectively than any individual customer.

There are several considerations when deciding whether to completely or partially outsource the response program. These include:

- **Division of Responsibilities** The extent to which the organization is willing to give an outsourcer authority to make operational decisions that may affect staff and infrastructure, including the granting of administrative privileges to its information resources. If this is of particular concern, this issue can be mitigated by having the outsourcer provide data and recommendations to an internal team, which ultimately makes operational decisions.

- **Sensitive Information Sharing** Restricting access to sensitive information can sometimes limit the effectiveness of outsourcers. This usually is addressed through contracts and oversight similar to the ones where the organization outsources services that require that the third parties access or process confidential information. In cases where the organization cannot share certain internal information with the outsourcer, a mechanism should be established to transfer responsibility for that part of the response to an internal staff member.

- **Lack of Organizational-Specific Knowledge** Internal staff usually have much better knowledge of the organization's environment than an outsourcer would. Accurate analysis and prioritization of data security incidents can be dependent on such knowledge. The organization should provide the outsourcer regular updates about its operational environment and technical infrastructure and configuration. This issue can also be a concern with wholly internal teams if communications are inadequate or operational information is not appropriately collected. Lack of organizational-specific knowledge within an internal team can be addressed in a similar manner.

- **Lack of Correlation** Effective incident response may require access to and correlation among multiple sources and logs. The response process can be negatively impacted if the outsourcer does not have administrative access to certain resources or if these resources cannot be accessed remotely.

Situations may arise in which the outsourcer is unavailable, cannot perform efficiently, or does not have the skills to effectively manage the incident. Even when completely outsourcing response capabilities, the organization should maintain basic incident response skills internally and appoint a senior manager to manage the outsourcer and to be ultimately responsible for the program.

Developing the Response Plan
Overview

During the response phase, a number of activities and actions may occur rapidly and concurrently. An effective data breach response plan will help document and prioritize these steps. It will provide a reference road map and a structured approach for handling a potential or actual data compromise within the organization and for taking appropriate action when the organization is responsible for a third-party incident.

A data breach response plan will establish procedures for handing data incidents by defining the response phases to a data security breach. These procedures describe how the response policies will be implemented and will allow all concerned parties to determine what operational steps are needed to respond in a manner that upholds the organizational security objectives.

The plan will be shaped by the organization's mission, size, structure, and functions. It will document the approach to be used in the event of data compromise by helping to identify as many tasks as possible ahead of time and by ensuring that responsibilities are clearly assigned. It will also outline scenarios that address any high-risk areas identified in the risk assessment.

The plan will include reference information, potential internal and external contacts, contact workflow, breach assessment, and mitigation and recovery strategy, and specific instructions about policies, procedures, and legal requirements. It should also provide templates for any documents required during the emergency.

It is, of course, not possible to draft a data breach response plan that can address every possible scenario. Each incident is unique with specific characteristics that may not be addressed in the plan. In addition to providing a road map for dealing with these types of incidents, the response plan should include more general guidelines on handling unexpected events that may not have been detailed.

Development

The Data Breach Response Team will be tasked with developing and testing a documented response plan. The team should be complemented with subject-matter experts from each of the organization's major business processes, internal auditors, and legal advisors.

A starting point can include the collection of information about what other organizations are doing. This can provide an initial template of what the plan needs to include for a particular industry or information risk. Effective incidence response plans should reflect experience from external as well as from internal sources and incorporate the following elements:

- Description of the types of data the organization collects, stores, and processes
- Identified risks and vulnerabilities
- Data Breach Response Team contact information
- Roles and responsibilities
- Incident detection and reporting
- Breach assessment and response

- Incident closure process

- Evidence and record preservation

- Internal and external contacts, including regulators, law enforcement, and media

- Sample notification letters and press releases

Once an initial draft is created, it will be reviewed by response team members as well as other identified stakeholders and subject matter experts and feedback provided to the team director for incorporation before the final draft approval by appropriate management.

Approval

Senior business and security management should review and approve the response plan before distribution. Because of its criticality in case of a data incident, the response plan should also be reviewed and approved by an executive board comprised of members of the governance and audit committees.

Audience

The response plan addresses the responsibilities of various organizational staff and external parties. For end users and managers, it will cover the detection and reporting of data security incidents, and for members of the response team it will outline procedures for assessing, responding to, and closing incidents. It will also take into account contractors and vendors, since third-party vulnerabilities and incidents may trigger organizational response.

The distribution of the complete plan should be restricted to the response team, since it could contain operational and response details that may allow a malicious party to circumvent established controls and undermine response and recovery procedures. Additionally, it is generally not necessary for organizational personnel to understand the internal operation of the DBRT in order to interact with it.

If desired, a redacted publicly available copy of the plan can also be developed and distributed for reference.

Contents

Members of the Data Breach Response Team will usually be tasked with creating and approving the response plan. An effective data breach response plan should incorporate the following elements.

Strategies and Goals

Overview outlining the purpose and scope of the plan. This section will include the mission statement, the organizational approach to data incident response, and how the program fits into the overall organization. It will also include an overview of the Data Security Policy.

Statement of Management Commitment

Besides ensuring that all employees understand the importance placed by the organization on the protection of its sensitive information resources and on effective incident management, this statement will provide the authority to the team to take the necessary actions during an emergency without having to go through the regular hierarchical reporting channels.

Data Breach Response Team

A description of the nature, function, and structure of the Data Breach Response Team. This will include how the team will communicate with the rest of the organization, contact information, reporting protocols, and team level of authority. Additionally, this section will outline:

- **Mandate and Objectives** The objectives of the team, including incident evaluation, analysis, and response; incident impact mitigation; management of affected party and regulatory notification; and development of lessons learned documentation and follow-up control implementation.

- **Benefits** Benefits offered by the establishment of the team, including efficient response activity coordination, expertise in various incident management skills, and enhanced communication and bridging of organizational barriers.

- **Team Organization** General organization of the team, including the core and auxiliary groups, staffing, and reporting mechanisms.

- **Team Member Responsibilities** Team director and individual member responsibilities, including triage, escalation, incident reporting, identification, analysis; and response, notification and disclosure, incident closure, and coordination with other parties.

- **Skills** Required skills and areas of expertise, including knowledge and training in data breach incident response, as well as understanding of security principles, data classification, risk analysis, implemented controls, and the effect of various threats upon vulnerabilities.

- **External Expertise** Contacts and relationships with external consultants and experts in areas where the organization does not have the required internal expertise.

- **Training** Staff training to achieve the necessary skill levels and to ensure continuing knowledge of emerging trends, technologies, and best practices.

- **Team Support** Administrative and computing support to allow the team to perform its function.

- **Communications** Information flow, channels, and hierarchy to ensure effective communications during an incident.

Contact Information

Primary and backup contact information for team members as well as on-call information for the rotating team coordination function. Contact information also should be included for parties external to the team within and outside the organization, such as administrators, managers, help desk, regulators, law enforcement, and managed services providers. This will include the timeframes within which each party must be contacted as well as the primary responsibility for contact.

List of Critical Assets

Critical information asset documentation, including types of data processed, sensitivity, infrastructure, data owners, custodians, and users.

Assets can be identified through general asset management activities or through feedback received from data owners during the data classification process.

Safeguards and Controls

The safeguards and controls in place to protect sensitive data. These will include technical, procedural, and physical controls.

Incident Types

Definitions of data security incidents that will cause the invocation of the plan with the associated risk assessment. Types of incidents include loss of information confidentiality; compromise of information integrity; misuse of services, information, or assets; unauthorized access; unusual system behavior; and intrusion detection alarms.

Business Impact Analysis

A Business Impact Analysis (BIA) will provide an assessment of the impact of various types and severities of breaches upon the organization. For each scenario, the assumption will be that existing controls have been bypassed or are otherwise ineffective. This will help guide the development of response actions appropriate to the circumstances and effects of the incident.

The BIA should consider all major sources of compromise and their impact. Since this can generate extensive information, the results should be organized and summarized in a meaningful manner.

Reporting Mechanisms and Guidelines

Procedures for notifying the response team, including a list of contacts with contact priority. The guidelines will outline the kinds of events to report, the information needed based on the type of compromise, and specific procedures to follow for recording and reporting the event. Documentation requirements should also be specified.

This section will include an example of the incident reporting form with field instructions. This form should be available online on the information security web site as well as in any other easily accessible manner. The form will include date and time of report; the reporting party's name and contact; date and time the incident occurred and was detected; the manner in which it was detected; a description of the incident or suspicious events; sensitive data believed to have been compromised along with its type, confidentiality, and quantity; steps currently taken to mitigate the incident; and any supporting documentation and attachments.

Information Disclosure

General policy on disclosure restrictions placed on information provided to the response team or information that the team provides other parties. The factors that determine if and to what extent information will be disclosed include the purpose, recipient, and category of the information. Consideration should also be given to the risk of second-level disclosure where the recipient in turn discloses the information to other parties, which can generally be addressed through labeling.

Severity Classification

Methodology for severity assessment, priority, and urgency along with the priorities for the handling of individual incidents based on the criticality of the affected resources, the risk of misuse, the impact of misuse, and the current and potential effect of the incident. Other factors that can be considered include the type and manner of loss, the ease of misuse, and the number of parties affected.

This classification will define the threshold for the director to assemble the response team within specific time parameters.

Severity classifications usually fall into three broad areas:

- **Critical or High** Incidents where sensitive data has been compromised in a manner that represents a heightened risk of disclosure.

- **Medium** Passive attacks or monitoring as well as data compromises with a low risk of disclosure.

- **Low** Incidents that do not require immediate action but should be monitored to prevent future escalation.

Analysis and Assessment

Procedures for investigating the data breach, including the actuality of the incident, its source, its progress, the vulnerability that allowed the occurrence, the data or systems compromised, and the impact on the organization. These procedures will include:

- **Preliminary Determination and Assessment** Manner in which a preliminary incident determination will be made, such as type of breach, extent, magnitude, source, business functions and units affected, precursors, data sensitivity and incident severity level, extent of possible damage, impact on the organization should the compromised data be used for identity theft or fraud, and any indications that the comprised information is being used by an unauthorized party.

- **Team Escalation** Threshold for incident escalation to the team director, additional assessment, notification of core team members, and escalation timeframes.

- **Information Gathering** Additional information collection about the breach from parties within and outside the organization and the review of technical feedback from logs and intrusion detection systems. It will include event correlation among multiple sources, baseline comparisons, and gathered information confidentiality.

- **Incident Classification**   Classification of the incident into one or more types, including system intrusions, unauthorized access, external attacks, policy violations, and technical events.

- **Scope**   The scope of the incident to clarify the extent of the compromise and to determine the response actions.

- **Severity**   Incident severity based on the sensitivity of the affected data, the risk, ease, and impact of misuse, type and manner of loss, and the number of parties affected.

Containment

Necessity and possible methods of containment of ongoing incidents to isolate and to prevent the problem from spreading. Containment measures can include shutting down particular systems or connections, disabling or elimination of internal or external means of access to the compromised or other data, systems, and services, changing passwords, and controlling physical access.

This section will also review possible tradeoffs between system and data availability and damage limitation, especially when mission-critical systems are involved or when service agreements require certain levels of availability.

Isolation

Criteria and considerations for isolating compromised data or systems, especially if isolation will significantly disrupt operations. Such criteria will consider the balance between the criticality and sensitivity of the data and the degree, severity, and consequences of the compromise. This will also specify thresholds to notify users of the status of the response as well as the estimated time to recovery.

Isolation steps include physical or logical disconnection of the data or a possible retention of connection and access for certain administrative functions. Other steps can include continuing normal operations with activity and network monitoring.

Recovery

Corrective actions related to technology, policies, and/or processes to address the breach and the underlying threat and vulnerability, restore normal operations, and to enhance security controls to prevent a recurrence, including patching vulnerabilities, improving access controls, and changing passwords.

For data integrity issues, this would include recovery of the data from a verified and validated backup source. For data confidentiality issues, it will address reactive measures aimed at limiting the impact of the compromise. Since some incidents involve the exploitation of multiple vulnerabilities, it will address the identification of the vulnerabilities and strategies for correcting or mitigating each one.

System and data monitoring will indicate signs of continued unauthorized access, and log reviews will help determine if there were access failures prior to or just following the suspected breach.

This section will include the responsibilities of organizational and business units to undertake an assessment of corrective actions to address a particular incident and reduce the likelihood that it will recur.

Forensics

Requirements for retaining records related to the incident, as well as the methods to preserve and record evidence and examples of the kinds of evidence that need to be gathered and lists of witnesses compiled. These guidelines will specify the manner in which a formal examination can be conducted to ensure the evidence admissibility. Evidence preservation factors will include:

- **Authenticity** Documentation that the evidence originated from the identified source and has not been altered.

- **Reliability** Documentation that the system that generated the evidence was reliable and that the evidence accurately represents the state of an event.

- **Chain of Custody** Documentation of locations of evidence storage and of the parties who have handled the evidence.

Disclosure and Notification

Under certain circumstances where a risk assessment indicates that the breached information has a likelihood of misuse, legal and regulatory mandates require that timely notification is given to victims. This will also help in managing reputational and legal risk and enable the affected parties to take protective measures against the consequences of identity theft or fraud.

This section will provide guidelines covering the following criteria:

- **Threshold** The determination of whether a particular incident meets the threshold notification requirements. This is arrived at through a risk analysis that considers the nature of the relevant information and the likelihood of its misuse. This will include a jurisdictional breakdown of thresholds.

- **Timing** Jurisdictional requirements affecting timing of notification. This can also be affected by law enforcement needs.

- **Contents** Typical notification contents for various types of circumstances.

- **Offered Services** Services that can be offered to the affected parties depending on circumstances, including credit monitoring and identity theft insurance.

- **Delivery** Acceptable methods of delivery to ensure that the affected parties will receive the notification.

- **Follow-up** The procedures for handling inquiries from affected parties following the receipt of the notification.

Communications

Communications with internal and external parties, including:

- **Internal** Criteria for communicating about the breach with internal staff as well as users of any affected system and data.

- **Regulatory Agencies** Procedures and responsibility for communicating with regulators as well as guidelines to determine if the incident requires such communications.

- **Law Enforcement** Procedures and contacts for communicating with law enforcement if the incident involves illegal activity.

- **Media** Responsibility for media interaction, general guidelines, and sample press releases.

- **Credit Reporting Agencies** For a large number of affected parties, credit reporting agency notification requirements in order to prepare for a surge in inquiries as well as requests for fraud alerts.

Documentation

Types of documentation that should be preserved, including how the incident was discovered, its category, the specific response steps, and its effectiveness.

Documentation activities will begin as soon as an incident has been detected and will include the details of each action when dealing with the incident, logs, external and internal communications, and any other relevant information.

Effective documentation will provide the necessary records for any disclosure and notification. During the post-incident review, documentation will help determine how the situation was handled and provide directions for future improvement.

The documentation should be organized and retained for further analysis and potential legal evidential use.

Damage Assessment

Procedures to analyze and measure the direct and indirect incident costs. Losses can include the cost of responding to the incident, conducting a damage assessment, managing the incident, and any revenue lost, cost incurred, or other consequential damages incurred. They will also include more intangible costs such as reputational and opportunity costs.

The overall impact will be categorized in terms of regulatory or legal, customer and lost business, reputational, and financial. More specific costs will include:

- **Personnel Costs** Direct personnel costs including the time of response team members as well as others who participated in the response.

- **Staff Productivity** Loss in the form of decreased productivity of employees who were prevented from working or experienced a slowdown in work because of the incident.

- **Lost Business** Costs related to the inability to service customers, decrease in sales, customers modifying relationship with the organization, and opportunity costs of future business.

- **Victim Notification** This can be legally mandated if there is a significant probability that the breach will result in identity theft or fraud. This cost is directly correlated to the number of victims.

- **Victim Assistance** Costs of assistance to help minimize the impact of the breach on its victims. These costs include credit monitoring, data breach monitoring services, identity theft insurance, and other possible incentives.

- **Call Center** Costs associated with an incremental increase in an existing call center or the setup of a new call center to handle calls from affected parties.

- **Media Management** Increase in media management activity responsibility on the public affairs department's regular scope.

- **Consulting Services** Costs for services for specialties that the organization does not have in house or to supplement existing skills.

- **Legal Fees** Legal advice in managing the breach as well as fees to represent the organization during regulatory review or civil litigation.

- **Regulatory or Legal Penalties** Fines assessed by regulatory agencies as well as civil legal penalties.

- **Reputational Costs** This is one of the most serious effects of a data breach, including the actual costs due to the loss of current customers as well as the opportunity costs due to reluctance to do business with the organization.

- **Competitive Advantage** Business effect of competitors obtaining released sensitive information.

Lessons Learned

Incident review procedures for lessons learned, including root cause analysis, preventative actions, analysis of the security measures in place around the compromised data, changes to systems, processes, and policies, appropriateness and improvement of the response capability, effectiveness of communications, and incident closure. This will provide direction in monitoring operational and technical risks and into policy and procedural enhancements.

The response team members as well as other key cross-functional personnel should be involved in the postincident review. This feedback will help identify, evaluate, and make recommendations for any needed changes and actions for the overall security strategy, security architecture, policies and procedures, the incident response plan, technological and infrastructure enhancements, team model, communications, and awareness and training.

Relevant lessons learned will be included in the revised data security and incident response plans.

Diagnosis Matrix

A diagnosis matrix will list potential symptoms with the likelihood of compromise indication, along with a fuller description of entry and validation guidance. It can provide initial guidance and can be used as a training tool. The matrix can include examples of incidents with the described symptoms. The matrix can also be helpful for help desk staff, system administrators, and others who perform their own analysis of precursors and indicators.

Vendor Contacts

A list of contacts with required licensing and reference information to enable the team to rapidly reach vendors whose products suffered the compromise in order to obtain any needed assistance.

For various installed hardware, software, and databases, this section can also include links to reference material, particularly as it relates to security and vulnerabilities, in order to rapidly identify device and software-specific procedures to handle incidents and compromises.

Internal and External Resources

A list of internal and external technical and process vendors and consultants that can supplement the response effort in the areas the organization does not have specific expertise. If other teams operate within the constituency perimeter, their authority and relationship to the DBRT should be defined.

Related Documents

Like the data security policy, the data breach response plan will exist within a framework of other security policies and procedures. This section will reference other documents that may supplement the plan. These can include other internal policies and procedures as well as external reference documents.

Future Roadmap

A proposed roadmap for maturing the incident response capability. As the incident response team and process evolve from initial inception, they will mature through the various stages characterized by the improving status and sophistication of the process. Team directors and organizational management can monitor and measure progress on the basis of this maturity model.

Information from the Lessons Learned phase can help determine improvements to the incident management processes. Capability maturity goals can include optimal funding and training, appropriate support infrastructure, improvement of controls to secure the infrastructure, and full compliance with legal and regulatory requirements.

Update

Once a plan is developed, it should be reviewed and tested on a scheduled basis to determine whether it remains effective. The response plan may become inadequate over time due to changes in the operational and technological environment, new legal and regulatory requirements, and new threats and vulnerabilities identified through risk assessments.

Part of the review is the assurance that the plan is supported with appropriate resources and incorporates lessons learned and best practice developments in order to ensure continual maturing of the organization's response capability.

In addition to the scheduled review and update, the plan should be reviewed and updated immediately if an incident occurs or a significant vulnerability is discovered and needs to be addressed. This nonscheduled update will include feedback from simulations and walkthroughs in which the plan is used in simulated incidents, lessons learned or weaknesses discovered during the management of a data security incident, or based upon any significant and relevant new information or event.

It is the responsibility of the team director to initiate and manage the plan review. Changes to the plan should be made based on the organization's change management policies and procedures.

Simulations and Walkthroughs

Periodic exercises, simulations, and walkthroughs should be conducted to help the team understand the general incident management workflow and prepare for various response situations. This is important since unless the organization has been the victim of a recent previous breach, it is unlikely that most members of the team will possess the experience of having managed and actual incident.

These exercises will help improve performance during an actual incident, increase the organization's confidence in its ability to respond to an incident, and identify flaws with or necessary enhancements to policies and procedures, communication, and the response plan. The scope of a simulation or walkthrough can range from a simple review of the plan by individual team members to live simulations where test data and systems are purposely compromised.

During the simulation, team members should be able to answer the following questions for each particular scenario:

1. Would this activity be considered a data breach or compromise?
2. If so, which section of the data security policy does this activity violate?

3. What measures are in place to attempt to prevent this type of incident from occurring?

4. What measures are in place to attempt to limit the incident's impact?

5. What were the precursors or initial indications of the incident?

6. What are the consequences of the incident not being contained?

7. How would the Data Breach Response Team analyze this incident?

8. How would the Data Breach Response Team prioritize and rank this incident?

9. What actions would be taken to contain, mitigate, and resolve the incident?

10. If notification is necessary, what parties need to be notified of the occurrence of the breach? How would each report be made?

11. What could be done to prevent similar incidents from occurring in the future?

Simulations should particularly focus on high-sensitivity systems and databases using tests and exercises defined by the team in conjunction with the responsible business operating unit.

After the simulation or test has concluded, an after-action review will focus on the tasks accomplished according to the plan as well as obstacles or deviations. Questions to consider include whether the response plan as well as any other necessary resources were readily available to the people involved in the test, the performance of the team members, and any deviations from the plan with explanations.

Summary

- An important step in responding to a breach is to engage in advance planning for this contingency by developing a data breach response program, since the ability to respond quickly and effectively is critical to efforts to minimize the effects of the breach.

- The data breach response program will outline a defined roadmap for responding to data security incidents, allow the organization to quickly and efficiently recover from incidents, help deal properly with legal issues, develop an organizational knowledge base, and establish an infrastructure of security professionals who can quickly respond to a security compromise.

- A key practice in preparing for a potential incident is the establishment of a Data Breach Response Team that is specifically responsible for responding to data security incidents.

- A structured team can provide coordination, expertise, efficiency, bridging of organizational barriers, and preparedness.

- Each team member will have particular duties depending on their background and role, including coordination, triage, escalation, investigation, response, documentation, root cause analysis, closure, and lessons learned.

- A team director will manage the team and coordinate the overall response and recovery activities.

- A team core group will include the Chief Security Officer, General Counsel, Director of Public Affairs, and a senior business line manager. Additional membership can include Human Resources, Chief Information Officer, and Internal Audit.

- In cases where the organization does not have the required internal expertise, it should develop relationships with external parties that can offer anticipated skill sets.

- Staff training is necessary to bring new and existing team members up to the necessary skill level to perform their function within the team and to ensure that the overall team skill set level is up to date with emerging trends, technologies, and best practices.

- A data breach response plan will establish procedures for handing data incidents by defining the response phases to a data security breach.

- The Data Breach Response Team will be tasked with developing and testing a documented response plan in conjunction with subject-matter experts from each of the organization's major business processes, internal auditors, and legal advisors.

- The response plan will define data security incidents that will cause the invocation of the plan, including loss of information confidentiality, compromise of information integrity, misuse of services, information, or assets, unauthorized access, and intrusion detection alarms.

- The response plan will include procedures for notifying the response team, including list of contacts with contact priority.

- A methodology for incident severity assessment, priority, and urgency will classify the incident and will define the threshold for the director to assemble the response team within specific time parameters.

- The response plan will include procedures for investigating the data breach, including the actuality of the incident, its source, its progress, the vulnerability that allowed the occurrence, the data or systems compromised, and the impact on the organization.

- Containment, isolation, and recovery strategies will be outlined for various types of data compromise incidents.

- Forensics guidance will outline the requirements for retaining records related to the incident, as well as the methods to preserve and record evidence and examples of the kinds of evidence that need to be gathered.

- Disclosure of the incident and notification of affected and other parties will be governed by threshold notification requirements. These will include timing, contents, and delivery of the notice.

- Guidelines for communicating with employees, regulators, law enforcement, media, and credit reporting agencies will be established.

- A damage assessment will allow the organization to determine tangible and intangible losses associated with the incident.

- The response plan must be reviewed and tested on a scheduled basis since it may become inadequate over time due to changes in the operational and technological environment, new legal and regulatory requirements, and new threats and vulnerabilities.

- Periodic exercises, simulations, and walkthroughs should be conducted to help the team understand the general incident management workflow and prepare for various response situations.

Chapter 6

Detection and Reporting

Solutions in this chapter:

- **Incident Life Cycle**

- **Detection**

- **Reporting**

☑ **Summary**

Incident Life Cycle

The incident life cycle includes several discrete stages and functions, from general pre-incident preparation through post-incident analysis. The initial phase involves establishing controls and safeguards to minimize the potential for an incident and the development of a response plan and response team. The other phases of the life cycle include:

- **Detection and Reporting** This phase covers the initial recognition or detection of an incident, whether by organizational personnel, automated means, or external parties, and its reporting to the appropriate parties.

- **Evaluation** This phase covers the collection of information on the incident and actions taken to categorize and prioritize it based on the determination of what occurred and its resulting impact, threat, or damage.

- **Response** This phase includes the steps taken to resolve or mitigate an incident and to restore the integrity of compromised data or systems.

- **Notification** This phase includes the coordination and dissemination of information about the incident to relevant parties, including internal constituents, external parties, or clients affected by the incident, regulators, law enforcement, and the media.

- **Closure** This phase provides closure for the incident by taking action against its cause and implementing follow-up strategies to minimize the risk of incident recurrence.

Detection

A data security incident is the suspected or confirmed compromise, unauthorized disclosure, acquisition, or access where parties other than authorized users and for an other-than-authorized purpose have access or potential access to sensitive and non public information in usable form.

The ability to detect that an incident is occurring or has occurred is an important component of the incident response process. This is especially relevant with respect to technical threats, since these are generally more difficult to identify. If an organization is not positioned to quickly identify incidents, the overall effectiveness of the response program may be affected.

Incidents may be detected through various means, including automated capabilities as well as direct reporting by employees or other parties. A particular incident may exhibit one or more symptoms, or may not exhibit any symptoms at the time of occurrence. The ability to detect an incident and recognize its symptoms will vary, especially since the volume of events that may indicate potential incidents is typically high in even a moderately sized organization.

In the Detection phase, information about potential incidents and vulnerabilities is gathered either reactively or proactively. This phase includes the identification of a potential data security incident and its reporting to the organizational Help desk or to the Data Breach Response Team. Accurate and timely detection can be complicated and challenging because alerts may arrive from a variety of sources and suspected incidents may be detected through a variety of avenues.

Incident indications, which are signs that an incident may have occurred or may be currently occurring, can be detected through a variety of means. Incident identification, however, is not strictly reactive, since in some cases, activities that are likely to precede an incident can be detected. These precursor activities indicate a possible future occurrence.

Many incidents will not be detected through precursors, since there may be no precursors, or possible precursors may not be detected. If precursors are detected, the organization may have an opportunity to prevent the compromise by altering its security posture through automated or manual means. In the most serious cases, the organization may decide to act as if an incident is already occurring, so that the risk is mitigated quickly. At a minimum, the organization can monitor certain activity more closely.

The most frequent means of detecting a data breach incident include a report from the party responsible for the data loss or compromise, reports from end users or administrators, or indications from automated detection systems.

In the case of an accidental compromise, the incident will generally be reported relatively quickly. The length and extent of the breach will usually be limited in scope. A malicious attacker, on the other hand, will attempt to disguise their activities. This will make it more difficult to ascertain both the length of time the breach has been occurring as well as the extent of the damage.

Party Responsible for Loss

In cases where a compromise occurs through the loss of a laptop or other portable device, the particular party responsible for the loss may alert management or the response team with information about the time, place, and circumstances of the loss, the sensitivity of the compromised data, and the likelihood of misuse.

Especially in the case of portable storage devices, it may be likely that the date and time the loss occurred differs significantly from the date and time it was discovered or reported. Obtaining an accurate estimate of that time span is important in ascertaining the risk of compromise, as this risk usually correlates with the amount of time the data is unaccounted for.

The person reporting or responsible for the loss must also provide an accurate indication of the types of data stored on the laptop or device and whether it was encrypted, since in addition to helping determine the risk of compromise, under certain laws and regulations this may drive the necessity to notify the parties whose information was compromised.

The manner of loss will also determine the risk involved. A stolen laptop present more serious data compromise circumstances than a lost one, since the motivation of the perpetrator is clearly malicious.

In order to encourage the prompt reporting of a loss or theft, deadlines should be specified for submitting a loss report. Prompt reporting will also be encouraged by minimizing penalties towards the responsible individual except in the most egregious circumstances.

System and Database Administrators

System and database administrators play an important role in the prevention and detection of security breaches. A regular security review of systems and databases should be part of the regular duties. Training and awareness in this area will help reduce complacency in this area, since it is possible that a system could have been compromised before a particular administrator took charge, or that it could have been compromised in such a way as to not provide obvious indications or alerts.

System or database administrators may notice unusual activity at the access and processing levels, including:

- Unexplained new user accounts, especially ones with administrative privileges.

- Activity from usually dormant accounts.

- Unusual activity or deviation from typical patterns in database or system logs.

- Unexplained modification or deletion of data.

- Unexplained or unauthorized new files, unfamiliar file names, or modifications to file lengths or dates. These can indicate backdoor programs or tools used to gain privileged access.

- Unauthorized installation of software or tools that present a risk of attack.

- Unexpected changes to files or folders, especially those to which access is normally restricted. Particular attention should be paid to changes or gaps in log files.

- Unexplained system crashes, poor performance, or unusual consumption of computing resources.

- Unexplained processes, processes running at unexpected times, and processes terminating prematurely. The goal is to verify that all processes are attributed to authorized activities of users, administrators, and system functions, and are operating as would be expected.

- Activity and performance statistics straying from a known baseline.

An area that administrators can provide help is in detecting suspect or unusual user behavior. These include:

- Repeated failed login attempts, especially to privileged accounts.

- Repetitive unsuccessful logon attempts within a short time interval.

- Unauthorized escalation of privileges on existing accounts.

- Unusual usage patterns or times.

- Unusual or unauthorized processes or commands executed by users.

Although no single symptom may conclusively indicate that an incident is taking place, observing one or more of these symptoms should prompt the administrator to investigate events more closely.

There are several steps administrators can take to make a system breach more noticeable and to lead to timelier discovery and reporting.

- **Entitlement Reviews** Regular entitlement reviews will ensure that any escalation of privileges or lack of appropriate segregation of duties is detected.

- **Logging** Enabling appropriate logging and then monitoring those log files will help identify any incidents or compromises. A log-monitoring tool can be used to parse log files and alert to any automatically notify of any suspicious events.

- **System Monitoring** System and database monitoring tools can detect performance issues and unusual processes that may be caused by a compromise.

- **Checksums** Using tools that take cryptographic checksums of system binaries and configuration files and notify of differences on subsequent runs can greatly minimize the amount of time required to detect intrusions.

- **System and Data Review** Ranking systems and data by sensitivity and establishing a regular review schedule based upon that.

End Users

An incident can be detected directly by an employee noticing unusual technical or procedural activity, or by users reporting problems with a particular system and data. User reports can include:

- Unauthorized persons in the business area or physical access attempts.

- Persons observed accessing information unrelated to their functional responsibilities.

- Data integrity issues.

- Data availability issues.

- Sluggish or non responsive system.

- Inability to access data with existing account.

- Presence of unfamiliar files in local or shared directories.

- Inaccurate time indication for last logon.

- Unfamiliar activity or access using their account.

Users are particularly important factors in incident detection, since they are aware of the normal behavior of their systems and environment and thus more apt to detect deviations from that norm. Some intrusions are not discovered until someone with day-to-day experience accessing certain data notices something unusual.

End users may report a suspected incident to their manager, the Help desk, or to the response team hotline. Employees should be trained in the basic steps regarding incident response, including the identification of events that are indicative of possible incidents and the reporting mechanism.

One particular type of incident that users should be aware of and promptly report is a social engineering attempt. This is any manipulation of a person, usually through social interaction, to obtain unauthorized information. By using persuasion, aggression, or other interpersonal skills, the unauthorized party will attempt to gain access or knowledge that will allow further discovery by encouraging legitimate users to provide sensitive information or authentication credentials.

Since sensitive information can be stored on physical media subject to compromise by theft, corruption, destruction, and unauthorized duplication, users should also report incidents of loss of this type of media.

In addition to data compromise or loss, users may be the recipients of unauthorized acquisition, such as the ability to access information for which he or she lack access or viewing authority. These instances should also be reported as they indicate a significant weakness in security controls that must be remedied.

External Parties

Mechanisms should be established for external parties to report incidents by publishing contact information on a public Web site or through other means. This can occur if an individual suspects or knows that their personal information has been breached, or if an external party believes that one of the organization's resources or users is compromising their systems or data.

Individuals may notice indications that their personal information was used by an unauthorized party, such as instances of identity theft, fraudulent accounts, unauthorized transactions, or even receipt of unsolicited e-mails to addresses only known to the organization. They may also report a phishing attempt, which is an e-mail fraud method in which a perpetrator sends legitimate looking e-mail appearing to come from the organization in an attempt to gather personal and financial information from recipients. If a breach determination is made, the organization should provide interim updates to the reporting party until resolution.

External entities, including business partners and outsourcers, may find direct or indirect evidence that the organization's systems were attacked from their systems, or attacks on their systems originated from the organization. These reports may originate from a response team that coordinates the response effort of the external entity or may be received through other means.

Other warning indicators include reports of incidents that have occurred at other organizations. Such incidents should be investigated and security controls implemented or reinforced to minimize any potential impact. One advantage of the public reporting of such incidents is that it allows the organization to keep track of new and developing trends and educate staff members about the continuing threat.

Malicious Party

The malicious party who accessed or obtained the data may notify the organization directly. In cases of financial motivation, the notice may contain an extortion attempt. Malicious parties can include current or former employees or consultants, competitors, business partners, or individuals and groups without any affiliation to the organization. These parties can have various levels of knowledge regarding the organization's infrastructure, and may sometimes be able to plan an attack based on publicly available information.

There are several motivations that will drive a malicious party:

- **Financial** Financial motivation includes an expectation of direct profit or the compromise of the organization's resources under the direction and pay of a third party. Additionally, sudden financial need may prompt an employee or external individual to engage in certain activity. This motivation can lead to extortion attempts or the exploitation of intellectual property and other information for personal gain.

- **Personal** Personal motives may include the need for revenge for a perceived slight or injustice by the organization, whether directed at the individual or at another group to which the individual feels kinship. The intent will be to damage the organization's reputation or competitive position. Disgruntled employees with personal motives present a particular risk since their knowledge and motivation can help them more easily circumvent existing controls.

- **Informational** Simple curiosity or the need for prestige may drive certain individuals to attempt to breach organizational systems and data. These individuals will usually want to focus attention upon themselves and may or may not attempt to damage the infrastructure. This type of motivation can also be transformed into a financial one.

For several reasons, insider malicious parties such as employees and consultants can be the most damaging since they may have detailed knowledge of the organizational data, systems, infrastructure, and security controls. They may also have authorized access to the data in question.

Antivirus Software

Malware refers to a variety of unauthorized hostile and intrusive software designed to infiltrate or damage a system. It includes computer viruses, worms, Trojan horses, rootkits, spyware, and other malicious and unwanted software.

Antivirus and similar software may indicate the existence of such malicious code whose purpose can include harvesting sensitive information. Antivirus tools will alert when any such code attempts to penetrate or does penetrate the security perimeter.

It is possible for new malware whose signature is not in the virus scanner's database to infect the organization's systems. In such circumstances, rapid action must be taken, including the isolation and rebuilding of infected systems, in order to contain the spread.

Information that will help determine the extent of compromise will include the origin of the malware, the data and systems affected, and the type of suspicious activity. Additionally, vendors of Antivirus and similar tools may have recent information about this particular malware and any containment methods.

Intrusion Detection Systems

Intrusion detection systems (IDSes) can identify suspicious events and behaviors caused by external attackers attempting to access organizational data and systems, as well as authorized users attempting to gain additional data access privileges to which they are not authorized or who misuse their current privileges. The IDS will detect and analyze these events, record pertinent data regarding them, including the type of event, date and time, and source, and display or send alerts to designated parties.

An IDS can detect attacks and other security violations that are not prevented by other security measures, and can also detect precursors to an attack. The detection of precursors is particularly important since malicious parties can attack in stages, initially probing for vulnerabilities. The IDS can identify suspicious probes, block the attacker's access, and alert appropriate personnel who can block any subsequent access by the attacker.

The IDS management console receives the input from various agents and serves as the interface for policy creation, alert notification, and reporting. Network and host agents analyze network traffic or audit logs to identify activity that could indicate an attack.

The suspicious events that an IDS will detect and the information it will provide will depend on its type. These include:

- **Network-based IDS** This will detect malicious activity such as port scans or intrusion attempts by monitoring network traffic. It analyzes incoming and outgoing packets for suspicious patterns. Placed at network segments or switches, this IDS can monitor and analyze the network traffic on the network segment and report events to a management console. This will also identify attacks against multiple systems or databases that may not be detected by individual host-based IDSes.

- **Host-based IDS** This monitors the internals of a system rather than its external interfaces. It can analyze activities and determine which processes and users are involved in a particular attack on the operating system, data, or application. This IDS consults several types of log files and compares the logs against an internal database of common attack signatures. A host-based IDS can also verify the data integrity of sensitive files and executables by storing the attributes of each object and creating a checksum for the contents. This type of IDS should be distributed to all hosts processing sensitive data.

- **Application-based IDS** This monitors the events and communication on specific software applications by analyzing the application log files. It can detect suspicious behavior due to authorized users exceeding their authorization.

Most IDSes can detect several types of malicious activity, using a combination of signature-based detection for known attacks and anomaly based detection for previously unknown attacks. Anomaly detection flags detect statistically unusual behavior through comparisons with rolling statistical profiles.

Since IDSes can produce false positives or flag events that may have benign causes, alerts should be validated by reviewing the supporting data or obtaining related data from other sources.

Because of the amount of information produced by an IDS, determining which types of events to monitor should be based on the risk level of the data and systems to be monitored. Events that indicate signs of a possible attack include:

- Unexpected changes in network traffic or performance.

- Connections to or from unusual source or destination addresses.

- Connections made at unusual times.

- Repeated failed connection attempts.

- Unauthorized scans and probes.

- Packets with unusual protocol or addresses.

- Headers and contents matching common exploit signatures.

- Changes to key configuration or system files.

- Changes to registry keys.

- Missing or extra processes, unusual process behavior.

- Unexpected shutdowns and restarts.

- High resource utilization compared to baseline activity.

- Existence of unauthorized processes or missing processes.

- Repeated failed login attempts, especially privileged accounts.

- Logins from unusual locations or at unusual times.

- Unauthorized changes to user privileges.

- Access to restricted files and unauthorized access attempts.

- Violations of log file integrity such as unexplained time gaps.

Since the components of an IDS can be distributed across various nodes, it is important that alerts be provided to indicate if any of the components are unavailable leading to a quality or integrity compromise of the detection system. This can also occur if an attacker modifies the operations of the IDS in a manner that conceals activities that should be reported.

Firewalls

Firewalls regulate data flow between external and organizational networks. For breach detection purposes, they provide an important logging and auditing function through summaries about the kinds and amount of traffic passing in and out and any indications of unauthorized intrusion attempts.

Useful firewall log entries for intrusion detection are the accepted and denied connections that may indicate port scans and general probing. An examination of incoming traffic log fields will indicate the disposition of the packet, policy applied, as well as attacker's and target's address. This will verify that sensitive services on trusted hosts are protected from unauthorized access and that external hosts can reach only those systems that host publicly offered services.

Particular attention should be paid to unusual or excessive traffic from external addresses. This can detect instances where authorized accounts may have been compromised and used by a malicious party.

Firewall audit logs track all changes made from the console, including the user or administrator who logged in to the firewall itself, the originating device, the authentication method, and the change made. A review of these logs can alert to changes to firewall policy, configuration, or log changes made, and addition or promotion of administrative accounts. This is useful for general auditing and for forensics regarding a compromised firewall host.

Firewall logs should be backed up on a scheduled basis for future reference in case a breach is discovered at a future date and an investigation is needed to determine if it has been ongoing.

Honeypots

Honeypots are systems or data files which contain information that may look valuable to an attacker but which has no value to the organization, therefore providing an easy attack target and distracting away from actual valuable systems or data. They are isolated from the network and configured with specific vulnerabilities to serve as a trap to detect or counteract attempts at unauthorized access or use. A honeypot is a valuable early warning tool since it is not accessed by any legitimate traffic, and any activity it captures can be surmised as unauthorized.

Honeypots can indicate the origin of an attack, the tools used, the kinds of vulnerabilities probed, and the type of exploit launched. They can offer several benefits:

- They can distract an intruder by steering them away from sensitive production systems and data, minimizing the chance of actual attack on those systems and data.

- They can encourage intruders to remain on the system long enough for administrators to respond.

- The information gained from monitoring honeypot intrusions can be used to strengthen the infrastructure against attacks.

- In conjunction with other data, information collected through these systems can be used for forensic, investigative, and legal purposes.

One of the salient characteristics of a honeypot is its ability to detect attacks that are not caught by other security systems, or attacks whose evidence may be lost in the amount of information produced by IDSes and other warning devices. Since any activity a honeypot captures is by definition unauthorized, it can clearly indicate any preparation for or attempt at a breach.

Audit Logs

System, application, and database logs can indicate unusual or unexpected events by tracking account activity with time, date, and actions performed. They can indicate failed logon attempts, logon attempts from default system accounts, repeated attempts to access data to which the user does not have permission, unusual activity, especially during nonworking hours, elevated or changed access permissions, both on an account or data level, and unauthorized changes to log files.

- Logon attempts using a locked out, disabled, or expired account.
- Logon attempts outside of the allowed time.
- Logon attempts to systems or data to which the user does not have access permission.
- Attempts to use unauthorized accounts.
- Incorrect or expired passwords.
- Creation or changes in account privileges.
- Attempts to perform privileged operations not within a permission profile.
- Unusual traffic to and from the host.
- System configuration changes.
- Loading, unloading, or existence of unauthorized programs or services.
- Unexplained account usage.
- Significant changes in expected resource usage.
- New files or directories with unusual names.

Even though these events can occur as part of normal organization activity, they can also represent misuse of an account or attempts at password guessing.

One of the clearest indications of an attack is the deletion of logs or particular log entries. An administrator will be able to detect such an event as well as any missing or modified log entries.

Creating and implementing a log retention policy that specifies how long log data should be maintained is important, since older log entries may show reconnaissance activity, previous instances of similar attacks, or the occurrence of an actual incident that is not discovered until later. The length of time to maintain log data is dependent on the organization's data retention policies and the volume of data.

Event Correlation

Since evidence of an incident may be captured in a different manner in several sources, correlating events among these multiple sources will help present a succinct and high-level view to detect whether a particular incident occurred, as well as provide any details that may be unavailable from a single source.

Event log consolidation is the process of merging disparate event logs from many sources into one consolidated log in a consistent format. The event correlation engines can rapidly recognize malicious activity and interpret its level of risk by aggregating and correlating similar or logically connected low level alerts from heterogeneous devices and provide a higher level view of the alerts. This will involve consolidating event data by removing duplicate information and redundancies, eliminate redundancy in the data, finding patterns and causes in the events, tracking large-scale attacks that have multiple stages over an extended period of time, and producing notifications or reports.

One auxiliary advantage of consolidation is that it provides secure storage for logs, which reduces the impact of attackers disabling logging or modifying logs.

All systems that produce or maintain log files should use synchronized clocks in order to allow an administrator to compare events and establish what actions were taken by an attacker. Without synchronized time, it is difficult to determine exactly when specific events took place and how they interlace.

Variance from Baseline Profile

One method to detect anomalies is to create and maintain profiles or baselines of system and database activity. Profiling is measuring the characteristics of expected activity so that changes and variances can be more easily identified. These profiles can be particularly effective for dedicated systems with a limited number of functions. A list of typical programs and processes, performance characteristics, or access patterns can be maintained, and significant or atypical deviations from these baselines can indicate suspicious activity.

A baseline profile can be created by analyzing current processes and performance and uninstalling unnecessary programs or services. The resulting configuration and performance characteristics will serve as a guide to determine if something has changed or is outside the range of expected values.

Baselines profiles can be updated on a rolling basis to reflect the current expected state of a system or database. Audit trails can provide typical usage over time as well as metrics to use for a quantitative comparison. Profiles can also be updated based on configuration and activity models, which will describe the profile of an uncompromised system or different compromise scenarios.

For users performing related or repetitive tasks, a particular method of detecting anomalous behavior is through the creation of user activity profiles, which are statistical models of usage created from audit logs and expected activity. Deviations from usage patterns may then indicate unauthorized activity or the use of an account by other than the authorized individual.

Multiple Steps

More complex data compromise incidents can occur in several steps, with reconnaissance activities to identify exploitable vulnerabilities preceding and preparing for the actual incident. Once specific vulnerabilities have been identified, an attacker can exploit one or more to access systems or data, or use one permitting a lower level access to gradually escalate access privileges. Since this is a multi-step process, such an attack may be detected at an intermediate step and stopped before further compromise.

Multiple-step attacks can be detected and analyzed through multi-step correlation, which identifies high-level attack patterns that are composed of several individual attacks or probes. This uses the concept of attack scenarios, which are specific sequences of actions and interactions performed by a single source to one or several targets with some particular malicious intention. By analyzing alerts for attack scenarios rather than individually, the strategy or intention of the attacker can be determined at each step.

If the attack is detected at an intermediate or later step, a systematic backward analysis may help determine the initial step and possibly identify the perpetrator.

Reporting

Incident reports may originate from several sources, including employees, external or affected parties, perpetrators, and technical means. A designated team member, or coordinator, should be available on a continual basis to respond to any incoming alert and receive initial information relating to the incident. Even though the coordinator role will rotate among team members on a scheduled basis to allow continual coverage, it is best to provide the constituency set contact information that does not vary based on the coordinator on duty at a particular time.

Contacting the Response Team

In order to ensure the reporting and the collection of all relevant information, employees as well as any other relevant constituency must be provided with simple and efficient procedures and mechanisms for reporting suspected or actual incidents. These include clear guidelines on the kinds of events to report, defined points of contact with details and availability, a general hotline or other means of contact, and specific procedures to follow for recording and reporting the event. Intrusion detection tools and automated reporting mechanisms should also be configured to notify the DBRT in cases of significant alerts.

Whatever the source, any person who detects the incident or who knows or reasonably believes that a data security breach has occurred, is responsible for initiating the reporting process. The person should follow the procedures specified by the response plan to report the event to the Help desk or the DBRT. All personnel should be aware of, and have access to, the guidelines for reporting possible information security incidents. In addition to suspected incidents, the constituency should be encouraged to report perceived vulnerabilities that could possibly be exploited in the future.

At a minimum, and regardless of specific guidelines for contacting the DBRT, all employees should have contact information. This includes the name of the DBRT, the location, the phone or hotline number, the e-mail address, the team member on duty, and other team members.

Help Desk

In order to avoid confusion and maintain one communication channel with the user community, it may be advisable to designate the Help desk as the single point of contact for incident reporting by end users. This would preferably be an internally staffed Help desk because of the sensitivity of a data breach, privacy issues, and ability to attract undesired attention. If the Help desk determines that the report is for a data breach incident, it will then be transferred to the DBRT coordinator.

All Help desk personnel should know how to recognize the symptoms of a data breach, understand the incident reporting process and procedures, and know how to contact the response team coordinator. They should also be trained and authorized to take certain preliminary action to mitigate severe threats in cases where the incident response team cannot be immediately contacted.

Reporting Form

In addition to direct verbal or e-mail contact, a reporting form that identifies the information needed to investigate and track an incident should be available to all members of the organization. This form can be available online on a security Web site, or included in information security policies or procedures. Constituents should be encouraged to report any suspected event as rapidly as possible so that the proper level of response can be initiated, even if some of the requested information is not available. If the reporting person is not confident about particular report data, it should be submitted with appropriate notes and revisions communicated later.

The form will collect the following information:

- Date and time of report.
- Reporting party's name, title, contact information, and contact information for manager and data owner.
- Date, time, and duration of the potential incident.
- Date and time the potential incident was detected.
- If not the reporting party, who initially detected the incident with contact information.
- The manner in which the potential incident was detected.
- Description of the incident or suspicious events observed.
- Type, confidentiality, and quantity of sensitive data believed to have been compromised.
- Storage medium from which data was lost or compromised,
- Countermeasures enabled when the loss or theft occurred, such as encryption.
- If paper documents are lost in transfer, shipping company and package tracking number.
- How widespread the internal or external knowledge of the incident is.
- Any steps taken to mitigate the incident or to isolate the data or system from further compromise.
- Incident severity based on the reporting party's judgment.
- Any recommendation or comments from the reporting party.

The form should include a section for supporting documentation and attachments, such as excerpts of audit logs or suspicious e-mails.

Initial Follow-Up

Upon receipt of the initial notification, the coordinator or a designated team member will initiate follow-up communications with the person submitting the report to gather further details. This is important in order to be able to collect any other relevant and timely information, and to remind the person reporting the incident to remain vigilant and forward any additional information that they may notice at a later time. A follow-up should be initiated even for benign events in order to encourage users to report incidents in the future.

The follow-up can include interviews with other relevant employees, vendors, and other parties involved in the breach. At this time, the DBRT's response process should be explained and the reporting party's feedback expectations outlined. This may include being informed about progress or changes in incident status. Any additional steps to be taken by the affected users should be clearly outlined. In general, it is advisable to discourage further investigation by the reporting party or others outside the response team in order to preserve volatile data and avoid further unintentional compromise. In addition, employees should not take any corrective or restorative actions unless advised by a member of the team.

Summary

- The incident life cycle consists of several discrete stages and functions, including detection and reporting, evaluation, response, notification, and closure.

- The ability to detect that an incident is occurring or has occurred is an important component of the incident response process.

- Incidents may be detected through various means, including automated capabilities, as well as direct reporting by employees or other parties.

- The most frequent means of detecting a data breach incident includes a report from the party responsible for the data loss or compromise, reports from end users or administrators, or indications from automated detection systems.

- In the case of a lost or stolen laptop or other portable device, the party responsible for the loss may alert management with information about the time, place, and circumstances of the loss, the sensitivity of the compromised data, and the likelihood of misuse.

- System and database administrators play an important role in the prevention and detection of security breaches by noticing and reporting unusual activity at the access and processing levels.

- An incident can be detected directly by an employee noticing unusual technical or procedural activity, or by users reporting problems with a particular system and data.

- External parties reporting incidents will include individuals who may notice that their personal information was used by an unauthorized party or external entities, including business partners and outsourcers, who may find direct or indirect evidence that the organization's systems were attacked from their systems, or attacks on their systems originated from the organization.

- The malicious party who accessed or obtained the data may notify the organization directly in case of financial, personal, or other motivation.

- Antivirus and similar software may indicate the existence of malicious code whose purpose can include harvesting sensitive information.

- IDSes can identify suspicious events and behaviors caused by external attackers as well as by authorized users attempting to gain additional access privileges or who misuse their current privileges.

- Firewalls logs provide summaries about the kinds and amount of traffic passing in and out and any indications of unauthorized intrusion attempts.

- Honeypots provide an easy attack target to an intruder and distract away from actual valuable systems or data.

- System, application, and database logs can indicate unusual or unexpected events by tracking account activity with time, date, and actions performed.

- Correlating events among multiple sources will help present a high-level view to detect whether an incident occurred and provide details that may be unavailable from a single source.

- Anomalies can be detected through profiles or baselines of system and database activity, which measure the characteristics of expected activity so that changes and variances can be more easily identified.

- A designated data breach response team member, or coordinator, should be available on a continual basis to respond to any incoming alert and receive initial information relating to the incident.

- Employees as well as any other relevant constituency must be provided with simple and efficient procedures and mechanisms for reporting suspected or actual incidents.

- Any person who detects the incident or who knows or reasonably believes that a data security breach has occurred is responsible for initiating the reporting process.

- In order to avoid confusion and maintain one communication channel with the user community, it may be advisable to designate the Help desk as the single point of contact for incident reporting by end users.

- A reporting form that identifies the information needed to investigate and track an incident should be available to all members of the organization.

- Upon receipt of the initial notification, the coordinator or a designated team member will initiate follow-up communications with the person submitting the report to gather further details.

Chapter 7

Evaluation and Response

Solutions in this chapter:

- Preliminary Determination
- Initial Assessment
- Team Escalation
- Information Gathering
- Classification
- Scope
- Length of Occurrence
- Severity Assessment
- Response Approach
- Containment
- Recovery

☑ Summary

Introduction

One of the challenges of the response process is the evaluation and classification of events as they occur. Some events are the result of routine activity while others may be indicators of a potential incident requiring response. A clear and efficient process is important since most organizations will normally be detecting many incident candidates, the majority of which will be false positives. An ineffective process may end up overwhelming organizational resources with the effort of dealing with noise and false positives and may lead to the occurrence of false negatives, where an incident requiring attention and response is not detected or managed.

The evaluation phase is the process of analyzing and evaluating the available data to determine if the incident needs further investigation and action and to assign a preliminary severity. The evaluation will result in a decision on whether to convene the complete team and implement the incident response plan. It will guide the development of an action plan and response strategy. The initial coordinator and subsequently the response team will confirm the incident's scope, origination, pattern, and severity in order to determine and prioritize subsequent activities. The result of this process is a course of action that represents the team's best judgment about how the incident should be addressed given the understanding of the circumstances.

Preliminary Determination

The coordinator who receives the first report of the incident will be tasked with making certain preliminary determinations, including:

- Is there sufficient information to make an initial assessment?

- Does an actual data security incident exist or is this a false positive?

- What is the type of breach, extent, magnitude, apparent cause, and source?

- Were there precursors, indications, or other correlating information?

- What is the data sensitivity level?

- What is the incident severity level?

- Does the severity of the incident justify escalation to the team director?

- What is the extent of any possible damage, and has it been contained or is it continuing?

If warranted, the coordinator may need to take immediate action to begin containing the damage and minimizing the risk. If other systems or data are at risk, the compromised system or database should be disconnected from the network or otherwise prevented from posing an extended threat. This will entail progressive steps that depend on the circumstances. They include:

- If the incident poses no immediate threat and analysis suggests that the activity may be legitimate, the reporting party or relevant administrator is contacted for determination or resolution.

- If the incident poses an extended threat, the coordinator will attempt to reach the designated administrator to have the system or database disconnected from the network.

- If the incident poses an immediate threat and the relevant administrator cannot be reached, the coordinator can take an immediate action of physically or logically disconnecting the system or database from the network.

All actions should be thoroughly recorded, as this will be used by the complete response team in managing the incident as well as for later documentation.

In order to effectively perform the preliminary determination and assessment, the coordinator must possess both technical and business awareness. This includes the understanding of data and asset need and criticality and the ability to determine the effect particular activity will have on the overall organization.

Initial Assessment

A preliminary assessment will assist in collecting and organizing information helpful in the formal assessment process as well as in assigning a severity. The assessment will help verify that an incident has truly occurred, identify the systems and data accessed without authorization, determine the methods of misuse or access, as well as any actions after obtaining access. Without such an understanding, it is difficult to select a course of action that will effectively correct and securely restore the affected data resources.

As part of the preliminary or formal team assessment, the following information shall be collected and addressed:

- Date, time, and duration of the potential incident.
- Date and time the potential incident was detected.

- Date and time the potential incident was reported.

- How and by whom the potential incident was detected and reported.

- Description of the suspicious events observed.

- Initial determination of whether the incident could be an actual or suspected breach of sensitive information.

- Determination of the internal or external origin of the breach.

- Determination of whether the breach is ongoing.

- Security measures in place and means by which the breach occurred.

- Type and quantity of sensitive data breached.

- Number of individuals potentially affected.

- Business functions and units affected.

- Ease or difficulty with which the compromised information can be used by an unauthorized party.

- Impact on the organization should the compromised data be used for identity theft, fraud, or other purposes.

- Whether the breach is public knowledge?

- Any steps that were taken to isolate the data or system from further compromise.

- Indications that the comprised information is being used by an unauthorized party.

Based upon the facts known at the time, the coordinator will make an initial impact scope and severity assessment of the event before it is reported to the director of the team. The assessment will be based on the likelihood and extent of harm caused by the incident and will take into account the following factors:

- **Nature of the Data** This is a key factor in assessing whether team escalation should occur. The severity of the breach will depend on the sensitivity of the breached data and the potential harm due to its disclosure to unauthorized parties.

- **Likelihood that the Data is Usable** An increased risk that the information will be used by unauthorized parties will influence the impact level. This risk is determined by whether the information has been lost or stolen, safeguards such as encryption, and the likelihood that the unauthorized party will know the value of the information.

- **Likelihood that the Incident May Lead to Harm** If the organization determines that the breached information has already been used or will likely be used by a malicious party, the incident can lead to significant harm.

- **Ability to Mitigate the Risk of Harm** This ability will be determined by the number of individuals affected and appropriate countermeasures such as monitoring to identify patterns of suspicious behavior.

The coordinator will categorize the risk level of each factor as follows:

- **Low** The likely risk of harm is low if the incident could result in limited or no harm, embarrassment, or inconvenience to any individual, or could have a minor or no adverse effect on organizational operations or assets. In particular, for personal information, the breach would not result in identity theft, the information was recovered and it was determined there was no access or distribution, or the information was encrypted.

- **Moderate** The likely risk of harm is moderate if the incident could result in significant embarrassment, or inconvenience to any individual, or could have a significant effect on organizational operations or assets. For personal information, if criminal activity is suspected, the sensitivity of the data will determine if the risk of harm is moderate or high.

- **High** The likely risk of harm is high if the incident could result in severe embarrassment, or inconvenience to any individual, or could have a catastrophic effect on organizational operations or assets.

After these factors have been evaluated, the coordinator will weigh the impact level of each factor to ascertain the severity of the incident. The nature and sensitivity of the data is a key factor in the risk analysis, and the impact level assigned to this factor should be the starting point for assessing the overall severity of the incident.

Whenever there is doubt as to the scope or severity level, the event should be escalated to the director for guidance.

As a result of this initial assessment, the coordinator will escalate the event to the team, reassign the incident outside of the response team process, or close the event. In cases where escalation is warranted, once the incident's severity level is assigned, the coordinator will adhere to the established notification timeframes.

Team Escalation

If it is evident or suspected that a data incident is significant and above a certain level of criticality, it should be reported by the coordinator to the team director or a designated alternate. Team escalation should occur in the following cases:

- **Reconnaissance** Probing activities that indicate a high level of skill or knowledge of sensitive resources.

- **Compromise** Attack showing knowledge of the organization, sensitive resources, or appears focused on a particular objective.

- **Exploitation** In all cases where there is evidence or indications that compromised information is being used without authorization.

Escalation should occur for incidents for which an initial severity determination cannot be made, since the possible escalation of false positives should not deter notification, as it is always preferable to act on a false positive than to fail to act on a genuine incident.

Escalation should also occur if the organization does not own the affected data but is a licensee. In these cases, the team director, in addition to invoking the response process, will immediately inform the owner of the affected data about the breach and discharge any obligations the organization has under its contract with the owner. The report will include any event or incident information as well as any descriptive information added by the coordinator such as category and severity. This can also include a preliminary analysis, the decision rationale for forwarding the information, and any information discovered by correlating the incoming event report with other past or current reports.

The director performs a preliminary analysis of the facts and assesses the situation to determine the nature and scope of the incident. This will include reviewing the incident record to ascertain whether it constitutes an actual data security incident, and whether the initial severity ascribed accurately reflects the risk to the impacted sectors and/or the franchise. If it is determined that the incident does not constitute an actual data breach, or if there is no possibility of unauthorized access, it will be referred to the appropriate internal group for action, including addressing any vulnerabilities that led to the incident.

The director will make any necessary adjustments to the severity level based on the incident report and any additional information that might have been gathered. This may further change in the course of the investigation or due to the impact of the event.

If a determination is made that the nature of the incident requires the gathering of the team, the director shall notify the core members of the team. Based on the circumstances, the director may also include subject matter experts and business users, especially data owners of the impacted data or systems. Based on the response plan, the director should clearly delineate responsibilities based upon the capability, expertise, and authority of each team member in order to avoid duplicative efforts.

A pre-defined notification and team response time window can be specified based on the assigned severity. This includes timeframes for director notification, director response, team escalation assessment, team member notification, and team member response. The process should state how long a person should wait for a response and what the person should do if no response occurs, such as re-contact or alternate contact activation.

Information Gathering

A more formal team assessment will be based on the information provided, the initial assessment, further information obtained, and analysis performed. Additional information about the breach can be obtained through parties within and outside the organization as well as through the review of the technical information. At this stage, the team will be able to determine with a degree of certainty that an incident has occurred, the data compromised, and the potential impact.

Since it may be necessary to discuss the incident with an end user, administrator, or other individual outside the response team, the interviewer should keep in mind the possibility that the particular individual may be the source of the compromise. As such, no information should be shared that may have the potential to compound the harm of the initial breach.

Party Responsible for Loss

In cases where a compromise occurs through the loss of a laptop or other portable device, the particular party responsible for the loss will provide the following information:

- What is the time and place where the loss occurred?
- What is the sensitivity of the compromised data?
- Was the data encrypted or masked?
- What were the circumstances of the loss?

- If the device was stolen or there is a possibility that it might be obtained by an unauthorized party, what is the likelihood of misuse or that the unauthorized party will know the value of the information?

Data Owners

The Data Breach Response Team (DBRT) should have access to classification documentation, which includes identification of all data owners. This will help rapidly identify the compromised data or system owner, who may then be able to provide further clarification on the type and exact determination of the compromised data, affected parties, and a possible context for the incident. Additionally, data owners must be kept closely informed about all the facts since they are responsible for the data and will eventually be reporting to their stakeholders about any significant events surrounding that data. Information to be collected from data owners includes:

- What is the level of sensitivity surrounding the compromised data and system?

- Who are the affected parties?

- Have there been any recent personnel issues in regards to the affected data or system?

- Is there any auditing or testing scheduled at the time of the event? If so, who is performing this audit?

- Are there any scheduled or unplanned maintenance activities occurring and could they be providing the suspicious indications?

System and Database Administrators

System or database administrators might have insight into the technical details of an incident and can provide information that confirms the suspicious nature of the incident or conversely can indicate that nothing is faulty, especially if a false positive is produced by a firewall or intrusion detection system (IDS). Information to be collected from administrators includes:

- Has there been any unusual activity?

- Has there been any unusual deviation from typical access?

- Have there been any administrative changes made recently?

- Who has administrative access to the system?

- Who are the users with access to the data or system?

- What are their access levels?

- Is there remote access to this system or data or connectivity to an external host outside the security perimeter?

- What are the logging capabilities and what do the database or application logs show?

- What security safeguards are implemented?

Network Administrators

Network administrators will be able to determine at which point or node in the network the attack may have originated as well as how it may have spread. The location of the compromised system can be pinpointed on a network topology diagram and will allow the administrator to arrive at certain conclusions regarding the mechanics of the attack. Any device on the network between the compromised system and the attacker should be investigated.

The connectivity of the compromised system or data to other devices will indicate the likely transmission across devices. A lack of connectivity will be even more indicative since the conclusion can then be drawn that the attack originated internally or at the system console.

End Users

The type of user report will dictate the appropriate analysis of an event. User reports can include:

- **Social Engineering Attempt** A determination should be made of what resources the attacker was interested in and the particular data should be examined for indications of compromise. Log-based activity should also be examined in case the attempt was a precursor to an actual attack.

- **Physical Access Attempt** The purpose of the activity should be determined and the physical security controls should be verified.

- **Data Integrity Issues** A review of logs and backup data may indicate the time and source of a possible compromise.

- **Access Issues** A user may be unable to access the system or data with their regular account, or may notice unusual activity with the account such as inaccurate last logon time or data access. This may indicate that the account was used by a malicious party with the legitimate user's knowledge.

- **Availability Issues** A sluggish or non-responsive system may indicate the presence of malicious code.

In any type of analysis requiring access and review of a user's system, care should be taken not to further damage the environment. This can be accomplished by making a logical copy that mirrors the original environment and performing the analysis on a separate system. This can be performed by a member of the response team or an administrator.

Help Desk

The Help Desk will provide the information initially submitted by the individual reporting the incident as well as any additional input received from various parties. This may include a direct confirmation of the incident or reports of technical issues that upon further analysis may indicate the occurrence of a breach.

The Help Desk may also be asked to review previous trouble tickets for signs of similar attacks or for precursors to the current incident. A malicious party can compromise multiple systems, and there may be telltale signs of intrusive activities at each compromised system. Although a single user report to the Help Desk may not be sufficient evidence of a compromise, analysis of several reports may reveal a pattern of attack and help determine a scope.

Malicious Party

It is possible that the malicious party responsible for the incident may notify the organization directly. It is generally not advisable to respond in order to try to obtain further information, as such information may be unreliable or purposely misleading and thus may expose the organization to downstream liability if acted upon.

Intrusion Detection Systems

IDSes can provide data that would support that an incident has occurred and indicate which data or system might have been affected, the methods of attack, the time and length of attack, and the overall extent of potential damage.

Evidence from an IDS residing on a system being inspected should not be relied upon unless it can be positively verified that the software and its supporting configuration files have not been modified.

Log Analysis

Application and database log files should be examined for failed logon attempts, logon attempts from default system accounts, repeated attempts to access data to which the user does not have permission, unusual activity, especially during nonworking hours, elevated or changed access permissions, both on an account or data level.

A particular sign may include gaps in or the absence of logs. The source of the deletion should be established and may provide an indication of an attempt to conceal malicious activity.

Historical data from older logs can indicate reconnaissance activity since it is possible that a number of different attacks or scans were performed prior to the current event.

Device-Based Information

In some cases, important information about the incident may be volatile or ephemeral and may be lost when the relevant device is powered down. The volatile data provides a snapshot of a system at the time of response and can include:

- Memory contents
- The currently established network connections
- Running processes or processes set to run
- Active users logged on
- Open files
- Browser cache and history folder, cookies folder, and Favorites list
- Temporary files created by applications, including word processing or spreadsheet programs.
- E-mail program temporary folder can contain copies of file attachments received with e-mail.
- Clipboard

After volatile data is collected, the team should collect persistent data, including storage contents. This may help determine if the sensitive data itself was compromised in addition to the system. It may be necessary to perform a forensic duplication of the data in order to obtain working copies for analysis without altering or destroying potential evidence.

Any tool used to collect data will by nature change the state of the target system by being loaded into memory and creating one or more processes which can overwrite volatile data by allocating space in memory. One workaround to this limitation is using tools that can dump the whole physical memory to an external storage device without the assistance of the operating system.

In addition to the device in question, other systems with similar attributes should be checked as they are more likely to have been compromised through a vulnerability common to both.

Baselines and Variations

In system and data environments with predictable and stable activity, creating a baseline for normal activity can quantify organizational processes and help detect deviations from a previously recorded baseline that may indicate adverse activity. A baseline is a snapshot of the state and configuration of a system or data under normal circumstances and operations. This can involve a statistical profile of normal activity for systems and data with boundaries based on that profile. Particular activity outside the boundaries may indicate a potential incident.

In addition to activity baselines, data and system state baselines will identify additions, deletions, modifications, and permission and control modifications to the data.

Root Causes

The response team will also need to determine whether the characteristics of the incident and circumstances surrounding it have a known or previously observed cause. Diagnosis can involve matching characteristics and circumstances with known conditions, or it could be a process of eliminating unlikely causes.

Classification

The classification, along with the severity assessment, will dictate the type of response and subsequent actions. Incidents may be classified into several types, including the following:

- **System Intrusions** Unauthorized access or activity, including password sharing, on one or more systems. Responses to these types of IS Incidents will be categorized on the basis of the criticality of the system that has been breached.

- **External Attacks or Abuse Reports** Incidents related to external parties that attempt to breach information security measures, in an attempt to obtain sensitive information.

- **Breach of Sensitive Information Assets** Incidents related to a breach of sensitive or confidential information, by either an internal or external source, either inadvertently or with intent to do harm.

- **Policy Violations** Even though a data or other information security policy violation does not necessarily imply a compromise or breach, it should be investigated and addressed since it can expose the organization to internal or external threats.

- **Technical Events** Incidents that involve the inadvertent exposure of sensitive information as the result of a system or application failure.

Scope

After an incident has been detected, it is important to promptly determine its scope in order to understand the extent of possible compromise to affected data, help in determining the intervention actions, and assign an appropriate priority. Scope considerations include:

- The internal or external origination or entry point of the incident and the extent of penetration.

- The location of the affected data within the security perimeter.

- The extent of compromise for a particular system or database.

- The level of access and privileges that the unauthorized party gained.

- The number of simultaneous or closely related incidents.

- The number of attack avenues being used.

- The number of hosts or databases that were compromised.

- The amount, sensitivity, and protection of data compromised.

- The number of parties affected.

- The number of people who know about the incident.

- The extent of the exploited vulnerability and its presence in other systems or databases.

- The potential damage of the incident.

Length of Occurrence

Determining how long the incident has been going on is important since there is an obvious correlation between the length of time a vulnerability exists undetected and the amount of data that can be compromised. In certain cases, such as the loss of a storage device, the time occurrence can be rapidly and accurately determined. In other cases, database, application, or IDS logs may help pinpoint the actual time. If that information is not available or does not provide the required indication, it may be necessary to systematically review backup copies of the data until a starting point can be determined.

In case the compromise has been going on for an extended period of time, it may be difficult to determine the exact start time and date. The response team should endeavor to narrow the range to the most specific extent and then select a likely start date prior to that to ensure that the investigation covers any possible time span.

Severity Assessment

A severity assessment can be arrived at by considering the sensitivity of the affected data, the risk of misuse, and the impact of misuse. Other factors to consider include the type and manner of loss, the ease of misuse, the amount of time between disclosure and discovery, the number of parties affected, and any mitigating factors.

Even though severity assessment may in some cases be difficult to determine until more extensive analysis has been conducted, it should be done at this stage and if necessary, refined later with input from the response team in order to allow the charting of an initial course of action based on best available information.

When determining severity, in addition to the sensitivity and criticality of the affected data and resources, the current and likely future impact of the incident must be taken into account, since a particular compromise and unauthorized access can lay the groundwork for a more severe compromise and the impact may become more severe without intervention.

In dealing with breaches of personally identifiable information, an increased number of data elements compromised will increase the severity and risk of harm. The factors to consider include harm to reputation, embarrassment, inconvenience, harassment, and prejudice, particularly when health or financial information is breached.

The correlation of similar events may result in a higher severity rating than that of any particular event in the group. Additionally, if an event is determined to be part of an ongoing incident, its severity may be automatically set to be that of the parent incident.

Severity 1: Critical

A Severity 1 incident represents an incident that is at the most critical level. Any sensitive information or data classified as "Confidential" is seriously impacted due to theft, malicious intent, accident, and/or negligence that may cause disclosure. Any incident classified with this severity level will require immediate intervention. One or more of the following parameters should be met:

- Involves the possible breach of one or more critical systems.

- Unauthorized disclosure, modification, destruction, or deletion of information classified as Confidential.

- Involves a large monetary amount, a significant amount of sensitive data, or could result in the notification of a significant number of affected parties.

- Is likely to be the subject of media coverage.

- Is likely to result in a non-routine notification of a regulator.

- Is likely to impact public long-term perception of the organization.

- Could otherwise pose a serious threat to the organization.

This severity should also be considered for less critical incidents that are spreading in an uncontrolled manner and whose impact could escalate with time.

Severity 2: Medium

Level 2 severity levels are identified to have non-intrusive impacts and represent passive attacks or monitoring, possibly in an effort to gain information for future attacks. One or more of the following parameters should be met:

- Could possibly result in the breach of a critical system.

- Has resulted in the breach of a low or medium criticality system.

- Results in the compromise of information classified as Internal Use and/or represents an attempt to harvest information classified as Confidential.

- Passive interception of critical plain-text communications.

- Has disrupted non-critical business processes.

- Represents an effort to gain further information for future attack.

- Unauthorized use.

- Unexplained system failures or outages.

The data owner or operator of resources involved in a Severity 1 or 2 incident should be explicitly instructed not to use the resources until the DBRT director provides further instruction.

Severity 3: Low

Even though low severity incidents may not require immediate action, they should be monitored in case they are an indication of future attempts at escalation. Such incidents can include random unsuccessful attempts to breach systems or lost or stolen data or equipment that is appropriately protected according to organizational guidelines.

Need to Know

Protecting information about an incident in progress is essential, not only to a successful response, but because it can have serious and long-term legal, privacy, security, and other ramifications. Limiting knowledge about an incident and securing it against security breaches will help ensure that sensitive information remains in the hands of those who need it to perform their duties.

Response Approach

Based on the incident analysis, including type, severity, and current state, a response can be developed to interrupt further damage, contain actual damage, and begin recovery and forensics activities. The goal of the response phase is to take technical and procedural measures to limit the scope of the incident and to return the organization to a secure status.

A data breach incident is a dynamic event and can evolve based on external events or on the actions of the response team itself. Since the information at any particular point in time is likely to be incomplete, the response team should continually gather and process facts about the incident to guide the attempt to resolve it.

Mitigation and response are not necessarily linear processes, but may occur concurrently with other processes, such as reporting, escalation, and investigation, or repeatedly during the incident-handling process itself.

Containment

If the incident is ongoing, it is important to contain it to prevent further unauthorized access to or use of sensitive information and before any additional spread overwhelms resources and increases damage. Containment essentially means limiting the compromise and its impact to the system or data already affected.

Criteria

Containment will help ensure that the affected data is no longer at risk from the threat of the incident. Criteria for determining the appropriate containment strategy include the potential damage to resources, the need for service and data availability, the time and resources needed to implement the strategy, and the effectiveness of the solution. Ideally, such strategies and procedures should be predetermined based on the type of breach, the criticality and sensitivity of the affected system or data, and acceptable risks.

Containment measures can include shutting down particular systems or connections, disconnecting or disabling access to data, systems, and services, reconfiguring firewalls, changing access accounts and passwords, and modifying physical access controls.

In certain cases, containment may be delayed in order to monitor suspicious activities or gather additional evidence. The value of collecting as much information as possible needs to be balanced against the risks of such a delay. This course of action should only be done under the direction of legal counsel and should generally be avoided since it can expose the organization to greater downstream liability from affected or other parties for any perceived delay or inaction. Additionally, it provides additional time for the malicious party to undertake actions that will cause further damage to the affected system or data as well destroy useful tracking information.

During containment, the DBRT should consider the tradeoff between availability and damage limitation. The organization should identify the availability requirements of specific data assets should they become involved in an incident. In particular, service agreements might require keeping systems and data available even with the possibility of further damage. Options include maintaining full availability, offering limited availability, or accepting any penalties specified in the service level agreements if the impact and scope of the incident justifies it.

Isolation

In order to prevent further intrusion or exposure of sensitive information until the breach is contained and can be prevented from recurring, the DBRT may consider isolating the compromised data or system. However, this may affect access for legitimate users and may significantly disrupt operations if the compromised data is mission-critical or the incident affects multiple systems or databases. Additionally, this course of action will necessarily alert users that a compromise has been detected. This may lead a malicious user to take action to conceal evidence or otherwise impede the investigation.

An evaluation of this course of action will consider the criticality and sensitivity of the data as well as the degree of compromise. The balance between those needs and the needs to isolate the data will have to be evaluated based on the severity and consequences of the compromise. If the organization does not own the data and is a licensee, any contractual obligations with the external party which is the primary owner must be considered.

The purpose of the isolation step is to prevent the corruption of other data or systems through a cascading compromise, and to maintain the state of the data or system for further analysis or use as evidence. It will also prevent an intruder from using the organization's systems to attack other systems and protect from liability as a result of damage claims by other organizations.

The simplest approach is to disconnect the affected system or data from network access to prevent any further compromise. Isolating the system or database may require that it be physically or logically disconnected from any network components or possibly from all access points so that only console access is maintained. It may also comprise retaining connection and access for certain limited administrative functions with minimal connectivity to the network.

If the system console is located in the same physical environment as the affected system, actual physical access should be restricted to the authorized administrator paired with a member of the response team.

Disconnecting a system or database from access will necessarily disrupt operations, so the team should consider more moderate solutions that focus on mitigating the risks to the extent practical rather than shutting down the environment. An evaluation of the appropriate course will include the type and criticality of system or data compromised and the activities of the malicious party. These steps can include continuing normal operations with activity and network monitoring.

The authority as well as the procedure for any disconnection should be predefined based on the criticality and sensitivity of the system or data. This is important in order to provide individual administrators with the management authorization to take actions that will necessarily disrupt operations. However, depending on the nature of the response, certain courses of action may need approval from senior management.

A notification process should be established for users, business partners, or any other party dependent on the system or data. For a prolonged disruption, users should be advised of the status of the response as well as the estimated time to recovery, especially when sensitive data has been compromised or destroyed.

Other Measures

Now let's discuss some other measures for evaluating or responding to an intrusion on your system.

Powering Off Affected Systems

Compromised systems should generally not be powered off or rebooted, since important data stored in volatile memory may be lost and session-only log files may be overwritten on reboot. Data lost can include memory contents, currently established network connections, queues of connection requests, open ports, running processes or processes set to run, clipboard contents, program images running in memory, and temporary files created by applications.

This course of action also poses the risk that a routine that destroys important data will be triggered during shutdown .This routine can occur either as part of normal shutdown or as an attempt by a perpetrator to destroy evidence.

Disabling Services and Processes

If an attacker is using a particular service to gain unauthorized access, containing the incident may include temporarily or permanently disabling the service. By disabling only the specific services used by an intruder, it is possible to continue providing users with access to all other services and to the system itself.

All processes running should be analyzed and any new or unknown process terminated. It is possible that certain processes will be disguised as normal operating processes or may not be detectable without extensive examination of the system. The system or database administrator will make these determinations in conjunction with a member of the response team.

Ideally, the response plan should outline defined circumstances that warrant disabling services and designate the authority to disable such services. The circumstances and levels of approval will depend on the business value and sensitivity of the service.

Securing Access

The attacker's route into the domain must be eliminated both in order to stop the current breach and to prevent the access of other resources. Firewalls may need to be reconfigured on a temporary or permanent basis to prevent access from certain external sources.

Integrity Checks

If it is suspected that any system configuration or particular data has been modified without authorization, a system or data integrity check should be initiated. In the case where the integrity of the system is compromised to a degree that makes it impractical or impossible to eliminate the compromise, it may be necessary to rebuild the system from scratch and securely configure it before returning it to production. This will include disabling unnecessary services, ensuring that the latest patches have been applied, recreating accounts with strong passwords, and continuing monitoring for a period of time until the administrator is confident that the threat has been removed.

Additionally, intruders may install programs to trigger certain malicious actions or to allow for alternative points of access. A full vulnerability assessment of the targeted system or database will help identify avenues through which the attack may have occurred and any new vulnerabilities that may have been introduced.

Disabling Accounts

Any account that may have been used in the attack should be disabled and a new account assigned. All accounts accessing a compromised system or database should be re-authenticated and checked for evidence of tampering. These accounts must be disabled and require positive identification and a new password before being re-enabled.

In certain cases, it may be necessary to disable all accounts, with the possible exception of administrative accounts that may allow further analysis, on or to change the passwords for those accounts. In any case, passwords for administrative accounts should always be changed since these accounts permit a higher access level in the event of compromise.

If the system or data compromised are part of a larger trust environment, it is possible that common accounts and passwords are sometimes used across systems and databases. It may be necessary to disable these accounts and passwords until all devices and data across the environment have been investigated and recovered.

The complete account file for a compromised system or database should be reviewed and a trusted version reinstalled. Particular attention should be paid to new user accounts that may have been created without authorization.

Enhancing Physical Security

If an unauthorized access incident involves a breach of physical security, additional containment strategies should be followed. This can include a complete review of authorized access, a re-issuance of access badges, a change in physical access mechanism, and the installation of additional physical access security measures.

Reconfiguring Detection Systems

Detection devices such as IDSes and other types of intrusion reporting tools should be updated to ensure that similar attacks are detected by these devices in the future. This can include:

- Determining if the devices need to be configured differently, such as adding new attack signatures or changing logging options.

- Determining if the devices need to be placed in a new or additional location on the network or on additional applications and hosts.

- Changing the number and type of alerts generated to better reflect the possible threats and vulnerabilities.

Preserving Data and Logs

Once a particular system or database has been compromised, a backup should be promptly performed to maintain the current state to the largest extent possible in order to facilitate subsequent review and forensic investigation. If the breach is ongoing, the backup may need to be repeated on multiple occasions in order to provide a timeline of the compromise and of the data affected.

At least two full backups should be made of the compromised data. One of the backups may be reinstalled on another system for further analysis and may eventually be used for recovery. The second backup will not be used for any operational task, but will be preserved as evidence with the appropriate security and chain of custody.

It is important that log files and all other records pertaining to the breach be preserved in a manner that prevents modification or loss. Administrative personnel should be notified to preserve all relevant logs.

Recovery

In recovery, systems are restored to normal mission status and a secure operational state and security measures and controls are enhanced to prevent a similar occurrence. Depending on the characteristics of a particular incident, corrective actions could be related to technology, policies, and/or processes. Business units, through their participants on the response team and with involvement of other team members as appropriate, will undertake an assessment of corrective actions that would address a particular incident and eliminate or reduce the likelihood that it will recur. Similarly, where a particular incident implicates organization-wide data, systems, or processes, the organizational function responsible will undertake a similar assessment.

Restoration

The process of restoring and returning a compromised system or database to normal operation is best accomplished after all means of intruder access are eliminated. This will reduce the risk of a similar breach occurring and ensure timely detection and notification by updated intrusion detection mechanisms.

Certain business-critical systems and databases, however, may need to be returned to production before the full breach analysis is completed and corrections made. The production requirements and priorities should be determined with the involvement of senior management. In this case, the risk needs to be carefully managed by continuing analysis and remediation in parallel and increasing the level of monitoring and intrusion detection to ensure that a new intrusion does not go unnoticed.

Restoring the integrity of compromised data will generally be performed from a verified and validated backup source. Any changes to the data from the time of the last backup to the present must be recreated. Users should be encouraged to review all restored data and check for unexpected changes to ensure it was not affected by the intruder's activities.

If data confidentiality has been breached, it is generally impossible to restore. If the compromise is limited to one or a small number of unauthorized parties, it may be possible to limit the spread of the data to those parties. In either case, reactive measures will aim to limit the impact of the compromise.

A full restore, including changes to every password, should be performed if an unauthorized party has gained administrative access to a system. The restoration to a secure operational state may be achieved through the application of patches, data restoration, or by disabling any compromised element. If the entire extent of the incident is unknown, then a complete system or database restore may be necessary.

One of the goals of the recovery process is to eliminate the cause of the incident and minimize the possibility of a similar event. Some incidents involve the exploitation of multiple vulnerabilities, so it is important to identify all vulnerabilities that were used and to determine strategies for correcting or mitigating each one. Similar systemic vulnerabilities should be identified and addressed across the organization.

Operational capability can be restored as soon as measures have been taken to address any vulnerability that led to the breach.

Monitoring

Systems and databases should be monitored for signs of continued unauthorized access. The priority should be to eliminate such access before any recovery operations can be effective. Additionally, audit logs must be reviewed to determine if there were access failures prior to or just following the suspected breach. On a longer term basis, in order to ensure that the compromise has been remediated, continual monitoring should be performed for system, database, intrusion detection, and firewall logs. Continual monitoring may also reveal other access paths not previously identified and will allow their rapid disablement.

Data Compromise

Monitoring is particularly critical to ensure that all compromised data is identified. If compromised data remains so after incident closure, it could continue to affect internal processes as well as victimized individuals without any organizational response to mitigate its effects.

The ability of an organization to monitor for and prevent attempts to misuse the breached information can be a factor in mitigating the effects of the breach. If the compromised information relates to internally maintained records, the organization can monitor these records for change requests which may signal attempts to misuse the information.

System Compromise

Compromised systems will generally be readily identified. However, systems with similar characteristics will run an increased risk of being similarly compromised through the exploitation of common vulnerabilities. Similarities can include the same network segment, the same trusted domain, and the same operating system or database management system. Beyond technical and processing similarities, human factors such as having the same system administrator can contribute to a common vulnerability due to common administrative errors.

Account Compromise

If an access account has been compromised, or if an unauthorized escalation of privileges has occurred, the account can be used to access other systems or data or to provide unauthorized access to other users. Any such account needs to be monitored to ensure that it is properly utilized by authorized users.

In addition to monitoring, a complete vulnerability assessment scan should be performed on the affected system to help detect and assess residual security weaknesses and risks. The scan should also be performed on similar systems since the same vulnerability may exist and be exploited.

Identifying the Attacker

Although the desire to identify an unknown attacker may be strong, the team should remain focused on containment and recovery, since identification can be a time-consuming and potentially futile process that can take valuable time from activities to minimize the impact of the breach.

Documentation

The DBRT is responsible for ensuring the secure retention of all information pertaining to an information security incident for further analysis, and potential legal evidential use. As soon as the DBRT suspects that an incident is occurring or has occurred, it is important to begin documenting all information related to the incident. All steps taken from the time the incident is detected to its final resolution should be documented. This will ensure a firm basis for decisions made and actions taken, provide the necessary records for any upcoming internal or external notifications, and ensure that adequate steps are taken to make the appropriate changes to the relevant business processes or technology.

During the management of the incident itself, thorough documentation will be used as a basis for reports on the current status and will ease any transition or handing off of responsibility to another staff member. After the completion of the response, during the Lessons Learned exercise, documentation will help the team determine how the situation was handled and provide directions for future improvement.

To reduce the risk of sensitive information being released inappropriately, the team should ensure that access to incident documentation is restricted to authorized parties. Any documentation containing sensitive information shall not be maintained longer than required by applicable records retention schedules to minimize risk of exposure. Such documentation should be destroyed in accordance with approved and secure methods designed to ensure against inadvertent disclosure, theft, or other compromise of personal or other non-public information.

The DBRT should document the details of each action when dealing with the incident. This should be done as events occur or are being observed. Each member of the response team should be responsible for documenting their own events and actions. Each of these logbooks will present the situation from the individual's perspective. Each entry should include the date and time, specific event or observation, actions, conversations, as well as any notes. Opinions and reasons for particular actions are useful to provide a context and fuller explanation of a particular event, but should be clearly marked as such to distinguish them from the facts. This is important in case the logbook entries are used in a legal proceeding and to make clear distinctions during the Lessons Learned exercise.

At the end of the active response phase, the individual logbooks will be consolidated into an incident timeline, which will include the detailed description of the events that took place. This will be a chronological and normalized consolidation that will be distributed to members of the team and any other relevant parties in order to review the incident. Cross-references to the original source should be noted.

Help Desk logs for any call or action concerning the incident should also be collected. In addition, all other logs, such as network, system, database, physical access, firewall, and IDS logs, external and internal communications, notification to impacted individuals, and any other relevant documentation should be maintained.

During the incident, the team should identify and implement appropriate steps to preserve documentation and evidence consistent with needs to restore availability. Since it is possible that systems and data may not be brought back online until evidence collection is completed, this should be performed as rapidly as possible to restore the availability of critical business processes in a timely fashion.

The documentation should be organized and reviewed with management and legal representatives. The DBRT is responsible for ensuring the secure retention of all information pertaining to an information security incident for further analysis, and potential legal evidential use.

Forensics

Although the primary reason for gathering evidence during an incident is to resolve the incident, it may also be needed for legal proceedings, both in order to prosecute a perpetrator or to defend the organization if subject to a lawsuit. A forensic investigation should ensure that the examination is conducted in a systematic, formalized, and legal manner to ensure the admissibility of the evidence, especially since both the integrity of the evidence and the integrity of the investigation process may be scrutinized. Several factors can affect the admissibility and value of the evidence, including:

- **Authenticity** The organization must be able to demonstrate that the evidence originated from the identified source in question.

- **Reliability** The organization must be able to demonstrate that the system that generated the evidence was reliable and that the evidence accurately represents the state of an event at a given point in time.

- **Integrity** The organization must be able to demonstrate that the evidence has not been altered during and since collection.

- **Chain of Custody** The organization must be able to produce verifiable documentation of the sequence of parties who have handled a piece of evidence from the moment it was collected, as well as the dates, times, and locations of evidence storage. This is to ensure that the evidence has not been accessed by unauthorized individuals and has been handled in a proper manner.

There are several sources from which forensic evidence can be retrieved:

- Intrusion detection software
- Firewalls
- Routers and other network devices
- Servers, workstations, and laptops
- Help Desk applications
- Corporate applications such as accounting and ERP software
- Hardware, software, and database logs

- Data backups
- Physical sources and security monitoring devices

The types and amounts of evidence to collect will depend upon:

- The impact of the collection process on normal business operations and the need to minimize disruptions.
- The cost of collection compared to the possible potential benefits of the collected evidence.
- The likely impact of particular evidence on the success of a formal action.
- Any legal collection requirements and constraints.

It is important to clearly document how all evidence has been preserved. Evidence should be collected, transferred, and stored according to procedures developed with the help of legal staff and appropriate law enforcement agencies. For a proven chain of custody to occur, the evidence must be stored securely, accounted for at all times, and the passage of evidence from one party to the next must be fully documented. Procedures must be followed to demonstrate that evidence integrity is preserved whenever it is used, moved, or combined with new evidence. Any other information that can demonstrate the objectivity and logical nature of analysis should also be documented.

Any investigation or manipulation should not be performed using the evidence collected for legal proceedings, but on a copy of that evidence in order to preserve the integrity of the evidence.

Since a wide range of staff will be involved with or responsible for evidence, specialized training should be conducted in general forensic principles, with more detailed training for specific members of the response team. This type of training is important to help reduce any errors in evidence handling and other forensic issues and minimize the chance that the expected scrutiny during legal and administrative proceedings may invalidate the evidence.

Records of the information security incident and forensic analysis should be stored in a physically secure environment, and controlled by appropriate procedures to prevent access by unauthorized parties.

Summary

- Some events are the result of routine activity, while others may be indicators of a potential incident requiring response.

- An ineffective event evaluation process may end up overwhelming organizational resources with the effort of dealing with noise and false positives, and may lead to the occurrence of false negatives, where an incident requiring attention and response is not detected or managed.

- The response team coordinator who receives the first report of the incident will be tasked with making certain preliminary determinations, including sufficiency of information, incident occurrence, the type of breach, extent, magnitude, apparent cause, and source of breach, data sensitivity level, and escalation.

- A preliminary assessment will assist in collecting and organizing information helpful in the formal assessment process as well as in assigning a severity.

- The preliminary assessment will be based on the likelihood and extent of harm caused by the incident and will take into account the nature of the data, the likelihood that the data is usable, the likelihood that the incident may lead to harm, and the ability to mitigate the risk of harm.

- As a result of the initial assessment, the coordinator will escalate the event to the team, reassign the incident outside of the response team process, or close the event.

- If it is evident or suspected that a data incident is significant and above a certain level of criticality, it should be escalated by the coordinator to the response team director.

- If a determination is made that the nature of the incident requires the gathering of the team, the director shall notify the core members of the team.

- Additional information about the breach can be obtained through parties within and outside the organization, as well as through the review of the technical information. These sources include the party responsible for the loss, data owners, system, database, and network administrators, end users, Help Desk, malicious party, IDSes, and audit logs.

- Protecting information about an incident in progress is essential, not only to a successful response, but because it can have serious and long-term legal, privacy, security, and other ramifications.

- The incident classification will dictate the type of response and subsequent actions. Incidents may be classified as system intrusions, external attacks or abuse reports, breach of sensitive information assets, policy violations, and technical events.

- The scope of the incident will depend on the extent of possible compromise to affected data, and will help in determining the intervention actions and assigning an appropriate priority.

- Determining how long the incident has been going on is important, since there is an obvious correlation between the length of time a vulnerability exists undetected and the amount of data that can be compromised.

- A severity assessment can be arrived at by considering the sensitivity of the affected data, the type and manner of loss, the risk and ease of misuse, the amount of time between disclosure and discovery, the number of parties affected, and the impact of misuse.

- If the incident is ongoing, it is important to contain it to prevent further unauthorized access to or use of sensitive information and before any additional spread overwhelms resources and increases damage.

- Containment measures can include shutting down particular systems or connections, disconnecting or disabling access to data, systems, and services, reconfiguring firewalls, changing access accounts and passwords, and modifying physical access controls.

- Isolation from the network can prevent further intrusion or exposure of sensitive information until the breach is contained, but may affect access for legitimate users and may significantly disrupt operations if the compromised data is mission-critical or the incident affects multiple systems or databases.

- Compromised systems should generally not be powered off or rebooted, since important data stored in volatile memory may be lost and session-only log files may be overwritten on reboot.

- If an attacker is using a particular service to gain unauthorized access, containing the incident may include temporarily or permanently disabling the service.

- The attacker's route into the domain must be eliminated in order to stop the current breach and to prevent the access of other resources.

- If it is suspected that any system configuration or particular data has been modified without authorization, a system or data integrity check should be initiated.

- Any account that may have been used in the attack should be disabled and a new account assigned.

- Once a particular system or database has been compromised, a backup should be promptly performed to maintain the current state to the largest extent possible in order to facilitate subsequent review and forensic investigation.

- Restoring and returning a compromised system or database to normal operation is best accomplished after all means of intruder access are eliminated. This will reduce the risk of a similar breach occurring, and ensure timely detection and notification by updated intrusion detection mechanisms.

- Restoring the integrity of compromised data will generally be performed from a verified and validated backup source.

- If data confidentiality has been breached, it is generally impossible to restore, but it may be possible to limit the spread of the data.

- Recovered systems and databases should be monitored for signs of continued unauthorized access.

- The organization should ensure the secure retention of all information pertaining to an information security incident, for further analysis and potential legal evidential use.

- All steps taken from the time the incident is detected to its final resolution should be documented.

- A forensic investigation should ensure that the examination is conducted in a systematic, formalized, and legal manner to ensure the admissibility of the evidence, especially since both the integrity of the evidence and the integrity of the investigation process may be scrutinized.

Chapter 8

Disclosure and Notification

Solutions in this chapter:

- **Notification Threshold**
- **Identifying Notification Recipients**
- **Timing**
- **Source**
- **Contents**
- **Protection Recommendations**
- **Offered Services**
- **Method of Delivery**
- **Other Notifications**
- **Legal Issues and Requirements**
- **Preparing for Follow-Up**

☑ **Summary**

Introduction

All organizations have an affirmative duty to protect sensitive information against unauthorized access or use. Notifying affected parties of a security incident involving their information is a key part of that duty. Once the organization becomes aware of an incident of unauthorized access to sensitive information, and once an investigation determines that misuse of customer information has occurred or is reasonably possible, it should, on the basis of legal advice, expeditiously notify the affected parties. Similarly, it should also notify entities in a position to either assist in informing affected parties, or to prevent or minimize the harm from the breach.

Despite the potential for embarrassment or inconvenience, timely notification is important to comply with legal requirements, manage an organization's reputation and legal risk, assist in maintaining good client relations, and enable the affected parties to take protective measures against the consequences of identity theft or fraud, or become vigilant about unauthorized activity. Despite the importance of timely notification, any decision concerning disclosure to external parties should be postponed until an internal investigation reveals the nature, extent, and severity of the breach.

The precise steps to take must be decided in light of the particular facts, as there is no single response for all breaches. However, the following criteria can provide the outline of the necessary approach:

- **Threshold** Since not all breaches will require notification, the determination of whether this particular incident meets the threshold notification requirements.

- **Timing** Timing can be affected by jurisdictional requirements, law enforcement needs, and whether the breach has been completely contained.

- **Contents** Notification contents based on the particular circumstances of the breach.

- **Delivery** The delivery mechanisms to ensure that the affected parties can reasonably be expected to receive the notification.

- **Follow-up** The procedures for handling inquiries from affected parties following the receipt of the notification.

Notification Threshold

Care is needed in defining appropriate criteria for incidents that merit public notification, since notification of a breach when there is little or no risk of harm might create unnecessary concern and confusion, and since the organizational costs associated with notification can be significant. The costs also include the financial expense and inconvenience to the affected parties that can arise from the actions taken by them to mitigate the effects of any potential identity theft. Other entities also incur costs in servicing these actions. In addition to direct financial costs, a notification may cause anxiety and confusion in the recipients, and potentially a loss of confidence in the organization.

Additionally, as a public policy consideration, the sending of too many notices based on overly strict criteria could render all such notices less effective, because affected parties could become desensitized to them and fail to act when risks are truly significant.

While legislation may require formal reporting and notification of affected parties in certain cases of data compromise, the organization should take a broader approach by defining an internal notification threshold when the possibility of unauthorized data acquisition has been discovered. As an example, most legislation exempts encrypted data from the notification requirement; however, if encrypted information is acquired and the organization believes that there is a reasonable possibility that the encryption can be breached whether through the compromise of the encryption key or other methods, then that can be a determining factor in the notification decision.

The decision of whether notification is appropriate can be arrived at through a risk analysis by the members of the Data Incident Response Team (DIRT) that considers the nature of the relevant information and the likelihood of its misuse.

The initial step will be to determine whether notice-triggering information is reasonably believed to have been compromised. The following factors should be considered:

- Is there evidence that sensitive information has been accessed by or is in the possession of an unauthorized user?

- Was a user account with access to sensitive information compromised?

- Was a database or system containing sensitive information compromised?

- Has equipment such as a laptop or other media containing unencrypted sensitive data been lost or stolen?

- Has a department or business unit not properly disposed of records containing sensitive information?

- Has a third-party service provider experienced any of the above incidents affecting the organization's sensitive data?

- Are there indications that the information was used or that the breach was publicized by the unauthorized party?

These factors will establish whether there is a reasonable likelihood that sensitive data was compromised. Once that determination has been made, additional factors to consider include:

- The nature of the information compromised, as well as any context or combination of information that might raise the sensitivity level.

- The type of loss, whether an intentional theft, an incidental theft (where theft of sensitive information may have been inadvertent and not have been the primary factor, such as in the case of stolen laptops), or an accidental loss. The risk is greater if data was stolen by a malicious party who was targeting the data, than if the information was inadvertently lost or if the data storage device rather than the information itself was the target. However, an opportunistic party may exploit information once it comes into their possession.

- The manner of loss, such as lost or stolen media, systems compromise, unauthorized disclosure or dissemination, improper disposal, or missed delivery.

- The likelihood of misuse, with special consideration given to whether the unauthorized party will know the value of the information.

- The ease of misuse, including whether the information was encrypted or masked. In cases of encrypted information, consideration should be given to whether the encryption key was also compromised.

- Any mitigating factors, such as whether the organization is able to retrieve the sensitive information, and based on an investigation, reasonably concludes that retrieval took place before the information was copied, transferred, or misused.

- The likelihood that the breach may lead to harm, such as the effect of a breach of confidentiality on affected parties or on fiduciary responsibility.

- The identity of the unauthorized party.

- The amount of time between disclosure and discovery.

- The number of individuals or parties affected.

- The residential jurisdiction of the affected parties, since different jurisdictions may have specific notification requirements.

- Relevant laws, regulations, and contractual obligations.

- The potential damage to affected parties if notification is not given.

- The potential reputation damage to the organization, in the case of notification or in the case of failure to notify.

In the event of an unauthorized disclosure by an unaffiliated third party, an additional set of factors will be considered in determining the appropriateness of notification:

- The manner in which the breach was discovered.

- Whether the affected parties are identified or identifiable.

- Whether the third party has already notified the affected parties, regulators, or the press.

The team director, legal counsel, and senior organizational executives will make a joint and final decision as to whether, how, and when external notification will be provided. If the results of the analysis indicate that misuse of the information has occurred or is reasonably possible, the organization should notify the affected parties as soon as possible. This is especially the case when the misuse would cause substantial harm to the parties, including the possibility of identity theft or fraudulent transactions.

Even if notification is not necessary, such as in the case where the investigation indicates that misuse of the information is unlikely to occur, appropriate steps should be taken to safeguard the interests of the parties, including monitoring affected records or accounts for unusual or suspicious activity.

Identifying Notification Recipients

If a determination can be made of precisely which parties' sensitive information has been improperly accessed, notification can be limited to those parties. However, if a grouping of sensitive data has been compromised, and it is not possible to identify which specific parties' information has been accessed, then all parties in the group must be notified.

The determination of which recipients to notify is also affected by jurisdictional requirements, which include timing and notification contents. Jurisdictional requirements may be overlapping since they may apply for the affected parties' residential location as well as the location where the breach occurred. Even if not required by law, the organization should provide notice for breaches involving higher-risk personal information if being notified would allow individuals to take action to protect themselves from possible harm.

While the desire to be inclusive will generally drive the determination of the population of recipients, it is important to avoid false positives, where the notice of a security breach is sent to individuals who should not receive it because their personal information was not acquired as part of the breach. Before sending individual notices, the organization should make reasonable efforts to include only those individuals whose notice-triggering information was acquired. The process for determining inclusion in the group to be notified should be documented, and the notification list should be checked to ensure it is not over-inclusive.

If it can be determined that the affected individuals are not English speaking, the notification should also be provided in the appropriate language. Special accommodations should be made for individuals who are visually or hearing impaired by providing alternative means of access to the information.

Timing

Once a decision to notify has been made, the notification should be sent in the most expedient time possible, but without compounding the harm from the initial incident through premature announcement based on incomplete facts or in a manner likely to make identity theft or fraud more likely to occur as a result of the announcement.

Since various jurisdictions have legal requirements regarding timing, care should be taken that each affected party is notified within the time limits of their local jurisdiction. Jurisdictional timing and other notification requirements should be included in the incident response plan for quick reference.

There are circumstances where a notification should be delayed even after the decision to notify has been made. They include:

- An appropriate law enforcement agency determines that the notification will interfere with an investigation and provides a written request for the delay. In this case, the law enforcement agency should be asked to inform the organization when it is safe to send the notification without impeding the investigation. It should not be necessary for an investigation to be completed before notification can be given.

- The data breach has not been contained and controlled and the affected systems have not been safeguarded and secured. The organization may need time to analyze the scope of the breach, secure the data, remediate the damage, and coordinate with external parties.

- A public announcement may alert the perpetrator of the value of the information or otherwise compound the harm of the initial breach.

- A brief delay to allow implementation of a consolidated announcement strategy as opposed to a hasty public announcement without detailed guidance on steps to take. This will permit public statements, Web site postings, and a call center staffed with individuals prepared to answer the most frequently asked questions, all to be made simultaneously available.

Any decision to delay notification will be made by a senior organizational executive in consultation with legal counsel.

Source

Given the serious security and privacy concerns raised by data breaches, notifications should generally be issued by a senior-level business manager. This will signal that the organization recognizes the concerns raised by the breach. In the case of a significant incident affecting a large number of parties, the notification should be issued by the chief executive of the organization.

If a subcontractor or third-party vendor with access to the sensitive information suffers the breach, the organization is responsible for ensuring that its subcontractor or partner promptly notifies it of any data loss. Notification responsibilities should be rapidly established if they have not already been done as part of the initial contract. Unless notification responsibilities are clear, an affected party could get multiple notification letters, likely with inconsistent details, and possibly not realize that multiple notices pertain to a single incident.

As a general best practice, regardless of which party is responsible for the breach, the actual notice should come from the party that the affected parties are reasonably likely to perceive as the entity with which they have a relationship.

Contents

In a simple and conspicuous manner, the notice should describe the incident, the information that was or is believed to have been acquired by an unauthorized party, and the organization's actions in investigating the breach, mitigating losses, and protecting against any further breaches. In addition, it should include a means of contact for further information and assistance. More specifically, a notice can include:

- A description of the breach in general terms.

- The date and time of the breach, or the best possible estimate, as well as the date and time the breach was discovered.

- The source of the breach, either the organization itself or a third party that maintains or processes information on its behalf.

- The manner in which the breach or compromise was detected.

- The approximate size of the affected population.

- The types and amount of personal information disclosed or potentially compromised, and the reason the affected party is being notified.

- An assessment of the risk of identity theft or fraud as a result of the breach, including whether any data is known to have been fraudulently used.

- Any mitigating factors.

- A description of the measures taken or that will be taken to manage the breach and to protect the affected parties' information from further unauthorized access. This can including engaging a third party to conduct a data breach analysis to determine whether a particular data loss appears to be resulting in identify theft.

- Information and advice on what the affected parties can do to protect themselves.

- An apology or statement of commitment to security. Regardless of the circumstances of the breach, an assumption of responsibility will increase the perception that the organization is seriously committed to resolving the issue.

- Anticipated next steps, if any.

- Contact information to obtain more information and assistance.

The notice should be crafted in a manner that provides the maximum information possible while avoiding the inclusion of any sensitive or personal information, thus potentially compounding the initial breach with a careless additional disclosure.

In certain circumstances, the public announcement of the breach could itself cause criminals, under the guise of providing legitimate assistance, to use various techniques to deceive the affected parties into disclosing personal information. If the organization determines that this could result from the announcement, specific instructions should also be included in the notification letter to help the affected parties guard against this.

Protection Recommendations

The protection recommendations will include the steps that affected individuals should take to protect themselves from the risk of fraud or identity theft. These should commensurate with the risk and the perceived or actual consequence of the data compromise, and strike a balance between being comprehensive and limiting unnecessarily the alarm and inconvenience of the affected parties. One or more of the following are appropriate:

- Remaining alert to possible identity theft or fraud for a specified period of time.

- Reviewing accounts or other documentation for suspicious activity.

- Steps for reporting identity theft and fraud to the organization and the appropriate authorities.

- Taking advantage of any credit monitoring or other service the organization intends to offer.

- Periodically obtaining credit reports to detect and request the deletion of information on fraudulent transactions.

- Placing fraud alerts or freezes on credit reports to notify creditors of the possibility of being a victim of fraud.

For all recommendations, proactive guidance should be provided with specific directions on additional steps to minimize the damage or rectify the situation. This includes links to appropriate resources or any relevant forms to fill out.

Offered Services

It may be necessary to offer certain services to the affected parties to assist them in minimizing the impact of the breach. These services can include credit monitoring and identity theft insurance.

Credit Monitoring

Credit monitoring services provide automatic monitoring and reporting of credit report activity and alert of any significant changes. By allowing the early detection of unexpected or unauthorized activity and limiting the amount of financial damage, they can become an important part of identity theft prevention and detection. Most credit monitoring includes:

- Credit file inquiries.

- New account activity to monitor any new accounts that are opened in the affected party's name.

- Changes to account information and credit limit increases.

- Address changes.

- Changes to public records.

- Closed accounts.

Determining when to offer credit monitoring requires risk-based management decisions, since such services are costly for the organization (both as a function of the number of affected parties and the length of time the service is offered), and require continual attention by the affected parties as each monitoring notice is received. A particular determinant of elevated risk is if there are indications that the compromised information has already been misused. In addition, the organization should consider the characteristics of the affected individuals. Some affected populations, because of duties or location, may have more difficulty in taking self-protective steps and self-monitor for identity theft.

If this service is something that the organization would consider offering in the event of a security breach, various options should be researched before an actual incident in order to understand the providers, services, and pricing.

Data Breach Monitoring

Technology-based data breach monitoring services offered by certain companies can help analyze whether a particular data loss appears to be resulting in identity theft. This may be a useful protective action when the organization is uncertain about whether the risk warrants implementing more costly credit monitoring services or when the organization wishes to do more than rely on individual actions by the affected parties. These services have the advantage of reducing or eliminating the protection effort of affected parties.

In addition, subsequent to any large data breach that is reported publicly, it is likely that an organization will get reports of identity theft directly from individuals in the affected class. However, it is statistically predictable that a certain number of the identity theft reports will originate through events other than the data security breach in question. Data breach monitoring can assist in determining whether the particular incident is truly a source of identity theft, or whether any such reports are the normal by-product of the routine incidence of identity theft.

Identity Theft Insurance

Depending upon the policy terms, identity theft insurance can provide assistance in detecting and reporting incidents of identity fraud as well as reimbursement for expenses and direct losses arising from identity fraudulent. Under certain circumstances, expenses will include lost wages for the time spent reclaiming financial identity as well as legal expenses.

Incentives

Acknowledging the risk that victims may opt to cease doing business or interacting with an organization following a data breach, it may be prudent to also offer incentives to lessen the possibility of such action. Such incentives will depend on the nature of the relationship between the organization and the affected parties.

Method of Delivery

The best means for providing notification will depend on the number of parties affected, what contact information is available about the affected parties, and the urgency with which they need to receive notice. The notification should be delivered in a manner that is designed to ensure that the affected parties can reasonably be expected to receive it. The notice should be sent separately from any other mailing so that it stands out to the recipient. If using another organization to facilitate the mailing, care should be taken that the organization that suffered the loss is identified as the sender, not the facilitating organization.

Generally, the primary means of notification is through a mail message or letter to the last known mailing address. E-mail can be used for parties for whom there is a valid e-mail address, who have agreed to receive communications electronically, and for whom a mailing address is not available. However e-mail notification is discouraged, as the affected individuals may have changed his or her e-mail addresses or could encounter difficulties in distinguishing the organization's e-mail from spam or a phishing e-mail. In emergency cases, where urgency may dictate immediate and personalized notification, telephone communications might be appropriate in addition to the e-mail notification.

If the number of parties affected is large, the cost of notification is prohibitive, or the organization does not have sufficient contact information for those to be notified, it may be necessary to use substitute means such as public announcement through the media, Web site postings, and distribution to public service and other membership organizations likely to have access to the affected parties. This course of action should be cleared by legal counsel, to ensure that all relevant laws and regulations are adhered to. These substitute means can also be used in conjunction with the primary notification.

Other Notifications

Other key constituencies must also be kept appropriately informed and updated and receive consistent and reliable information. All stakeholders should be identified to ensure complete and appropriate communications. Where appropriate, they include organizational management, regulatory agencies, consumer reporting agencies, employees, third-party vendors, the media, and law enforcement. Communications with each constituency will be coordinated through a designated Data Loss Response Team member.

For each constituency, a communications list should be assembled in advance. In addition to actual contacts, it will include an outline and examples of the type of information that each constituency will be seeking. The contents of the communication should be as appropriate and thorough as possible, in order to aid in the rapid acknowledgement and understanding of the problem. If particular members of a constituency are asked to perform certain actions to help with the incident response, the instructions should be as detailed and self-contained as possible to ensure that they are performed according to the response team's expectation.

A communications team comprised of the DBRT director, a senior corporate manager, the director of public affairs, and a legal representative should be identified to manage information dissemination. Since a data breach might require communications expertise not usually found within the organization, it may be prudent to engage an external agency or consultant to supplement the team.

In a crisis, there may be a natural conflict between the advice provided by various members of the team regarding the extent of information to provide various constituencies. This conflict should be resolved by a senior business manager, taking into account the need for open communications balanced by the requirements of the investigation and management of the incident.

Internal Disclosure

It is important to communicate not only externally, but also internally. Rapid internal notification of appropriate management is critical, since internal delays can prevent key personnel from being aware of the data breach in a timely manner and can delay the response.

Where appropriate, employees should also be notified, since inaccurate or fragmentary information and rumors can circulate and demoralize staff. Employees, especially those with consumer contact, can serve as important community ambassadors during a breach. In addition, employees might be contacted by the media or other parties and may provide inaccurate or incomplete information that might negatively affect the organization's efforts to manage and resolve the breach.

More particularly, users of an affected system or data must be notified and kept apprised of incident resolution progress in order to remain vigilant against further compromise attempts, and since the need may exist to restrict access to the system or data while remediation measures are being implemented.

One of the particular risks of internal disclosure before external notification or general knowledge of the breach is the possibility of insider trading. If the severity of the breach is likely to result in a substantial change in the price of the organization's stock or security, an internal knowledge of the breach would constitute material nonpublic information. Such nonpublic information used by an organizational insider for the purchase or sale of a security can constitute a serious legal violation. A delay in notification or public disclosure of a breach, even at the request of a law enforcement agency, will not negate the organization's obligations regarding insider trading.

In cases where external notification is warranted, reasonable advance notice should be provided to senior management of the decision before external notification is made.

Depending on the stage of the incident, internal notification can take several forms, from information related to specific ongoing activity, to longer-term information for improving awareness and system security. A preliminary alert can be sent when detailed information is unavailable, to inform users of an indication of a potential issue or threat. It will allow users to be on the lookout to recognize the issue and its importance. It will also encourage feedback from users who may have noticed the issue but underestimated its importance. Further alerts or incident status reports can follow as the incident unfolds.

As in the case of external disclosure, care should be taken not to disseminate any information that would provide the malicious party with any knowledge that could compound the harm of the breach. More generally, any information disseminated should be approved by the team director before distribution.

Regulatory Agencies

Certain regulated organizations, especially in the financial or communications industries, are required to report breaches or other suspicious activity to the appropriate regulatory or other governmental agency. Any contact with primary regulators should be managed by legal counsel and is usually initiated through the filing of a Suspicious Activity Report (SAR). This can be preceded by direct in-person or telephone communications with the primary contact within the regulatory agency. Additional regulators may be notified as required and appropriate.

Even if not required by applicable regulation, the organization may find it advantageous to notify its primary regulator to avoid misunderstandings that may develop through incomplete information received from other channels.

A primary concern of regulators will be that incident response decisions and notifications were documented and appropriate to the circumstance. This will provide an early warning to allow them to assess the effectiveness of the response plan, and, where appropriate, to direct that notice be given to the affected parties if the organization has not already done so.

The incident should be described in detail, explaining the origin, type, scope, severity, current status, and actual or potential consequences. Any relevant security policies and procedures utilized during this incident should be listed, as well as the names and titles for the incident management team that authorized and made decisions regarding the incident and resolution. If the incident resulted in a notification effort, regulators will be notified that notification is proceeding under applicable laws. A copy of the letter should be included as well as the number of parties impacted. One central contact, usually legal counsel, should be listed if the regulatory agency has additional questions.

Law Enforcement

If there is suspicion or confirmation that the incident may involve illegal activities or may be related to other breaches or other criminal activity, it should be reported to the appropriate law enforcement agencies in a manner consistent with the requirements of the law and the organization's procedures. This contact should be managed by a designated individual who is familiar with the reporting procedures for all relevant law enforcement agencies, and understands potential jurisdictional issues in order to determine which agency, if any, should be contacted. Points of contact should have previously been established in order to facilitate any investigation and the incident resolution. Additionally, since it may sometimes be difficult to determine which law enforcement agency will assume jurisdiction in any given incident, making contacts and finding the proper channels beforehand can expedite any necessary involvement.

Legal counsel should be involved in the decision to contact law enforcement to facilitate multi-level coordination and provide guidance. Consideration should be given to the fact that once this step is taken, it is likely that the organization may lose control of the incident management process as well as of proprietary information that may become part of the public record. Even though any investigation will have as its primary purpose the apprehension of a suspect, most law enforcement officials dealing with this type of crime will be cognizant of the impact of their actions on the organization, and will preserve the confidentiality of any information to the maximum possible extent.

Additionally, should law enforcement request a notification delay to conduct the investigation, the organization can be exposed to greater downstream liability from affected or other parties for any perceived delay in the incident management and notification. Liability can also increase due to possible law enforcement monitoring of customer accounts and data without customer knowledge.

There are, however, specific advantages to engaging law enforcement help. Law enforcement agencies possess a legal authority to subpoena external records and piece a perpetrator's anonymity that is not available to the organization. An auxiliary benefit is that this, along with certain other aspects of the investigation, can be done at no cost to the organization. Law enforcement agencies may also be aware of other similar concurrent intrusions and much more rapidly identify the source through the correlation of this knowledge.

Media

Prompt public media disclosure is generally desirable, since delayed notification can erode public trust. However, a decision to notify the media requires careful planning and execution so that it does not unnecessarily alarm the public or disseminate information that might compound the damage of the breach.

Media communications procedures should be established in accordance with the organization's policies on appropriate interaction with the media and information disclosure. A list of media contacts should be readily available and interviews or interactions should be limited to those contacts to avoid possibly discussing the breach with parties that do not belong to legitimate media organizations.

For incidents where the private information of a large number of parties is compromised, the media attention can consume a substantial amount of time and affect the progress of the investigation, especially if response team members are contacted directly. In order to allow team members to more effectively focus on the recovery process, a single media point of contact and a backup should be designated, usually from the Public Affairs department.

Even though all senior members of the response team should be prepared to interact with the media, team members or others contacted directly by the media should refer questions to the designated media contact. This will help ensure that consistent communication can take place while controlling rumors and misinformation.

A senior member or the head of the department, working under the direction of counsel to ensure legal privileges apply, will take responsibility for developing the press plan and crafting key communications to ensure consistent messages. This will include managing the preparation of a press statement (modified as additional information becomes available), interacting with members of the media, and provid-ing talking points for use by those who may be communicating about the issue with external constituencies. A media contact log with follow-up actions should be kept to ensure that accurate and timely information is disseminated.

If the severity of the breach should reach a national or crisis level, a news conference may have to be held with selected media representatives in order to proactively provide information to a larger audience.

In general, the following guidelines should be used when interacting with the media:

- Notification should focus on providing information to aid the affected parties in responding to the breach.

- Any technical information should be easily understood by the general public.

- The level of detail should not allow a malicious party to duplicate or compound the breach.

- Only established facts should be communicated since speculation about perpetrators or motives may be in error and may cause an inflamed view of the incident.

- Any impact of the breach should be presented in a balanced manner, and should not be minimized in order to prevent a perception of a lack of concern or commitment to security.

These guidelines should be followed even in the case of unsolicited media attention, to allow the organization to take a proactive stance in communicating the incident.

Under all circumstances, a member of the Public Affairs department should monitor media coverage and attempt to promptly respond to any inaccurate information that may hinder recovery efforts or cause unwarranted concern among affected parties.

Incident Reporting Agencies

Based either on legal obligation or on internal practice, the incident may be reported to a governmental or industry incident reporting and control agency that can assist in breach handling and mitigation efforts. These agencies do not replace the internal team, but can provide possible assistance based on collective experience. From a public policy aspect, one of their major responsibilities is to identify trends and precursors of attacks as well as produce data breach statistics, which can only be developed by collecting and analyzing data from multiple organizations.

A primary contact should be designated to report an incident, its impact, and corrective actions. This person should be familiar with reporting requirements and timeframes for the relevant agency.

Credit Reporting Agencies

A breach involving a large number of individuals can potentially have a significant impact on credit reporting agencies and their ability to respond efficiently due to the high volume of calls that may follow the notification. Additionally, agencies may be contacted by victims of identity theft resulting from the breach, to review credit files and to dispute negative information.

Depending on the nature of the incident and the number of parties affected, major credit reporting agencies should be notified prior to sending a large number of notices that include contact information for the reporting agencies. The agencies should be notified of the type of breach, the timing and distribution of notifications, and the number of affected parties in order to prepare for a surge in inquiries as well as requests for fraud alerts.

Financial and Other Institutions

If the breach involves organizationally issued or authorized credit cards, the organization should promptly notify the issuing bank or financial institution. The response teamshould coordinate with the organization's finance or human resources department regarding such notification and suspension of the account. If the breach involves individuals' bank account numbers used in employment-related transactions such as direct deposits for payroll, expense reimbursements, or benefit payments, the organization should coordinate with the affected individuals to notify the financial institution or processing entity that handles the particular transaction.

Additionally, an incident involving medical information may warrant notification to health care providers and insurers. In general, any institution that may be affected by the incident or may play a role in mitigating the potential harm stemming from the incident should be notified.

Other External Parties

Several other external parties may need to be contacted or notified depending on the incident. These include:

- **Owners of Attacking Domains** If an attack or compromise originates from an external organization's domain, the response team may want to communicate with the designated security contacts for the organization to alert them to the activity and to collect additional information. If an intruder has gained access to organizational resources through an external party, administrators at these parties may provide valuable logging and tracing information. For obvious reasons, caution should be exercised with unfamiliar external organizations.

- **Hardware or Software Vendors** If the compromise seems to have occurred because of a vendor hardware or software vulnerability, the specific vendor may need to provide information about any known or unknown vulnerability, as well as any similar types of compromises of their product that they may be familiar with. Additionally, the availability of patches or fixes may need to be determined.

- **Other Incident Response Teams** Groups that promote security and breach-related information sharing among incident response teams can sometimes offer needed assistance based on the experience of other members of the group. These groups can also facilitate more effective and efficient incident handling for all teams involved, provide access to advice from security professionals, and improve knowledge of security best practices. As part of the ongoing response planning, the response team can join such a group or subscribe to relevant information resources.

- **Other Organizations** If it can be determined whether other organizations have experienced a breach with a common point of compromise or other similar characteristics, a coordinated response may be advantageous depending on the circumstances. Even if that is not possible, such sites should be alerted to allow them to take appropriate action. It is sometimes possible to identify other affected sites through the review of log files.

Information Requests

If the scope and magnitude of the breach and of its consequences are significant, a number of information requests from various parties can be expected. An information dissemination plan should be created outlining the type of information that will be released to each party as well as the contact point for that release. This is important since non-responsiveness in this situation may lead to unwarranted and inaccurate conclusions being drawn about the seriousness of the breach and the organization's ability to respond.

Beyond that, requests for information regarding a security incident from any external party without a clearly defined need to know must be directed to legal counsel. The decision to release information based on these requests will be made on a case-by-case basis, consistent with the organization's legal, regulatory, or policy obligations.

There are several factors that determine if and to what extent information can be disclosed:

- **Purpose** A legitimate need-to-know or underlying purpose for obtaining the information.

- **Recipient** The type of recipient and whether they are internal or external.

- **Type** The category and sensitivity of the information as determined by the data classification scheme.

Correspondence created during the discovery or investigation phase of a security incident may be considered a public record subject to release under certain legal obligations. Information that is not appropriate for release based on the protection of privacy interests or security considerations, should not be included in this correspondence.

Legal Issues and Requirements

Various jurisdictions have enacted legislation governing disclosure and notification requirements. These laws are primarily designed to help protect individuals who might be adversely affected by a breach of their personal information. They provide definitions of the types of information compromises that require notification to affected parties residing or located within the jurisdiction, and can provide specific obligations concerning thresholds, timing, language, and methods of delivery.

Organizations doing business or conducting operations in multiple jurisdictions will likely be subject to several security breach notification laws. As a practical matter, the strictest standard will have to be applied to all the notification practices to minimize the negative public perception of notifying only certain affected parties and not others. This approach, however, may not always be practical, since specific provisions in the law of one jurisdiction may conflict with those of other jurisdictions.

Legal counsel will determine which laws and regulations are applicable based on the locations of the affected parties, the type of entity suffering the breach, the type of information compromised, and the purpose for which the information was initially collected.

If the affected person does not reside in a jurisdiction with a data breach law, the organization must make a business decision as opposed to a legal determination regarding notification. As a good business practice and to minimize legal liability, notification should be provided if it will allow individuals to take action to protect themselves from possible harm.

Preparing for Follow-Up

Those notified can experience considerable frustration if in the wake of an initial public announcement they are unable to find sources of additional accurate information. The organization should prepare for follow-on inquiries by establishing call centers prepared to answer the most frequently asked questions. If the breach is confined within the organization or if the number of affected parties is relatively small, this can be an existing internal Help Desk whose members have been updated on the breach. In cases where the number of inquiries is likely to exceed the organization's native capacity, it might be advisable to briefly delay the public announcement until the implementation of dedicated customer care center staffed by trained personnel.

The customer service team should be briefed on the circumstances of the breach, what the organization is doing to protect the affected parties and to prevent further unauthorized access, and what the affected parties can do to protect themselves. In addition, the team should be apprised of issues that must be referred to other responsible parties as well as of the escalation path for dissatisfied callers, callers that have been victimized, or for questions that it cannot answer.

Since some callers may not be satisfied with the information that the call center can provide, an escalation procedure will ensure that such inquiries receive appropriate attention. The escalation path will most likely be a designated manager from the line of business where the incident occurred. This can be followed in select cases by further escalation to a top-level executive, to demonstrate the organization's understanding of the seriousness of its responsibility for the safeguard of sensitive information.

Summary

- Notifying affected parties of a security incident involving their information is a key part of the organization's affirmative duty to protect sensitive information against unauthorized access or use.

- Care is needed in defining appropriate criteria for incidents that merit public notification, since notification of a breach when there is little or no risk of harm might create unnecessary concern and confusion, and since the organizational costs associated with notification can be significant.

- The decision of whether notification is appropriate, can be arrived at through a risk analysis that considers the nature of the relevant information and the likelihood of its misuse.

- The determination of which recipients to notify is affected by jurisdictional requirements as well as a positive determination of which parties were affected.

- The notification should be sent in the most expedient time possible, but without compounding the harm from the initial incident through premature announcement based on incomplete facts or in a manner likely to make identity theft or fraud more likely to occur.

- Given the serious security and privacy concerns raised by data breaches, notifications should be issued by a senior-level business manager or by the head of the organization.

- The notice should describe the incident, the information that was or is believed to have been acquired, the organization's actions in investigating the breach, the mitigating losses, and protecting against any further breaches, and a means of contact for further information and assistance.

- The protection recommendations will include the steps that affected individuals should take to protect themselves from the risk of fraud or identity theft.

- It may be necessary to offer certain services to the affected parties, to assist them in minimizing the impact of the breach. These include credit monitoring, identity theft insurance, and other incentives.

- The notification should be delivered in a manner that is designed to ensure that the affected parties can reasonably be expected to receive it. This is usually done by mail.

- Rapid internal notification of appropriate management is critical, since delays can prevent key personnel from being aware of the data breach in a timely manner and can delay the response.

- Certain regulated organizations are required to report breaches or other suspicious activity to the appropriate regulatory or other governmental agency.

- If there is suspicion or confirmation that the incident may involve illegal activities or may be related to other breaches or other criminal activity, it should be reported to the appropriate law enforcement agencies.

- A decision to notify the media requires careful planning and execution so that it does not unnecessarily alarm the public or disseminate information that might compound the damage of the breach.

- Depending on the nature of the incident and the number of parties affected, major credit reporting agencies should be notified prior to sending a large number of notices that include contact information for the reporting agencies.

- Organizations doing business or conducting operations in multiple jurisdictions will be subject to several security breach notification laws.

- The organization should prepare for follow-on inquiries by establishing call centers prepared to answer the most frequently asked questions.

Chapter 9

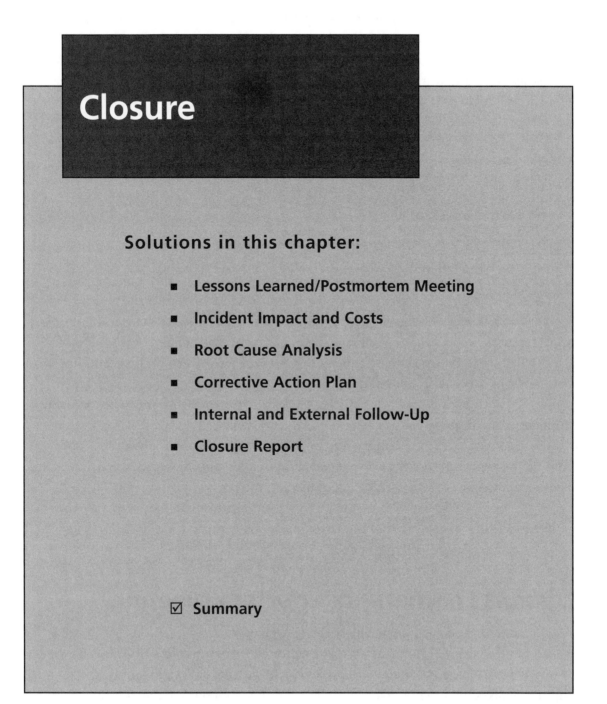

Closure

Solutions in this chapter:

- **Lessons Learned/Postmortem Meeting**
- **Incident Impact and Costs**
- **Root Cause Analysis**
- **Corrective Action Plan**
- **Internal and External Follow-Up**
- **Closure Report**

☑ **Summary**

233

Introduction

An incident can be closed upon the completion of the investigation, the issuance of external notifications if warranted, and the implementation of all suitable security remediation measures. This phase provides closure for the incident by taking action against its cause and learning from it to improve current processes and procedures. The successful close of a data security incident involves several steps:

- Lessons Learned and Postmortem
- Cost Analysis
- Root Cause Analysis
- Corrective Action Plan
- Follow-Up Reporting and Management Briefing
- Documentation

Once all the closure activities have been completed and approved, the incident can be formally closed, as no further action is required of the response team, unless the incident is reopened due to new evidence, new activity, or a reoccurrence of activity that appears to originate from the same source. Even though closure implies a connotation of finality, the effects of an incident may be felt for a substantial amount of time after its end, especially if legal or regulatory action is triggered and reputational damage occurs.

Post-incident evaluation will enable the organization to learn appropriate lessons from the incident and to ensure the remediation of any control or response deficiencies. The Team Director is responsible for coordinating the post-incident review and subsequent closure activities. This is conducted after sufficient time has elapsed after the incident such that effectiveness of the response can be evaluated. The same individuals involved in the security breach response process should be involved in this phase.

Lessons Learned/Postmortem Meeting

After a major data security incident has been handled, the organization should hold one or more Lessons Learned or post-incident review sessions with all involved parties, to review how effective the incident management process was, and identify necessary improvements to existing policies, processes, controls, awareness, training, risk analysis, and other organizational practices. The purpose of a Lessons Learned meeting is to provide insight and recommendations for mitigating contributing factors by providing direction in monitoring specific operational and technical risks, and in providing insight into policy and procedural enhancements, which may serve to mitigate certain risks.

The entire incident and its response should be reviewed to determine which parts of the process and response plan were effective and which need improvement for increased efficiency and effectiveness. Other reviews will include the security measures in place around the compromised data to determine if security approaches should be changed, and the result of communication to affected and other parties to determine the effectiveness of the communication.

A Lessons Learned meeting should also be held for lesser data breach incidents. The information accumulated can be used to identify systemic security weaknesses and deficiencies in policies and procedures. These sessions can also be held in response to a major incident at another organization to apply any possible information to the internal processes and procedures.

The post incident review process should be conducted after sufficient time has elapsed after the incident has taken place and been resolved, to provide a more objective view of the effectiveness of the response and communication. The team members involved in the security breach management process should be involved in the post-incident review. Additionally, other key cross-functional personnel should attend to ensure a full range of feedback, since insights can come from interaction between parties and groups. This provides a chance to review what occurred, what was done to intervene, and how well intervention worked, and will allow team members to critically analyze their performance and deliverables.

By reviewing the current security measures and controls and the process by which the incident was handled, the meeting can help identify, evaluate, and make recommendations for any needed changes and actions for specific updates to the following:

- Overall security strategy
- Security architecture, tools, and resources
- Policies and procedures
- The incident response plan
- Technology, configuration, or system enhancements
- Personnel resources, including response team resources
- Team model and structure

- Incident documentation and reports
- Communication procedures
- Awareness and training

Questions to be answered in the Lessons Learned meeting include:

- What were the early warning signs of the incident?
- Were precursors and indications appropriately recorded and logged?
- Could any signs have been recognized sooner or were any signs ignored?
- What information may have been needed sooner?
- What security measures were in place around the compromised data?
- Were there any measures that could have prevented the incident?
- Was there enough information available to analyze the incident? If not, what else would have helped and how could that have been obtained?
- Did the incident cause damage before it was detected?
- What were the timeline and details of the incident?
- What was the root cause of the incident?
- How well did staff and management perform in dealing with the incident?
- Were the documented incident response policies and procedures followed?
- Were the procedures outlined in the response plan adequate and work as intended?
- Are there any additional procedures that would have aided in the detection and management of the incident?
- Were all appropriate parties kept informed of the status of the incident response?
- How effective were the communications to different audiences?
- Were any steps or actions taken that might have inhibited the recovery?
- Were the response efforts appropriate? Was the selected course of action effective?
- Were significant problems encountered during the response process and how they can be addressed?

- What would be done differently the next time a similar incident occurs?

- What were the monetary, reputational, or other costs?

- What corrective actions can prevent similar incidents in the future?

- Do affected controls, policies, and procedures need to be revised beyond what was implemented during the response phase?

- Might other data or systems be vulnerable to the same compromise? If so, what steps can be taken to mitigate the risks?

- What was done right? What can be improved?

- What steps have been taken to prevent a recurrence of the incident?

- What additional tools or resources are needed?

- Were the right people on the response team? If not who should be included?

The Lessons Learned meeting will enable both an objective assessment by analyzing the response based on pre-determined criteria to determine how effective it was, as well as a subjective assessment, where response team members and data owners may be asked to assess their own performance, as well as that of other team members and of the entire team.

Any relevant lessons learned should be included in the revised data security and incident response plans for reference, and the updated documents should be communicated to all relevant personnel.

Incident Impact and Costs

The response team should develop a procedure by which it can analyze and measure the direct and indirect costs associated with a data breach incident, in order to determine the value of information and assets lost. This will provide a cost/benefit analysis of the incident response process, justify the implementation of new safeguards and controls, and help determine a monetary amount if the organization pursues legal actions to recover damages, as penalties are directly tied to the amount of damage done and the cost of responding, restoring, and business resumption along with revenue and productivity losses.

The loss will include the cost of responding to the incident, conducting a damage assessment, managing the incident and, if necessary, restoring data to its prior condition, and any revenue lost, cost incurred, or other consequential damages incurred.

Overall Impact

The overall impact that the incident has had on the organization can be categorized in one or more of the following terms:

- **Regulatory or Legal** Will the incident likely result in regulatory attention or penalties, civil or governmental prosecution?

- **Customer** Did the incident result in a disruption of customer service, visibly affected customers, and/or resulted in a loss of customer accounts?

- **Reputational** Did the incident result in negative publicity and/or negatively impact the reputation of the organization?

- **Financial** Did the incident result in or is likely to result in a financial loss?

Personnel Costs

Among the most measurable costs in dealing with the incident are usually direct personnel costs, including the time of response team members as well as others who participated in the response. Ideally, response team members and others should document time, resource costs, and expenditures. A simple calculation will allow the determination of the personnel costs. The time will include initial response, analysis, incident management, information recovery, time spent on notification activities, and closure.

Staff Productivity

Loss in the form of decreased productivity must also be considered. This is tabulated by considering the number of employees who were prevented from working or experienced a slowdown in work because of the incident, as well as the attributable downtime. A productivity impact can also be attributed to the need to quickly redeploy resources to contain a breach and mitigate its consequences. The productivity impact on a particular resource may have collateral and downstream damage if the unavailability of that resource affects the work of other dependent resources.

Another source of lost productivity is employee distraction and concern caused by breach publicity and internal efforts to manage the incident.

Lost Revenue

There may be costs related to the inability to service customers and the attendant loss in sales. There may also be losses attributable to data integrity compromise, especially billing and financial data that may result in inaccurate accounting.

A major consideration when considering revenue loss is the opportunity cost of customers terminating or modifying their relationship with the organization, and the attendant impact on future business.

Victim Notification

Victim notification is generally mandated if a risk analysis indicates that there is a significant probability that the breach will result in identity theft or fraud. Based on the number of victims and the availability of contact information, notification costs are generally not negligible, especially since most jurisdictions require mail notification. For particularly severe breaches, telephone notification can also add significant cost. In all cases, the time and expense required to determine the affected parties, collect, analyze, and normalize the contact information, and send the notification should also be considered.

Victim Assistance

It may be necessary to offer certain types of victim assistance to help minimize the impact of the breach. The cost of these services will depend on the nature of the breach, its severity, the number of victims, and the length of time the services are offered. Typical services include:

- Credit monitoring to provide automatic monitoring and reporting of credit report activity and alert of any significant changes.

- Data breach monitoring services to analyze whether a particular data loss appears to be resulting in identity theft.

- Identity theft insurance can provide assistance in detecting and reporting incidents of identity fraud, as well as reimbursement for expenses and direct losses arising from identity fraudulent.

- Other incentives that depend on the nature of the relationship between the organization and the victims.

If victim assistance services are being considered in the event of a security breach, various options should be researched before an actual incident in order to understand the providers, services, and pricing.

Call Center

The organization will need to prepare for the natural increase in calls from affected parties, by establishing call centers prepared to respond to victim inquiries and questions. This will either entail incremental existing help desk costs if the number of affected parties is relatively small, or the cost of establishing and maintaining an internal or external customer care center staffed by trained personnel. It may also entail the time of senior business line or technical managers to whom certain calls may need to be escalated.

Media Management

Media management activities are generally within the media relations department's regular scope. However, an incident may greatly increase such activities, including the effort to develop the press plan, craft key communications, managing the preparation and release of a press statement, increased interaction with members of the media, talking points development, and other public relations activities.

Additionally, the Investor Relations department may also need to become involved in communications where investors and analysts are warranted.

Consulting Services

Consulting services may need to be procured for specialties that the organization does not have in-house, or to supplement existing skills. These services include technology consultants, forensics experts, legal advice, and public relations management.

Legal Fees

These include fees associated with legal advice in managing the breach, as well as fees to represent the organization during regulatory review or civil litigation, whether initiated by the organization against the malicious parties or by victims against the organization.

Regulatory or Legal Penalties

Fines may be assessed by regulatory agencies if it is determined that the organizational security infrastructure or incident response process was not consistent with mandates or best practices. Fines will be determined by the extent of loss, the number of affected parties, and the degree of deviation from the standard.

Potential compensatory and punitive penalties that may be assessed civilly against the organization as a result of action by victims are harder to tabulate, but experienced counsel can usually determine a range of exposure. These penalties can include actual loss by the victims, as well as damages for failure to exercise an adequate standard of due care when sensitive data is compromised or when the organization's systems are inadvertently or intentionally used to attack others.

Additionally, certain regulatory agencies have the authority to impose stricter audit requirements on organizations that were subject to a breach and that were found to have failed to adequately secure customer data. Such audits can be rigorous and complying with them can be costly.

Reputational

Reputational damage is one of the most serious effects of a data breach. Its effects consist of the actual costs due to the shift of current customers to competitors due to loss of trust and turnover, as well as the opportunity costs due to an increased reluctance of potential customers to do business with the organization. It can usually be measured as follows:

- **Turnover Cost** The value of each particular class of customer multiplied by the estimated number of current customers in that class who will terminate their relationship with the organization as a result of the breach.

- **Cross-Sell Cost** The value of potential additional products and services that an existing customer may purchase, multiplied by the estimated number of current customers who will desist from purchasing due to the loss of trust.

- **New Customer Acquisition Cost** The value of products and services that a potential customer may purchase, multiplied by the number of potential customers who will not form a relationship with the organization as a result of the breach.

Competitive Advantage

A general range of loss of competitive edge due to the business effect of competitors obtaining released sensitive information should be determined. This can be developed through the input of the business units suffering the breach, as well as ones who may possibly suffer adverse competitive consequences due to the breach.

Credit Rating and Stock Price

For publicly traded firms, it is conceivable that the reputational damage from a serious data breach can negatively affect the stock price, due to both direct concern by investors or to analyst recommendations. In certain instances, credit rating agencies may also downgrade the creditworthiness of the organization due to the effects of the breach, thus increasing costs of capital.

New Controls and Safeguards

In general, incident cost estimates should not include the cost of putting in place or strengthening technology, processes, and controls to ensure similar breaches do not occur in the future, or more stringent audits for the affected units.

Root Cause Analysis

The Data Breach Response Team (DBRT) in cooperation with the impacted business unit or sector, should perform a Root Cause Analysis (RCA) to determine and document the root cause or underlying causal factors. Root causes are the underlying reasons that allow the apparent causes to trigger an incident. Even though specific conditions that allowed a compromise to occur must be corrected, they form the basis for further analysis to reach fundamental root causes.

Root causes can be related to process or technology failures, malicious intent, or human error, which contributed to the occurrence of the incident or series of incidents. Often the root causes are previously identified areas of concern whose impact was not fully recognized.

The RCA will include an overview, the methods and approach used, initial and final understanding of the incident, cause and effect analysis, causal statements in order of priority, and main, associated, and incidental findings.

Corrective Action Plan

Based on the Lessons Learned and Root Cause assessments, and once the successes and failures of the controls, processes, policies, and technology have been identified, any changes in organizational practices should be implemented. Whether organization-wide or at a unit level, these changes are initiated through a documented Corrective Action Plan (CAP) derived from any accepted recommendations detailed in the Lessons Learned documentation in order to assist in preventing a recurrence.

The CAP should focus on immediate actions taken to stabilize the situation that led to the incident, as well as medium- and long-term actions that will be undertaken to mitigate the underlying factors that contributed to the occurrence. CAPs can include changes to controls, processes, technical infrastructure, monitoring and detection, training and awareness, data security policy, and breach response plan.

- **Controls and Safeguards** A data breach represents a significant failure in the controls and safeguards implemented around data security. As an immediate step, all ineffective controls that led to this particular incident should be thoroughly analyzed and any deficiencies remediated. Additionally, similar controls in other systems or data should also be remediated if appropriate. In cases where no controls existed or were enforced, the organization should implement appropriate remediation to address identified vulnerabilities and prevent recurrence.

- **Organizational Processes** Any organizational process that may have contributed to the security breach must be reviewed and redesigned in order to eliminate any vulnerabilities that it may contain or expose. During the redesign, particular attention should be paid to implementing security best practices such as segregation of duties and least privilege.

- **Detection** Improved detection activities and mechanisms should be implemented in order to reduce the risk and impact of a future incident. These measures can include new firewall rules, improved host- and network-based intrusion prevention technologies, and upgrades to more secure applications. Part of an improved detection process will include increased monitoring of particular systems or data to rapidly detect unusual and suspicious symptomatic activity.

- **Training and Awareness** Lessons Learned should be incorporated into security awareness and training programs for users as well as response team members. Furthermore, if the breach was due to a failure in a process involving people, such as a social engineering attempt, training and awareness of controls mitigating that risk should be incorporated.

- **Data Security Policy** Depending on the nature of the breach, the relevant sections of the Data Security Policy should be reviewed and updated. For significant breaches, the policy should be redistributed in a timely manner to ensure that all organizational areas are aware of any new measures.

- **Response Plan** The effectiveness of the response is directly linked to the procedures in the response plan. Whether a particular procedure was judged effective or not, the response plan should be completely reviewed after a major data breach. Improvement focus should include availability of the plan and effectiveness of implementation, with particular attention paid to plan procedures that were not effective during the incident. In addition, any other improvement identified in the Lessons Learned should be implemented.

Once issued, it is the responsibility of the affected business and technical units to develop action plans and assign responsibility to track and implement any CAPs required for remediation. Change implementation must be planned by considering the resources needed, the cost, the short-, medium-, and long-term priorities, and the timeframe.

Within this framework, the priority of a particular remediation will drive the effort and allocation of resources. A project plan should be developed based on the prioritized tasks, taking into account availability of resources and impact on other controls and processes. Regular progress reports to appropriate management will ensure that there is organizational awareness and oversight of the change process.

Internal and External Follow-Up

Once the organization determines that the response phase of the incident has been completed, it may be necessary to notify internal and external affected parties of the status. This will help set appropriate expectations and avoid confusion. The team should encourage correspondents to provide any relevant feedback. This is important, since this new information may indicate a premature closure and result in the reopening of the incident.

For widespread breaches or those that have gathered publicity, a general announcement to employees will outline the final disposition and, if necessary, a summary of lessons learned and precautionary actions. This will help prevent any concern and confusion from causing additional disruption to operations. Users of the specific data or system compromised will need a more extensive briefing and possibly a management presentation.

External parties to notify may include regulators, whether or not they have been previously apprised of the breach. This could be through an update to the Suspicious Activity Report.

If the incident caused severe adverse publicity, it may also be advisable to contact the victims of the breach with the final disposition.

Closure Report

Another important post-incident activity is the creation of a closure report. This is developed by the team director and will include a description of the incident, the response process used, the notification process used, actions taken to prevent further incidents, tangible and intangible damage and cost, suggested policy and control changes, and, if appropriate, a statement from organizational counsel that the incident was handled in a manner consistent with policy and applicable law.

In addition to providing appropriate management and the board a detailed incident response accounting, the report will serve as a reference to assist in handling similar incidents, to identify potential areas of improvement in incident handling and reporting procedures, and to train new response team members. Portions of the closure report can also be used for the following purposes:

- To provide supporting information in legal matters.
- To support a report to a regulatory agency.
- To support an insurance claim.
- To justify disciplinary action.

Much of the data for the Closure Report will come from the Lessons Learned meeting as well as other documentation already collected. It will provide a mechanism to organize the information and present to a managerial audience. It will also include a timeline of the events from initial identification to final resolution.

At a summary level, the report should include the following information:

- A description of the incident.
- The method of discovery and reporting.
- A description of the sequence of events, including the timeline of key turning points.
- The number of individuals impacted.
- The type and sensitivity of the data compromised.
- The severity of the incident and whether it is deemed to represent a significant risk to the organization.

- The relationship of the attacker to the organization and possible motives if applicable.

- A description of the response including all actions taken with the person involved.

- A preventive measure put in place, including policy, process, and technical changes implemented at the business and technical level to mitigate risk.

- An assessment if the recovery steps taken were sufficient and what other recommendations need to be considered.

- Follow-up items with completion status.

- The identification and analysis of the process and technology root causes, including operational and technical risks that contributed to the incident.

- The types and descriptions of impact, including reputational, regulatory, legal, and financial.

- Confirmation that all appropriate parties have been contacted and have no pending issues.

The Closure Report should incorporate an incident technical summary outlining the technical aspects of the breach, including detection and recovery, for use by other areas of the organization to determine the applicability of the security issues to their environments.

In addition to the summary provided, the report may need to describe the detailed actions and steps for each phase of the incident response life cycle. This would be appropriate for more significant incidents or breaches that attracted public attention. For each phase, the report may include:

Preparation

- The security measures that were in place around the compromised data.

- An analysis of whether these safeguards and controls were appropriate.

- An analysis of whether these safeguards and controls were working properly.

- A description of measures that could have prevented the incident.

- The conditions that allowed the incident to occur.

- The adequacy of user training and awareness.

- The adequacy of the response plan.
- The appropriateness of the team composition and assignments.
- The familiarity of team members with the response plan.

Detection

- The time elapsed between incident occurrence and detection.
- The time elapsed between detection and reporting.
- The time elapsed between reporting and response team activation.
- The early warning signs of the incident.
- Recording and logging of precursors and indications.
- Whether any signs were undetected or ignored and why.
- Whether the incident was reported in an appropriate timeframe.

Evaluation

- The amount and type of information available to analyze the incident.
- Any information that was unavailable but that could have aided in the analysis, and the means by which such information could have been obtained.
- The initial and subsequent severity assignment.
- Factors that determined severity assignment.
- Availability of the response team.

Response

- Whether the response plan included the breach scenario.
- The degree to which the response plan was followed.
- Appropriateness of selected course of action.
- Effectiveness of response efforts.
- Determination of relative priorities if the response involved multiple simultaneous actions.
- Steps or actions that have hastened the recovery.
- Steps or actions that have inhibited the recovery.

- Disruption of service to internal or external users.

- Disruption of service decision factors, including number of systems and users affected by and length of disruption.

- Affected party, regulatory, or law enforcement notification.

- Effectiveness of communications.

Closure

- Incident root cause.

- Appropriateness of team model, structure, and personnel.

- Problems encountered during the response process.

- Direct and indirect financial, regulatory, and reputational costs.

- Other data or systems vulnerable to the same compromise, including risk level of compromise.

- Short-term and long-term need for revision to policies, processes, procedures, as well as to the response action plan.

- Short-term and long-term need for strengthening of current or implementation of new controls and safeguards.

- Need for enhance or additional training and awareness.

- Other changes to prevent a similar incident.

- Completeness of incident documentation and reports.

- Metrics including the total amount of direct and indirect labor spent working on the incident, the elapsed time from the beginning of the incident to its resolution, the elapsed time for each stage of the incident handling process, the time between occurrence and detection, the time between detection and reporting, and the time between reporting and response team activation.

This final section of the Closure Report can be an opportunity to present a cost-benefit analysis to management regarding future safeguards and changes to achieve a more secure organization. The costs of the improvements and controls to systems, data, policies, and processes can then be measured against the losses that these changes would have prevented and thus justify an increased investment in them.

Any relevant documents should be attached to the report, including assessment documentation, communication to affected parties, management, and other entities.

The closure report may be accompanied by an After-Action Briefing, which is the presentation made to senior managers where they are briefed about the incident, effects, response team actions, legal actions, restoration, and current status. In this briefing, senior managers deliver their views about the organization's efforts, expectations, and results.

Summary

- The closure phase takes action against the causes of the incident and helps the organization learn from it to improve processes and procedures.

- After a data security incident, the organization should hold one or more Lessons Learned sessions to review how effective the incident management process was, and to identify necessary improvements to existing policies, processes, controls, awareness and training, risk analysis, and other organizational practices.

- The post incident review process should be conducted after sufficient time has elapsed after the incident has taken place and been resolved, to provide a more objective view of the effectiveness of the response and communication.

- Any relevant lessons learned should be included in the revised data security and incident response plans for reference, and the updated documents should be communicated to all relevant personnel.

- The response team should develop a procedure by which it can analyze and measure the direct and indirect costs associated with a data breach incident, in order to determine the value of the information and assets that were lost.

- Among the most measurable costs in dealing with the incident are direct personnel costs, including the time of response team members as well as others who participated in the response.

- Loss in the form of decreased productivity can be tabulated by considering the number of employees who were prevented from working or experienced a slowdown in work because of the incident, as well as the attributable downtime.

- A major consideration when considering revenue loss is the opportunity cost of customers terminating or modifying their relationship with the organization, and the attendant impact on future business.

- Victim notification and assistance can represent significant breach-related costs.

- Legal fees include legal advice in managing the breach, as well as fees to represent the organization during regulatory review or civil litigation.

■ Fines may be assessed by regulatory agencies if it is determined that the organizational security infrastructure or incident response process was not consistent with mandates or best practices.

■ Experienced counsel can usually determine a range of exposure to potential compensatory and punitive penalties that may be assessed civilly against the organization as a result of action by victims.

■ Reputational damage is one of the most serious effects of a data breach. Its effects consist of the actual costs due to the shift of current customers to competitors due to loss of trust and turnover, as well as the opportunity costs due to an increased reluctance of potential customers to do business with the organization.

■ The organization should perform a RCA to determine and document the root cause or underlying causal factors of the breach.

■ Based on the Lessons Learned and Root Cause assessments, changes in organizational practices should be implemented through a documented Corrective Action Plan.

■ Corrective Action Plans can include changes to controls, processes, technical infrastructure, monitoring and detection, training and awareness, data security policy, and breach response plan.

■ It is the responsibility of the affected business and technical units to develop action plans and assign responsibility, track, and implement any remediation requirements.

■ A Closure Report will provide a detailed incident response accounting and serve as a reference to assist in handling similar incidents, to identify potential areas of improvement in incident handling and reporting procedures, and to train new response team members.

■ The Closure Report may be accompanied by a presentation by senior managers where they are briefed about the incident, the effects, the response team actions, the legal actions, the restoration, and the current status.

Appendix A

Relevant Legislation

Solutions in this chapter:

- United States—Federal Legislation
- United States—State Legislation
- Canada
- European Union

Introduction

Privacy and data breach legislation has been enacted and continues to evolve, both as a natural consequence of the amount and type of personal data stored by organizations, as well as in response to well-publicized security breaches and the heightened public concern about the loss of control over sensitive personal information.

Most legislation includes a breach notification provision, where organizations holding sensitive personal data are required to notify individuals in the event of a security breach of their personal information. The notice of breach provision usually takes into account the likelihood that the data may be misused in order to avoid over-notification. Some legislation includes a two-tier trigger requiring notification to individuals in cases where there is a material risk of the data being misused, and simple notification to a regulatory entity of any breach for which notification to individuals is judged unnecessary.

In addition to consumer notification, some legislation includes notice to regulators and to credit reporting agencies. Notice requirements are usually in writing via a letter, but alternate means are sometimes provided if the cost and number of affected individuals are above a certain defined threshold.

Since preventive measures are always preferable to a security incident and the possible ensuing notification, some legislation requires organizations to implement security safeguards to protect personal information from unauthorized access, alteration, or disclosure.

United States—Federal Legislation

In the United States, there is currently no federal legislation concerning data breach notification specifically. However, several federal laws mandate various levels of information security and disclosure for specific industries. These include the Gramm-Leach-Bliley (GLB) Act, the Health Insurance Portability and Accountability Act (HIPAA), and Sarbanes-Oxley (SOX). Each of these laws has an information security component, which mandates that organizations implement certain information security measures to protect sensitive personally identifiable information.

Gramm-Leach-Bliley (GLB)

The Financial Modernization Act, also known as the Gramm-Leach-Bliley (GLB) Act, applies to a wide range of financial institutions, including banks, securities firms, insurance companies, as well as other types of companies providing financial products and services to consumers. It includes provisions to protect consumers' private financial information, referred to as Nonpublic Personal Information (NPI). In order to secure the confidentiality of customer records and information, it requires financial institutions to develop an information security program that addresses the administrative, physical, and technical safeguards that are appropriate to organizational size and complexity, the nature and scope of the activities, and the sensitivity of any customer information at issue.

The GLB Act gives authority to several federal and state agencies to administer and enforce the Financial Privacy Rule, which governs the collection and disclosure of customers' personal financial information, and the Safeguards Rule, which requires the design, implementation, and maintenance of safeguards to protect customer information. More specifically, Title V of the GLB Act authorizes each of the agencies to establish and enforce guidelines to ensure the security of and protect against unauthorized access to or use of customer data. These agencies have issued Interagency Guidelines, which, through a combination of standards and regulations, require financial institutions to safeguard personal data by developing appropriate security programs and formal response plans to deal with data security breaches.

A financial organization must designate an employee to coordinate the information security program and to monitor compliance. A risk assessment must be performed to identify reasonably foreseeable internal and external risks to the security, confidentiality, and integrity of customer information that could result in the unauthorized disclosure, misuse, alteration, destruction, or other compromise of such information.

At a minimum, such a risk assessment should include consideration of risks in each relevant operational, including:

- Employee training and management.
- Information system design, processing, storage, transmission, and disposal.
- Detection, prevention, and response to attacks, intrusions, or other failures.

The organization should design and implement information safeguards and controls to manage and mitigate the identified risks, and regularly test or otherwise monitor the effectiveness of key controls, systems, and procedures. The security program should be evaluated and adjusted in light of the results of control testing and monitoring, any material changes to operations or business arrangements, or any other circumstances that may have a material impact on the program.

The guidelines also require the monitoring of third-party providers who have access to the organization's data for compliance to the guidelines, including the taking of reasonable steps to select and retain service providers that are capable of maintaining appropriate safeguards for the customer information at issue, and requiring the service providers to implement and maintain such safeguards.

The organization must also implement a security incident and breach notification program, which includes an immediate notification of the organization's oversight regulatory agency of an incident involving unauthorized access to or use of sensitive customer information. Individual consumers do not need to be notified of a security breach unless, upon reasonable investigation, the organization determines that misuse of the customers' personal information has or may reasonably occur. Information protected by encryption is not exempt based on its encrypted status alone.

Civil and criminal penalties for non-compliance include liabilities of up to $100,000 for each violation, personal officer and director liability of up to $10,000 for each violation, and criminal penalties that include fines and imprisonment. Other penalties include termination of Federal Deposit Insurance Corporation (FDIC) insurance, cease and desist orders barring practices deemed in violation, and removal of management, directors, and officers with a potential permanent prohibition from working in the financial industry.

Health Insurance Portability and Accountability Act (HIPAA)

The Health Insurance Portability and Accountability Act (HIPAA) protects the privacy of individually identifiable health information and medical records held by health care providers, health maintenance organizations, health records clearinghouses, and any third party that contracts with these entities to provider services that involve the use of this information.

The HIPAA is implemented through regulations issued by the Department of Health and Human Services, which provide guidance regarding the proper ways to protect personal health information through the Privacy and Security rules. The security regulations closely resemble those of the GLB Act, including the establishment of a security program and the implementation of policies and procedures to address security incidents.

The HIPAA mandates that a covered entity protects the confidentiality, integrity, and availability of all health information through administrative, physical, and technical safeguards and controls.

- Administrative safeguards are accomplished through the implementation of security policies and procedures that include an assessment of risks and vulnerabilities to the protected health information, the implementation and maintenance of security measures to mitigate the risks, workforce training and awareness, procedures to address security incidents, and contingency and disaster recovery plans.

- Physical safeguards include limiting physical access to the systems, data, and facilities to authorized individuals, as well as procedures governing the receipt, movement, and removal of hardware and media that contain protected health information. These safeguards include disposal procedures, media reuse procedures, and data backup and storage.

- Technical safeguards include regular and emergency access control procedures, appropriate account and password management, transmission security, and encryption to preserve data confidentiality and integrity.

Third-party providers that create, receive, maintain, or transmit personal information on the covered entity's behalf must also have similar safeguards. They must also report to the covered entity any security incident of which it becomes aware.

The HIPAA requires covered entities to appoint security and privacy officers, who may have personal liability in addition to the organizational liability. The Department of Health and Human Services has enforcement authority. Individuals can also bring an action.

Sarbanes-Oxley Act (SOX)

The Sarbanes-Oxley (SOX) Act, also known as the Public Company Accounting Reform and Investor Protection Act of 2002, requires publicly traded companies to implement a system of internal controls to prevent and detect unauthorized acquisition, use, or disposition of financial information whose compromise could have a material effect on the company's financial statements.

Section 404 of the SOX Act requires public companies' annual reports to include the company's assessment of internal control over financial reporting, and an auditor's attestation. These controls affect both financial and Information Technology (IT) processes and include physical, administrative, and technical safeguards. The SOX Act does not have a data breach management and notification mandate, but since employee, customer, and partner information is an organizational asset, its protection is a compliance requirement under Section 404.

Federal Information Security Management Act (FISMA)

The Federal Information Security Management Act (FISMA), which was created to strengthen U.S. government computer and network security, lays out a framework for annual IT security reviews, reporting, and remediation planning. It imposes a set of processes that must be followed for all information systems used or operated by a federal agency or by a contractor or other organization on behalf of the agency.

The FISMA requires federal agencies to improve the security of IT systems, applications, and databases in order to ensure the integrity, confidentiality, and availability of federal information systems.

The Risk Management Framework for FISMA successful compliance includes eight steps:

- **Asset Categorization** Information assets are categorized by sensitivity and based on the impact that a loss of security could have on the agency. This process includes asset definition, identification, and security prioritization.

- **Security Controls** A baseline of security controls and safeguards must be developed, implemented, assessed, and reviewed.

- **Refine Controls** Security controls must be defined from the initial baseline based on risk assessments to provide adequate protection.

- **Document Controls** Controls must be documented in an information security plan and policy.

- **Implement Controls** The security controls defined in the security plan must be implemented.

- **Assess Controls** Once the controls have been implemented, their effectiveness in meeting security requirements must be assessed, including whether they are implemented correctly and operate as intended.

- **Determine Risk** Before you authorize system operation, operational risks must be determined based on known vulnerabilities and any corrective actions.

- **Test Controls** Security controls must be monitored and assessed on a scheduled basis through a cycle of testing and update.

The FISMA also requires agencies to implement incident response procedures for detecting, reporting, and responding to security incidents.

United States—State Legislation
California

California's seminal data breach disclosure law, Senate Bill 1386, was enacted in July 2003. It has since become a benchmark for data breach notification, with most subsequent laws in other states following the basic tenets of California's original law.

SB 1386, also known as the Security Breach Information Act, requires public disclosure of security breaches, usually in writing, in which unencrypted confidential information of California residents has or is reasonably believed to have been compromised. It also provides a private right of action that allows individuals to seek judicial redress against any organization failing to comply with the law.

Because of the size of the California market, a breach affecting residents there will likely have nationwide consequences. Thus the California law has set the de facto notification requirements across the United States. It effectively requires government or business organizations to notify California consumers when a data breach has occurred, regardless of whether the information is suspected to have been used illegally or has contributed to identity theft.

The most important provisions of the California law include:

- **Applicability** Governmental and business organizations conducting business in California and/or that maintain or license personal information about California residents. SB 1386 also affects firms who provide outsourcing services for a company with customers or employees in California.

- **Security Breach Definition** A security breach is defined as an unauthorized acquisition of data that compromises the security, confidentiality, or integrity of personal information maintained by the organization.

- **Personal Information Definition** Unencrypted nonpublic personal information including an individual's first name or first initial and last name in combination with a Social Security number, driver's license or ID card number, account, credit, or debit card number in combination with a required security code, or password that would permit access to the account.

- **Notification** Disclosure and notification are mandated following discovery of a breach in the security of the data to any California resident whose unencrypted personal information was or is reasonably believed to have been acquired by an unauthorized person.

- **Timing** The statute does not set a notification timeframe, but requires that disclosure shall be made in the most expedient time possible and without unreasonable delay. The statute allows for delay in order to comply with a law enforcement criminal investigation or to determine the scope of the breach and restore the integrity of the data.

- **Method** Requires that notice be given in writing, but permits substitute forms of notice when the number of individuals affected exceeds 500,000 or the cost of notification would exceed $250,000. Substitute notice includes e-mail, conspicuous posting on the organization's Web site, or major statewide media.

- **Enforcement** Specific penalties have not been enumerated, but the law permits consumers to pursue a private right of action against an organization failing to comply with the law.

California legislation AB 1298, signed into law in October 2007, added medical information and health insurance information to the definition of personal information. Medical information is defined as "any information regarding an individual's medical history, mental or physical condition, or medical treatment or diagnosis by a health care professional." Health insurance information is defined as "an individual's health insurance policy number or subscriber information number, any unique identifier used by a health insurer to identify the individual, or any information in an individual's application and claims history, including any appeals records."

Other States

At least 39 states and the District of Columbia have enacted data security breach legislation requiring organizations that possess sensitive personal information to warn individuals of security breaches. California led the way in the creation of these laws, driven by concerns about identity theft and lax information security. Although most of those laws follow the California example, there are a number of significant deviations:

- The definition of a security breach as an unauthorized acquisition of and access to personal information, has been refined to require a likelihood of misuse or reasonable likelihood of harm to individuals. This is an important issue, since too many notices when there is no real danger of identity theft may desensitize consumers.

- In addition to accepting encrypted information from the statute, some states have also accepted redacted information, where the data is altered or truncated such that no more than the last four digits of a social security number, driver license number, financial account number, or credit or debit card number is accessible.

- Some states leave it to the organization itself to determine whether there is a likelihood of harm or misuse, while others involve a governmental agency in the determination.

- Many states apply the law to the state and municipal governments as well as private business. However, some states exempt government agencies from some of the sanctions associated with noncompliance.

- Some states require that consumer reporting agencies be notified if the security breach passes a certain threshold for the number of consumers affected.

- Some states have lowered the triggers for cost and number of affected parties for when substitute notice may be used.

- Although many states do not provide a private right of action, they do provide state enforcement jurisdiction and penalties for violations.

- Some states have expanded the types of data that are subject to the law, especially in the area of health information.

- Some states have accepted entities subject to the GLB Act or the HIPAA from the law or have substituted functional regulators for enforcement.

- Some states that did not have data destruction laws preceding the enactment of the security breach notification laws, added a data destruction requirement to their notification statutes.

Arizona

Legislation: SB 1338

Effective Date: December 2006

Requires notice of breach in the security of unencrypted, unredacted computerized personal information.

Does not require notice for immaterial breaches or if an investigation reveals that misuse of information has not occurred or is not reasonably likely to occur.

Allows substitute notification if the notification would cost more than $50,000 or the affected class of persons exceeds 100,000.

Financial instructions under the GLB Act are exempt.

Health plans or healthcare providers under the HIPAA are exempt.

Organizations maintaining procedures for a breach pursuant to the regulations established by a primary or functional regulator are exempt.

Penalties for failure to promptly disclose.

No private right of action.

Arkansas

Legislation: SB 1167

Effective Date: August 2005

Requires reasonable and appropriate security procedures and practices to protect personal information.

Requires notice of breach in the security of unencrypted computerized personal information and medical information in electronic or physical form.

Provides protection for additional categories of information, such as the date of birth and mother's maiden name.

Does not require notice for immaterial breaches or if an investigation reveals that misuse of information has not occurred or is not reasonably likely to occur.

Allows substitute notification if the notification would cost more than $250,000 or the affected class of persons exceeds 500,000.

Organizations maintaining procedures for a breach pursuant to the regulations established by a primary or functional regulator are exempt.

Penalties for failure to promptly disclose.

No private right of action.

Colorado

Legislation: HB 1119

Effective Date: September 2006

Requires notice of breach in the security of unencrypted, unredacted computerized personal information.

Does not require notice for immaterial breaches or if an investigation reveals that misuse of information has not occurred or is not reasonably likely to occur.

Requires notification to credit reporting agencies if more than 1,000 persons are affected.

Allows substitute notification if the notification would cost more than $250,000 or the affected class of persons exceeds 250,000.

Financial institutions under the GLB Act are exempt.

Organizations maintaining procedures for a breach pursuant to the regulations established by a primary or functional regulator are exempt.

Penalties for failure to promptly disclose.

No private right of action.

Connecticut

Legislation: SB 650

Effective Date: January 2006

Requires notice of breach in the security of unencrypted computerized data, electronic media, or electronic files containing personal information.

Does not require notice for immaterial breaches or if an investigation reveals that misuse of information has not occurred or is not reasonably likely to occur.

Allows substitute notification if the notification would cost more than $250,000 or the affected class of persons exceeds 500,000.

Financial institutions under the GLB Act or credit unions under the Federal Credit Union Act are exempt.

Organizations maintaining procedures for a breach pursuant to the regulations established by a primary or functional regulator are exempt.

Governmental entities are not required to provide notice.

No penalties for failure to promptly disclose.

No private right of action.

Delaware

Legislation: HB 116

Effective Date: June 2005

Requires notice of breach in the security of unencrypted computerized personal or medical information of Delaware residents.

Provides protection for additional categories of information, such as date of birth and mother's maiden name.

Does not require notice for immaterial breaches or if an investigation reveals that misuse of information has not occurred or is not reasonably likely to occur.

Allows substitute notification if the notification would cost more than $75,000 or the affected class of persons exceeds 100,000.

Organizations maintaining procedures for a breach pursuant to the regulations established by a primary or functional regulator are exempt.

Includes notification to the state Consumer Protection Division of the Department of Justice.

Penalties for failure to promptly disclose.

Includes private right of action.

District of Columbia

Legislation: 28–3851

Effective Date: January 2007

Requires notice of breach in the security of unencrypted computerized or other electronic personal information held by a business or a government agency.

Requires notification to credit reporting agencies if more than 10,000 persons are affected.

Allows substitute notification if the notification would cost more than $50,000 or the affected class of persons exceeds 100,000.

Financial institutions under the GLB Act or credit unions under the Federal Credit Union Act are exempt.

Penalties for failure to promptly disclose.

Includes private right of action.

Florida

Legislation: HB 481

Effective Date: July 2005

Requires notice of breach in the security of computerized, unencrypted personal information held by an organization that conducts business in the state.

Provides protection for additional categories of information, such as date of birth and mother's maiden name.

Does not require notice for immaterial breaches or if an investigation reveals that misuse of information has not occurred or is not reasonably likely to occur.

Determination must be documented in writing and maintained for five years.

Requires notification to credit reporting agencies if more than 1,000 persons are affected.

Organizations maintaining procedures for a breach pursuant to the regulations established by a primary or functional regulator are exempt.

Exempts state government from the penalty provisions of the bill.

Penalties for failure to promptly disclose.

No private right of action.

Georgia

Legislation: SB 230

Effective Date: May 2005

Covers only data brokers.

Requires notice of breach in the security of computerized personal information.

Requires notification to credit reporting agencies if more than 10,000 persons are affected.

Allows substitute notification if the notification would cost more than $250,000 or the affected class of persons exceeds 500,000.

No penalties for failure to promptly disclose.

No private right of action.

Hawaii

Legislation: SB 2290

Effective Date: January 2007

Requires notice of breach in the security of unencrypted or unredacted data containing personal information.

Requires notification to credit reporting agencies if more than 1,000 persons are affected.

Allows substitute notification if the notification would cost more than $100,000 or the affected class of persons exceeds 200,000.

Financial institutions under the GLB Act are exempt.

Health plans or healthcare providers under the HIPAA are exempt.

Penalties for failure to promptly disclose.

No private right of action.

Idaho

Legislation: SB 1374

Effective Date: July 2006

Requires notice of breach in the security of unencrypted, computerized personal information.

Does not require notice for immaterial breaches or if an investigation determines that misuse of information has not occurred or is not reasonably likely to occur.

Allows substitute notification if the notification would cost more than $25,000 or the affected class of persons exceeds 50,000.

Organizations maintaining procedures for a breach pursuant to the regulations established by a primary or functional regulator are exempt.

Penalties for failure to promptly disclose.

No private right of action.

Illinois

Legislation: HB 1633

Effective Date: January 2006

Requires notice of breach in the security of unencrypted or unredacted data containing personal information.

Allows substitute notification if the notification would cost more than $250,000 or the affected class of persons exceeds 500,000.

Penalties for failure to promptly disclose.

Includes private right of action.

Indiana

Legislation: HB 1101

Effective Date: July 2006

Requires notice of breach in the security of unencrypted or unredacted data containing personal information.

Requires notification to credit reporting agencies if more than 1,000 persons are affected.

Allows substitute notification if the notification would cost more than $250,000 or the affected class of persons exceeds 500,000.

Financial instructions under the GLB Act are exempt.

Health plans or healthcare providers under the HIPAA are exempt.

Organizations maintaining procedures for a breach pursuant to the regulations established by a primary or functional regulator are exempt.

Failure to comply with data destruction requirements is a criminal offense.

No penalties for failure to promptly disclose.

No private right of action.

Kansas

Legislation: SB 196

Effective Date: January 2007

Requires notice of breach in the security of unencrypted, unredacted computerized personal information.

Does not require notice for immaterial breaches or if an investigation determines that misuse of information has not occurred or is not reasonably likely to occur.

Requires notification to credit reporting agencies if more than 1,000 persons are affected.

Allows substitute notification if the notification would cost more than $100,000 or the affected class of persons exceeds 50,000.

Organizations maintaining procedures for a breach pursuant to the regulations established by a primary or functional regulator are exempt.

Penalties for failure to promptly disclose.

No private right of action.

Louisiana

Legislation: SB 205

Effective Date: January 2006

Requires notice of breach of the security of unencrypted computerized personal information.

Does not require notice for immaterial breaches or if an investigation determines that misuse of information has not occurred or is not reasonably likely to occur.

Allows substitute notification if the notification would cost more than $250,000 or the affected class of persons exceeds 500,000.

Financial instructions under the GLB Act are exempt.

No penalties for failure to promptly disclose.

Includes private right of action.

Maine

Legislation: LD 1671

Effective Date: January 2006

Requires notice of breach in the security of unencrypted, unredacted computerized personal information.

Requires notification to credit reporting agencies if more than 1,000 persons are affected.

Allows substitute notification if the notification would cost more than $5,000 or the affected class of persons exceeds 1,000.

Financial instructions under the GLB Act are exempt.

Penalties for failure to promptly disclose.

No private right of action.

Maryland

Legislation: HB 208

Effective Date: January 2008

Requires notice of breach in the security of unencrypted, unredacted computerized personal information.

Does not require notice for immaterial breaches or if an investigation reveals that misuse of information has not occurred or is not reasonably likely to occur.

Requires notification to credit reporting agencies if more than 1,000 persons are affected.

Allows substitute notification if the notification would cost more than $100,000 or the affected class of persons exceeds 175,000.

Financial instructions under the GLB Act are exempt.

Penalties for failure to promptly disclose.

Includes private right of action.

Massachusetts

Legislation: HB 4144

Effective Date: February 2008

Requires notice of breach in the security of unencrypted personal information or encrypted data where the encryption key has been compromised.

Provides notice to the attorney general and the director of consumer affairs.

Does not require notice for immaterial breaches or if an investigation reveals that misuse of information has not occurred or is not reasonably likely to occur.

Allows substitute notification if the notification would cost more than $250,000 or the affected class of persons exceeds 500,000.

Penalties for failure to promptly disclose.

No private right of action.

Michigan

Legislation: SB 309

Effective Date: July 2007

Requires notice of breach in the security of unencrypted, unredacted computerized personal information.

Does not require notice for immaterial breaches or if an investigation reveals that misuse of information has not occurred or is not reasonably likely to occur.

Requires notification to credit reporting agencies if more than 1,000 persons are affected.

Allows substitute notification if the notification would cost more than $250,000 or the affected class of persons exceeds 500,000.

Financial instructions under the GLB Act are exempt.

Health plans or healthcare providers under the HIPAA are exempt.

Penalties for failure to promptly disclose.

No private right of action.

Minnesota

Legislation: HF 2121

Effective Date: January 2006

Requires notice of breach of the security of unencrypted computerized personal information.

Requires notification to credit reporting agencies if more than 500 persons are affected.

Allows substitute notification if the notification would cost more than $500,000 or the affected class of persons exceeds 250,000.

Financial instructions under the GLB Act are exempt.

Health plans or healthcare providers under the HIPAA are exempt.

Penalties for failure to promptly disclose.

No private right of action.

Montana

Legislation: HB 732

Effective Date: March 2006

Requires notice of breach of the security of unencrypted computerized personal information.

A social security number alone constitutes personal information for purposes of record destruction.

Does not require notice for immaterial breaches or if an investigation reveals that misuse of information has not occurred or is not reasonably likely to occur.

Allows substitute notification if the notification would cost more than $500,000 or the affected class of persons exceeds 250,000.

Penalties for failure to promptly disclose.

No private right of action.

Nebraska

Legislation: LB 876

Effective Date: April 2006

Requires notice of breach in the security of unencrypted, unredacted computerized personal information.

Does not require notice for immaterial breaches or if an investigation reveals that misuse of information has not occurred or is not reasonably likely to occur.

Organizations maintaining procedures for a breach pursuant to the regulations established by a primary or functional regulator are exempt.

Allows substitute notification if the notification would cost more than $75,000 or the affected class of persons exceeds 100,000.

Penalties for failure to promptly disclose.

No private right of action.

Nevada

Legislation: SB 347

Effective Date: January 2006

Requires reasonable and appropriate security procedures and practices to protect personal information.

Requires notice of breach of the security of unencrypted computerized personal information.

Does not require notice for immaterial breaches or if an investigation reveals that misuse of information has not occurred or is not reasonably likely to occur.

Requires notification to credit reporting agencies if more than 1,000 persons are affected.

Allows substitute notification if the notification would cost more than $250,000 or the affected class of persons exceeds 500,000.

Financial institutions under the GLB Act are exempt.

Penalties for failure to promptly disclose.

No private right of action.

New Hampshire

Legislation: HB 1660

Effective Date: January 2007

Requires notice of breach of the security of unencrypted computerized personal information.

Does not require notice for immaterial breaches or if an investigation reveals that misuse of information has not occurred or is not reasonably likely to occur.

Notice not required if organization maintains own notification procedures established by primary or functional regulator.

Requires notification to credit reporting agencies if more than 1,000 persons are affected.

Allows substitute notification if the notification would cost more than $5,000 or the affected class of persons exceeds 1,000.

Organizations maintaining procedures for a breach pursuant to the regulations established by a primary or functional regulator are exempt.

No penalties for failure to promptly disclose.

No private right of action.

New Jersey

Legislation: AB 4001

Effective Date: January 2006

Requires notice of breach of the security of unencrypted computerized personal information.

Does not require notice for immaterial breaches or if an investigation reveals that misuse of information has not occurred or is not reasonably likely to occur.

Written documentation of the investigation must be kept for five years.

Requires notification to credit reporting agencies if more than 1,000 persons are affected.

Allows substitute notification if the notification would cost more than $250,000 or the affected class of persons exceeds 500,000.

No penalties for failure to promptly disclose.

No private right of action.

New York

Legislation: SB 5827 & AB 4254

Effective Date: December 2005

Requires notice of breach of the security of unencrypted computerized personal information or encrypted information with acquired encryption key.

Notifications must also be provided to the New York State Attorney General, the New York State Consumer Protection Board, and the New York State Office of Cyber Security and Critical Infrastructure Coordination.

Requires notification to credit reporting agencies if more than 5,000 persons are affected.

Allows substitute notification if the notification would cost more than $250,000 or the affected class of persons exceeds 500,000.

Penalties for failure to promptly disclose.

No private right of action.

North Carolina

Legislation: SB 1048

Effective Date: December 2005

Requires notice of breach in the security of unencrypted, unredacted computerized personal information or encrypted information with acquired encryption key.

Provides protection for additional categories of information, such as date of birth and mother's maiden name.

Does not require notice for immaterial breaches or if an investigation reveals that misuse of information has not occurred or is not reasonably likely to occur.

Requires notification to credit reporting agencies and the Consumer Protection Division if more than 1,000 persons are affected.

Allows substitute notification if the notification would cost more than $250,000 or the affected class of persons exceeds 500,000.

Financial institutions under the GLB Act are exempt.

Penalties for failure to promptly disclose.

Includes private right of action.

North Dakota

Legislation: SB 2251

Effective Date: June 2005

Requires notice of breach in the security of unencrypted, unredacted computerized personal information.

Provides protection for additional categories of information, such as date of birth and mother's maiden name.

Does not require notice for immaterial breaches or if an investigation reveals that misuse of information has not occurred or is not reasonably likely to occur.

Allows substitute notification if the notification would cost more than $250,000 or the affected class of persons exceeds 500,000.

Financial institutions under the GLB Act or credit unions under the Federal Credit Union Act are exempt.

Penalties for failure to promptly disclose.

No private right of action.

Ohio

Legislation: HB 104

Effective Date: February 2006

Requires notice of breach in the security of unencrypted, unredacted computerized personal information.

Does not require notice for immaterial breaches or if an investigation reveals that misuse of information has not occurred or is not reasonably likely to occur.

Requires notification to credit reporting agencies if more than 1,000 persons are affected.

Allows substitute notification if the notification would cost more than $250,000 or the affected class of persons exceeds 500,000.

Financial institutions under the GLB Act or credit unions under the Federal Credit Union Act are exempt.

Health plans or healthcare providers under the HIPAA are exempt.

Penalties for failure to promptly disclose.

Includes private right of action.

Oklahoma

Legislation: HB 2357

Effective Date: June 2006

Applies only to state agencies.

Requires notice of breach in the security of unencrypted computerized personal information.

Allows substitute notification if the notification would cost more than $250,000 or the affected class of persons exceeds 500,000.

No penalties for failure to promptly disclose.

No private right of action.

Oregon

Legislation: SB 583

Effective Date: October 2007

Requires notice of breach of the security of unencrypted, unredacted computerized personal information or encrypted information with acquired encryption key.

Determination must be in writing and kept for five years.

Does not require notice for immaterial breaches or if an investigation reveals that misuse of information has not occurred or is not reasonably likely to occur.

Requires notification to credit reporting agencies if more than 1,000 persons are affected.

Allows substitute notification if the notification would cost more than $250,000 or the affected class of persons exceeds 350,000.

Financial institutions under the GLB Act are exempt.

Organizations maintaining procedures for a breach pursuant to the regulations established by a primary or functional regulator are exempt.

Penalties for failure to promptly disclose.

No private right of action.

Pennsylvania

Legislation: SB 712

Effective Date: June 2006

Requires notice of breach of the security of unencrypted, unredacted computerized personal information or encrypted information with acquired encryption key.

Requires notification to credit reporting agencies if more than 1,000 persons are affected.

Allows substitute notification if the notification would cost more than $100,000 or the affected class of persons exceeds 175,000.

Organizations maintaining procedures for a breach pursuant to the regulations established by a primary or functional regulator are exempt.

Financial institutions under the GLB Act are exempt.

Penalties for failure to promptly disclose.

No private right of action.

Rhode Island

Legislation: HB 6191

Effective Date: March 2006

Requires notice of breach of the security of unencrypted, unredacted computerized personal information.

Does not require notice for immaterial breaches or if an investigation reveals that misuse of information has not occurred or is not reasonably likely to occur.

Allows substitute notification if the notification would cost more than $25,000 or the affected class of persons exceeds 50,000.

Organizations maintaining procedures for a breach pursuant to the regulations established by a primary or functional regulator are exempt.

Financial institutions under the GLB Act or credit unions under the Federal Credit Union Act are exempt.

Health plans or healthcare providers under the HIPAA are exempt.

Penalties for failure to promptly disclose.

Includes private right of action.

Tennessee

Legislation: SB 2220

Effective Date: September 2005

Requires notice of breach of the security of unencrypted computerized personal information.

Requires notification to credit reporting agencies if more than 1,000 persons are affected.

Allows substitute notification if the notification would cost more than $250,000 or the affected class of persons exceeds 500,000.

Financial institutions under the GLB Act are exempt.

Penalties for failure to promptly disclose.

Includes private right of action.

Texas

Legislation: SB 122

Effective Date: September 2005

Requires reasonable and appropriate security procedures and practices to protect personal information.

Requires notice of breach of the security of unencrypted computerized personal information.

Requires notification to credit reporting agencies if more than 10,000 persons are affected.

Allows substitute notification if the notification would cost more than $250,000 or the affected class of persons exceeds 500,000.

Financial institutions under the GLB Act are exempt.

Penalties for failure to promptly disclose.

No private right of action.

Utah

Legislation: SB 69

Effective Date: January 2007

Requires reasonable and appropriate security procedures and practices to protect personal information.

Requires notice of breach in the security of unencrypted, unredacted computerized personal information.

Does not require notice for immaterial breaches or if an investigation reveals that misuse of information has not occurred or is not reasonably likely to occur.

Organizations maintaining procedures for a breach pursuant to the regulations established by a primary or functional regulator are exempt.

Penalties for failure to promptly disclose.

No private right of action.

Vermont

Legislation: SB 284

Effective Date: January 2007

Requires notice of breach of the security of unencrypted, unredacted computerized personal information.

Does not require notice for immaterial breaches or if an investigation reveals that misuse of information has not occurred or is not reasonably likely to occur.

Requires notification to credit reporting agencies if more than 1,000 persons are affected.

Allows substitute notification if the notification would cost more than $50,000 or the affected class of persons exceeds 5,000.

Financial institutions under the GLB Act or credit unions under the Federal Credit Union Act are exempt.

Notice and explanation must be provided to the Attorney General or department of banking, insurance, securities, or health care administration.

Penalties for failure to promptly disclose.

Includes private right of action.

Washington

Legislation: SB 6043

Effective Date: July 2005

Requires notice of breach of the security of unencrypted computerized personal information.

Does not require notice for immaterial breaches or if an investigation reveals that misuse of information has not occurred or is not reasonably likely to occur.

Allows substitute notification if the notification would cost more than $250,000 or the affected class of persons exceeds 500,000.

Penalties for failure to promptly disclose.

Includes private right of action.

Wisconsin

Legislation: SB 164

Effective Date: March 2005

Requires notice of breach of the security of unencrypted, unredacted computerized personal information.

Covered information includes DNA and biometric data.

Does not require notice for immaterial breaches or if an investigation reveals that misuse of information has not occurred or is not reasonably likely to occur.

Requires notification to credit reporting agencies if more than 1,000 persons are affected.

Financial institutions under the GLB Act are exempt.

Health plans or healthcare providers under the HIPAA are exempt.

No penalties for failure to promptly disclose.

No private right of action.

Wyoming

Legislation: SB 53

Effective Date: July 2007

Requires notice of breach of the security of unencrypted computerized personal information.

Does not require notice for immaterial breaches or if an investigation reveals that misuse of information has not occurred or is not reasonably likely to occur.

Financial institutions under the GLB Act or credit unions under the Federal Credit Union Act are exempt.

Penalties for failure to promptly disclose.

No private right of action.

Canada

Personal Information Protection and Electronic documents Act (PIPEDA)

The Personal Information Protection and Electronic Documents Act (PIPEDA) sets out ground rules for how private sector organizations may collect, use, or disclose personal information in the course of commercial activities. Personal information is defined as any factual or subjective information such as name, address, telephone number, gender, identification numbers, income, and credit records. The legislation also covers sensitive personal information, including health or medical history.

The PIPEDA applies to all organizations engaged in commercial activities, unless the federal government exempts an organization or activity in a province that has substantially similar legislation to the Act. It is based on ten privacy principles developed by the Canadian Standards Association and is overseen by the Privacy Commissioner of Canada who is authorized to receive and investigate complaints. These principles include:

- **Accountability** Organizational responsibility for personal information under its control.

- **Identifying Purposes** Identification of the specific purposes for which the information is collected.

- **Consent** Knowledge and consent of the individual whose information is collected or used.

- **Limiting Collection** Collection limited to that which is necessary for the purposes identified by the organization.

- **Limiting Use, Disclosure, and Retention** Personal information shall not be used or disclosed for purposes other than those for which it was collected, and shall be retained only as long as necessary for the fulfillment of those purposes.

- **Accuracy** Personal information shall be accurate, complete, and up-to-date.

- **Safeguards** Personal information shall be protected by security safeguards appropriate to its sensitivity.

- **Openness** An organization shall make readily available, policies and practices relating to the management of personal information.

- **Individual Access** An individual shall be given access to personal information and be able to challenge the accuracy and completeness of the information.

- **Challenging Compliance** An individual shall be able to address a challenge concerning compliance to the designated individual accountable for the organization's compliance.

The PIPEDA dictates that personal information shall be protected by security safeguards appropriate to its sensitivity. These safeguards include physical, technical, and administrative controls.

In addition to PIPEDA, there are several federal and provincial sector-specific laws that include provisions dealing with the protection of personal information.

European Union
Directive 95/46/EC

Directive 95/46/EC is a directive of the European Union (EU) designed to protect the privacy and protection of all personal data collected about citizens of the EU, with regard to the collection, storage, use, modification, and transmission of that data.

Personal data is defined as any information that can directly or indirectly identify a person. The protection rules apply to organizations operating within the EU and/or use any equipment located in the EU to process personal data.

The Directive's guidelines protect individuals from the unlawful storage of personal data, the storage of inaccurate personal data, or the abuse or unauthorized disclosure of such data. These guidelines are based on seven principles:

- **Notice** All data shall be collected with the knowledge or consent of the subject and through lawful means.

- **Purpose** The purpose for which personal data is collected should be specified and the subsequent use limited to the fulfillment of this purpose.

- **Consent** Personal data should not be disclosed or shared with third parties without consent from its subject(s).

- **Security** Personal data should be protected by security safeguards against loss, unauthorized access, use, modification, destruction, or disclosure.

- **Disclosure** Personal data should not be disclosed or used for purposes other than those specified, except with the consent of the individual.

- **Access** Individuals have the right to obtain data relating to them and challenge and correct inaccuracies.

- **Accountability** A data owner is accountable for complying with measures to adhere to these principles.

Other national legislation that is patterned after the EU Directive includes:

- **United Kingdom** The Data Protection Act of 1998 implements Directive 95/46/EC.

- **Australia** The Federal Privacy Act contains eleven Information Privacy Principles, which apply to government agencies, and ten National Privacy Principles, which apply to parts of the private sector and health service providers.

- **Japan** The Personal Information Protection Law applies to any company with offices in Japan that holds personal data on 5,000 or more individuals.

Index

Syngress: *The Definition of a Serious Security Library*

Syn·gress (sin-gres): *noun, sing.* Freedom from risk or danger; safety. See *security*.

Syngress: *The Definition of a Serious Security Library*

Syn·gress (sin–gres): *noun, sing.* Freedom from risk or danger; safety. See *security*.

Syngress: *The Definition of a Serious Security Library*

Syn·gress (sin–gres): *noun, sing.* Freedom from risk or danger; safety. See *security*.

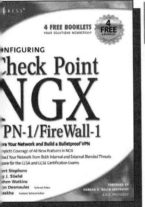

Syngress: *The Definition of a Serious Security Library*

Syn·gress (sin-gres): *noun, sing.* Freedom from risk or danger; safety. See *security*.

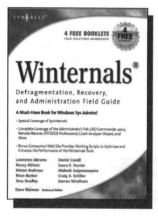

Syngress: *The Definition of a Serious Security Library*

Syn·gress (sin-gres): *noun, sing.* Freedom from risk or danger; safety. See *security*.

How to Cheat at Designing Security for a Windows Server 2003 Network

Neil Ruston, Chris Peiris

While considering the security needs of your organiztion, you need to balance the human and the technical in order to create the best security design for your organization. Securing a Windows Server 2003 enterprise network is hardly a small undertaking, but it becomes quite manageable if you approach it in an organized and systematic way. This includes configuring software, services, and protocols to meet an organization's security needs.

ISBN: 1-59749-243-4

Price: $39.95 US $55.95 CAN

How to Cheat at Designing a Windows Server 2003 Active Directory Infrastructure

Melissa Craft, Michael Cross, Hal Kurz, Brian Barber

The book will start off by teaching readers to create the conceptual design of their Active Directory infrastructure by gathering and analyzing business and technical requirements. Next, readers will create the logical design for an Active Directory infrastructure. Here the book starts to drill deeper and focus on aspects such as group policy design. Finally, readers will learn to create the physical design for an active directory and network Infrastructure including DNS server placement; DC and GC placements and Flexible Single Master Operations (FSMO) role placement.

ISBN: 1-59749-058-X

Price: $39.95 US $55.95 CAN

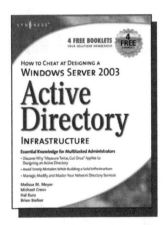
How to Cheat at Configuring ISA Server 2004

Dr. Thomas W. Shinder, Debra Littlejohn Shinder

If deploying and managing ISA Server 2004 is just one of a hundred responsibilities you have as a System Administrator, "How to Cheat at Configuring ISA Server 2004" is the perfect book for you. Written by Microsoft MVP Dr. Tom Shinder, this is a concise, accurate, enterprise tested method for the successful deployment of ISA Server.

ISBN: 1-59749-057-1

Price: $34.95 U.S. $55.95 CAN

SYNGRESS®

Syngress: *The Definition of a Serious Security Library*

Syn·gress (sin–gres): *noun, sing.* Freedom from risk or danger; safety. See *security*.

SYNGRESS